Resistance Advocacy as News

Resistance Advocacy as News

Digital Black Press Covers the Tea Party

Benjamin Rex LaPoe II
Victoria L. LaPoe

LEXINGTON BOOKS
Lanham • Boulder • New York • London

Published by Lexington Books
An imprint of The Rowman & Littlefield Publishing Group, Inc.
4501 Forbes Boulevard, Suite 200, Lanham, Maryland 20706
www.rowman.com

Unit A, Whitacre Mews, 26-34 Stannary Street, London SE11 4AB

British Library Cataloguing in Publication Information Available

Library of Congress Cataloging-in-Publication Data

Names: LaPoe, Benjamin Rex, author. | LaPoe, Victoria, 1977- author.
Title: Resistance advocacy as news : digital black press covers the tea party / Benjamin Rex LaPoe II,
    Victoria L. LaPoe.
Description: Lanham : Lexington Books, [2018] | Includes bibliographical references and index.
Identifiers: LCCN 2018000242 (print) | LCCN 2017057036 (ebook) | ISBN 9781498566865 (Elec-
    tronic) | ISBN 9781498566858 (hardcover : alk. paper)
Subjects: LCSH: African American press—History. | Tea Party movement—Press coverage. | Tea
    Party movement—United States. | Journalism—History—Political aspects. | Mass media—Polit-
    ical aspects—United States—History—21st century. | United States—Politics and government.
Classification: LCC PN4882.5 (print) | LCC PN4882.5 .L26 2018 (ebook) | DDC 071.308996073—
    dc23
LC record available at https://lccn.loc.gov/2018000242

♾™ The paper used in this publication meets the minimum requirements of American
National Standard for Information Sciences Permanence of Paper for Printed Library
Materials, ANSI/NISO Z39.48-1992.

Printed in the United States of America

Contents

Introduction

The result of the 2016 presidential election surprised many and engendered a popular hashtag and slogan—resist. Various derivations of the word frequently trend on social media and during the numerous protests that have followed. A diverse coalition of communities resisted, for valuable reasons, the administration on a wide spectrum of rationale and issues, one of those being a platform closely aligned with white supremacist ideologies. While the word "resist" may be trendy now, the black press has been advocating resistance to institutionalized white supremacy ideologies since 1827. Not too long ago, scholars believed the United States desired equality so much that making explicit racial comments in an attempt to disparage opponents, to ostracize communities, or to attract voters was taboo and one would be rejected as an illegitimate, incompetent, unintelligent bigot not worthy of an elected representative's public servant duties.[1] This was not the case in the 2016 presidential election. The GOP nominee made numerous explicit racial comments and appeals without being rejected, leaving priming experts to wonder what happened. We argue to understand how we got to this point, we need to look back, not far back—President Obama's first term. It feels as though the United States has changed a great deal culturally since the 2008 presidential election; following President Obama's election some even pondered if the United States was suddenly post-racial. It was during this time the GOP 2016 presidential nominee began to gain traction as a political figure, primarily through his affection for birthers and the tea party, and his disdain for President Obama. Examining media coverage of this period helps explain the aversion to diversity much of the United States embraced in 2016 and continues demonstrating.

On May 3, 2011, the *Chicago Defender* published an article titled "Sorry about the birth certificate I've been hunting Osama."[2] The author argued

President Obama had an "amazing and infuriating trait" for anyone following him in any fashion—"incredible timing." The writer for one of the historically prestigious black newspapers summarized a few political conflicts at the time dampening President Obama's political clout: continued verbal assaults from the white press and Republicans, a budget battle with Republicans where "Democrats had survived . . . without totally capitulating everything they claimed they stood for," rising gas prices, "sluggish economic outlook," and "even worse, race baiting reality T.V. toupee salesman Donald Trump was gobbling up all available airtime again dredging up the boogeyman that Obama wasn't born in the United States." Less than a year later, George Zimmerman fatally shot Trayvon Martin and Zimmerman was later acquitted in 2013. His acquittal sparked a hashtag #BlackLivesMatter and a social movement was born.

During every moment leading up to President Obama's election and after, traditional legacy newspapers struggled to accurately cover these events and their connections with black communities; the black press continued filling this void of misinformation online and advocating for issues salient to their communities. The black press began expressing black voices in 1827 and has continued advocating for equality by providing a presence for black voices and issues typically absent, ignored, and/or marginalized in traditional media.[3] Embodying an advocacy function, the black press also instructs communities about the vital importance of civil rights.[4] These traits are not prevalent in a mainstream press espousing rigid adherence to objectivity. Despite the black press's historical significance in helping shape civil rights victories, little scholarship examines the modern black press.[5] An overwhelming majority of academic media research focuses only on the mainstream press—not surprisingly given the mainstream press's larger audiences. This book advances our knowledge by examining online black press newspapers and comparing them to online mainstream press newspapers on the same topic—tea party dissent during President Obama's first term.

Black newspapers and mainstream newspapers still interpret issues relevant to black communities through much different lenses,[6] resulting in marked variances in the coverage of identical issues impacting the black community and reflecting ideologies frequently at odds with each other.[7] For instance, on the subject of reparations, mainstream newspapers offered two viewpoints—advocates and opponents; helpful deliberations on the substance of the subject were absent.[8] Mainstream newspapers interpreted the issue of reparations in an "us versus them" style, a zero-sum game where someone wins and someone loses, positioning African Americans as the "other" that would win while whites would lose. Black newspapers, on the other hand, offered only one viewpoint, advocacy, with this advocacy focusing intently on the substance of the issues and why they were important to their communities.[9] "The black press was less likely to use comparative coverage . . . their coverage more often focused on the Black experience in America."[10]

In another example, Mark Dolan sampled black newspaper coverage during the month after Hurricane Katrina and found the black press criticized the mainstream press for failing to investigate the hurricane's impact on the African-American communities. Instead, mainstream media focused on the illegal actions of some black New Orleans residents, ignored the conditions that invited such criminal behavior, and failed to cover the illegal actions of some white New Orleans residents.[11] Mainstream press coverage portrayed blacks as looters, while whites, conducting the same activities, were reported as innocents doing what was needed to survive.

Coverage of Supreme Court cases is another example. In decisions salient to the black community, the black press mediated the cases and rulings differently than the mainstream press.[12] "As an advocate for black interests, the black press focused on the implications of the ruling for minorities . . . and emphasized pro-affirmative action sources."[13] While the black press's stories also focused on the harmful impacts of some rulings, the mainstream press relied on legalistic and constitutional language portraying the Supreme Court as a politically neutral institution; while the black press frequently criticized justices who they perceived as negatively influencing race relations, the mainstream press refrained from criticism or praise of the judges— "choosing to quote from his concurring opinion" instead.[14]

The black press isn't as constricted by self-imposed white press strategic rituals of idolized objectivity, encompassing racial advocacy and educational responsibilities instead. This does not diminish the factual accuracy of the content in the black press, but frees it to amplify black perspectives ignored or oversimplified in the mainstream press. "It is not in spite of, but because of, their commitment to norms of objectivity and impartiality that [mainstream] journalists" are subservient to prevailing white ideologies.[15] Issues with a great deal of historical context, multiple cultural layers, and countless perspectives are difficult for the mainstream press to cover. They know their readers have short attention spans and don't want to expend a great deal of energy to digest a story, so they provide minimal context, typically a single layer, and usually only two sides to a story, if needed. The mainstream press's mission engenders this type of superficial reporting on race. We will show the black press's continued advocacy mission permits it to provide more context, more substance, and more layers on stories and issues connected to their communities during a time of much cultural friction.

February 7, 2007, marked the beginning of perhaps one of the more challenging modern narratives journalists constructed. On that day, then Illinois Senator Barack Hussein Obama announced his intentions to run for President of the United States of America. Senator Obama emerged as a legitimate candidate, with a serious chance of becoming the first African-

American president, when he won the Iowa caucus. Following that victory, race became the most salient issue in newspaper coverage of the democratic primaries.[16] Obama edged out then Senator Hillary Clinton and moved on to a general election against Senator John McCain. Race again emerged as a significant variable in journalists' coverage of the election.[17] During the general campaign, McCain, Alaska governor Sarah Palin (McCain's running mate), and other Republican surrogates called Obama everything in their repertoire of negative adjectives, such as socialist, illegal immigrant, monkey, witch doctor, and terrorist. Cries of "kill him" could be heard at rallies. Even for politics, the negativity and hostility seemed excessive.

When the electorate chose Obama as president on November 4, 2008, six African Americans had been senators in U.S. history. Blacks have seen a steady increase in proportional representation at local levels, but statewide and national positions are still far from being proportionate.[18] Even though President Obama became the first African American to reside in the Oval Office, black communities are just beginning to have their voices and perspectives heard at higher levels in the federal government.[19]

On November 4, 2008, the *Chicago Defender*, a black newspaper founded in 1905 and considered the first commercially successful black newspaper, published an article titled, "Barack Obama sweeps to victory: First Black U.S. President." The story's lead highlighted the historic moment of race in the United States: "Barack Hussein Obama, son of a Black Kenyan father and a white Kansan mother, swept into the White House as the first Black to win the race for President of the United States, riding a wave of votes from Blacks, Whites, Hispanics, women, youth, new voters and the elderly."[20] No one doubts the historical and symbolic significance of President Obama's election in a nation founded by a culture of slavery, but no communities enjoyed the victory more than black communities. Mainstream journalists, on the other hand, struggled to interpret his election, his historic and symbolic meaning, his policies and how they connected to the black community (if at all), and his *immediate* opposition, best represented by the tea party. The modern tea party was first reported in white media five weeks after President Obama's inauguration. Comprised mostly of whites, the tea party, with intense hostility and aggression, opposed virtually all policies the infant administration proposed.

From the inception of slavery, to the three-fifths compromise (legislation that considered slaves and free African Americans as only three-fifths of a person), to the civil war, to Jim Crow, to World War I and II, Vietnam, and civil rights, some voices have always insisted that race is not a significant consideration in the oppression of African Americans or the marginalization of their perspectives.[21] Some scholars and opinion leaders, in that same vein of logic, have argued that the tea party narrative is devoid of any racial undercurrents, insisting the group reflects a devotion to conservative ideology.[22] These voices struggle to explain race when it does emerge in the tea party narrative. For instance, one tea party pundit, on a blog, referred to black congressman and presidential candidate Herman Cain as a runaway slave. "I keep having images of Herman Cain barefoot, covered in sweat and mud, wearing an old patchwork shirt and hand-made burlap pants held up by a rope rather than a belt, out of breath and frantically running for his life."[23]

Initially, mainstream newspapers weren't convinced the tea party questioned equality values and hopes. Instead, they suggested protest was a core American value. An article in the *Virginia-Pilot* highlighted how not all press outlets criticized, or delegitimized, the tea party, "during this spring's anti-tax 'tea party' demonstrations, Goldberg said he found many network's coverage disgraceful. But he was also critical of Fox, which he said, 'didn't simply cover the Tea Parties, they championed them.'"[24]

The *Post and Courier* asserted, "the gist of President Barack Obama's proposed health care reform is the promise that by spending another trillion dollars over the next decade, the nation can bring down the future costs of health care that threaten to break the federal budget."[25] The *Palm Beach Post* argued, "they are very mission-driven and have very strong values combined with good business sense"[26] and the *Contra Costa Times* opined, "he's poisoned the well with Republicans who are disinclined to sign on to anything big, and he may have ruined his health-care brand."[27] An emergent theme of mainstream newspaper stories was a rationale attempt to justify the group's existence because anti-spending and anti-tax dissent does not question American norms and values. One could reasonably argue anti-tax and anti-spending values are sacred in American society, pervading the culture since, at least, the nation's founding. At the time, white newspapers were missing a much larger point salient to diversity issues in a pluralistic society: impact outweighs intent. Many white news narratives then followed interpreting the tea party as a group of "thousands" gathered for "disruptive, irrational, threatening" purposes. This narrative packaging began to infer the tea party was not a legitimate dissenting voice, but a horde of upset, irrational individuals, again, focusing on intent and ignoring the impact of their platform.

For instance, an article titled "Tea Party Protestors Stir Things Up; Thousands Turn Out in Albuquerque," stated:

> Several thousand people brandishing signs and carrying tea bags jammed a long Albuquerque boulevard on Wednesday as Americans protesting federal government tax and spending policies conducted tea parties across the country. . . . Traffic slowed to a crawl and some drivers—clearly fewer than those honking in approval—jeered at the demonstrators.[28]

The *State* commented, "[the] experience [that] came to mind as I watched news coverage of the vigorous, shrill and angry protests," as "I hear one news commentator say that she'd never before seen such a disruptive, irrational, threatening and rude behavior," is "the 2008 presidential campaign where McCain/Palin rallies almost became mob scenes and when so many of their rowdy and angry supporters responded to . . . Obama with shouts of 'terrorist' and 'kill him.'"[29] The *Kansas City Star* correlated, "fear is the most powerful enemy of reason. Both fear and reason are essential to human survival, but the relationship is unbalance. Reason may sometimes dissipate fear, but fear frequently shuts down reason."[30]

One headline for the *Connecticut Post* read, "Rabble-Rousers Target Himes' Town Hall Meetings." Protestors were not narrated as concerned citizens deliberating about legitimate policy concerns, but as "rabble-rousers." The same article continued:

> Audience members at a series of recent town hall meetings . . . have developed a playbook of their own, scripting a series of offensive plays designed to get the freshman congressman back on his heels on topics such as government spending and his support of a public option for health care reform . . . there's clearly sort of a movement nationally to be very aggressive . . . many agitators across the nation are spreading myths . . . this discussion about death panels and the public option is ridiculous. . . . You need to rock the boat early in the rep's presentation the memo said. Watch for an opportunity to yell out and challenge . . . early.[31]

The *Lowell Sun* highlighted the antagonist "party puppet" package with an article titled, "GOP Wants To Attack, Not Help," noting, "and disruption by right-wing hooligans of town-hall meetings" have not added useful information in the health care discourse, it has hurt and held back efforts to improve the country.[32] The *Chico Enterprise-Record* took this package one step further. The article described a town hall meeting where one participant described himself as "a proud right-wing terrorist."[33] Congressman Wally Herger of Chico replied, "Amen. God bless you. There is a great American." The article continued, saying the incident had found its way onto cable news channels, resonating with the public. Why claiming proudly to be a terrorist would resonate with the public wasn't asked. The man said it was a blunder, "he mistakenly said right-wing terrorist, instead of 'right-wing extremist.'"[34]

Some began to question the tea party's true motivations. For instance, former President Jimmy Carter, in the *Washington Post*, said:

> I think an overwhelming portion of the intensely demonstrated animosity toward President Barack Obama is based on the fact that he is a black man, that he's African American. I live in the South, and I've seen the South come a long way, and I've seen the rest of the country that shared the South's attitude toward minority groups at that time, particularly African Americans. And that racism inclination still exists. And I think it's bubbled up to the surface because of the belief among white people, not just in the South but around the

country, that African Americans are not qualified to lead this great country. It's an abominable circumstance, and it grieves me and concerns me very deeply.[35]

History supports the assertion race, knowingly or not, is a significant factor in the tea party narrative. A dissenting group, comprised primarily of whites, typically forms following the election of the first African American to a political office.[36] The groups' main goals, usually, are to oppose the newly elected officials' policies and thwart their reelections.[37] This is not to imply all groups who oppose black officials are racists, a massive oversimplification. We are interested in better understanding how all of these different components and layers fit together. How did journalists, both for the black press and the mainstream press, interpret the tea party? How did journalists disentangle and highlight the racial undercurrents of the policies the tea party opposed, the historical precedents, President Obama's symbolic representation, the nature of politics, and conflicts with ideology? How did journalists implicitly frame race while designing the arc of the tea party narrative, if at all?

With all these facets considered, one may reasonably argue constructing the tea party's anti-Obama story was challenging for any intuitive journalist, regardless of whether the journalist writes for the black press or the mainstream press. One of the professed requirements for journalism's storytelling art, even in different types of presses with different missions, is to interpret reality as accurately as possible. White media have a poor record of accurately interpreting race in the United States, a major catalyst for black newspapers forming; while the two tell different sides to the stories, they are tethered to each other by their profession.[38]

Stuart Hall identified the restless native framework as a historically consistent way mainstream journalists cover issues salient to black communities. Through this model, mainstream journalists portray blacks as a massive horde out to destroy white, innocent ideologies.[39] The black community is usually narrated as "other," with that other undesirable, less than, abnormal, and menacing.[40] To counter this framework, the black press works tirelessly to humanize their readers, their voices, their communities, their issues, and their stories; they tried to overcome the "other" stereotype and present people simply trying to enjoy the same freedoms so many whites take for granted.

Research on how the mainstream press[41] covered the inception of the tea party found that journalists cautiously debated and highlighted the possibility race may have been a key component in a mass of whites aggregating in fear of a black president, but the mainstream newspapers never conclusively stated it.[42] The initial tea party narratives somewhat inverted the restless native framework—whites were the wave of hostility seeking to demolish black ideologies being disseminated on a national stage by President Obama.[43]

Following the on-air "rant" of Rick Santelli, a broadcast commentator for CNBC, newspapers reported tea parties began meeting in February 2009. White newspapers interpreted the group negatively as uneducated hooligans who may have been motivated by racial prejudice, rarely as legitimately concerned citizens voicing constructive dissent, and never focusing on how their proposed policies, if they proposed any at all, would disproportionately marginalize black communities.[44] Mainstream newspapers continued debating the racial nature of the tea party during the health care reform debate highly visible in 2009.[45] For instance, one commentary described the tea party as a group of individuals terrified by the potential financial burdens resulting from health care reform. "Forget intent. . . . It's so easy to lie about that. . . . Health insurance reforms as applied to our present situation are where the scrutiny should be. I think the American people who are showing up at the town hall and tea parties realize that."[46]

Unconvinced of this interpretation, a *Palm Beach Post* reporter, highlighting the racial nature of tea party dissent, interviewed individuals on their thoughts about the tea party. The following was one response:

> "Sometimes it bothers me when the word civility comes up," said Brownstein, who said people on "the other side . . . are not civil to us." . . . Brownstein, who is White, said "White Southerners in this country are going nuts" because of the popularity of Black figures such as Obama and Oprah Winfrey. He said he raised the issue because "you have to know who your enemy is." . . . "The foundation of all of this is racism."[47]

Many voices existed during the debate examining the weight of the tea party's racially driven motivations. Initially, mainstream journalists interpreted race, ideology, and the nature of politics during the tea party's first three months without relying on the "zero-sum" traditionally used to tell race-related stories.[48] The coverage of the tea party was negative, but not because they posed threats to equality or because they were echoing oppressive white ideologies haunting US history books.

Instead, mainstream newspapers interpreted tea partiers pessimistically because they were perceived as excessively hostile, uneducated, and Republican pawns. The black press viewed the hostility aimed at President Obama as anger towards those who elected him, towards the step towards equality his administration symbolized, and towards non-hegemonic ideologies valuing diversity. Mainstream newspaper coverage reflected the belief the tea party symbolized continued conservatism discourse and race played a minimal role in their organization.[49] During 2010, the racial component of the tea party subsided in mainstream newspaper coverage as the group's traction increased. Race was almost entirely excluded from the narrative as a possible variable, but impact on race never stopped being an important variable for the black press. Tea partiers still were classified as extremist hooligans in the mainstream press, but the racial nature of their polarizing perspectives rarely emerged in those newspapers.[50] For instance, mainstream newspapers focused much of their tea party coverage on Sarah Palin and her power of backing candidates for the midterms.

Leading up to the 2010 midterms, Palin was immediately seen by many mainstream pundits as an intriguing and powerful force. *Time Magazine* wrote: "Sarah Palin has arrived in our midst with the force of a rocket-propelled grenade. . . . Our fascination with her—and it is a nonpartisan phenomenon—is driven by something more primal . . . Palin . . . illuminates the mythic power of the Republican Party's message."[51] During the midterms, the *Washington Times* offered: "In the most stunning results of the midterm season . . . Christine O'Donnell, backed with endorsements from tea party activists and former Alaska Gov. Sarah Palin, became the latest 'outsider' candidate to knock off an establishment-backed Republican."[52] Through their coverage of Palin's influential endorsements of unknown "outsiders" (or rogues), newspapers began crafting the de facto leader of the tea party's dissenting voice as a powerful rebellious Republican. Receiving an endorsement from the "Queen of the Tea Party," the "conservative superstar," could "catapult" the candidates "to the national stage."[53] These narratives afforded Palin a great deal of tea party influence and were, for the most part, devoid of discussions on how the policies Palin's picks proposed negatively impacted minorities. This was surprising because the 2010 midterm elections were an opportunity for mainstream journalists to interpret the tea party as an institutional challenge to racial solidarity, black political representation, and a stride towards equality. Instead, journalists returned to historical habits and ignored the racial components, and the black voices expressing them, of the tea party. Diverse newspapers such as the black press are still very much needed to amplify the perspectives of their communities often ignored by the mainstream media and marginalized by politics for a pluralistic society to function in an effective and equal manner.

The initial mainstream press coverage of the tea party was possibly an aberration. The early tea party narratives simultaneously highlighted suspicions of racially driven motivations and the ideological clash between autonomy and perceived handouts of resource allocations designed to level a playing field that, historically, favored whites and oppressed blacks.[54] This was a serious historical deviation from mainstream narratives of race nearly always presenting this type of discourse as zero-sum conflicts.[55] Given the mainstream press has done little, if anything, since civil rights to positively form a racial comity voice,[56] the answer might seem, yes, the initial mainstream tea party coverage was an aberration. This would seem to justify why the press ignored highlighting the racial component of the narrative in 2010. Or, was the coverage a positive societal marker? Had society progressed at that point groups motivated by or suspected of racial prejudice were no longer socially accepted voices? We argue if that happened, it didn't last long based on the 2016 presidential election outcome. The election of President Obama changed many whites' attitudes negatively towards issues salient to black communities.[57] Overt white supremacist ideologies, previously publicly scorned by many and somewhat lingering in hushed corners but still inferentially prevalent in many institutions, reacted quite strongly to President Obama's election. If the social desirability concept of priming is accurate, then it would seem logical for a more egalitarian mainstream press to emerge as well, theoretically resisting the re-normalizing of overt white supremacist ideologies.[58] But, *how would we know if/when the mainstream press in fact became more egalitarian and resisted*?

One possibility is mainstream newspapers' coverage of the racial nature of the tea party subsided because the discourse became more implicit.[59] Identified early as a group possibly motivated by race, the group's appeals became much more implicit in order to not entirely be rejected. This correlates with the formation of most groups aspiring to be social movements. During the infant stages of movements, the groups deliberately and explicitly demonstrate and protest aggressively because they know in journalism "what bleeds leads," acts of hostility and violence tend to dominate news coverage because that is what sells, and more media attention usually means more members for advocacy groups. As the group broadens its umbrella, attracting more people with different points of view, the aggressive nature of the movement sometimes dissipates as the dissenting group, now a recognizable brand, can offer constructive discursive input to more receptive ears aimed at achieving the group's goals. As the group becomes larger and more sustainable, it appeals to less polemic constituents and no longer needs to behave aggressively to attract media attention.[60] In other words, they recognized their ideas marginalizing others attracted media attention, so they became better at disguising that layer of their group. Mainstream journalism is not equipped or informed enough to sift through the costume; the black press has much experience in this area.

Understanding the relationships between media and protest groups "have come to be regarded, alongside resource mobilization and political opportunity processes, as a central dynamic in understanding the character" of social life in a representative democracy.[61] The first premise essential to exploring these relationships is that journalism is an occupation full of habits and traditions formed during a time when assimilation to white ideology was the preferred social model.[62] The second is recognizing protest groups and social movements tend to use these traditions to their advantage, as do political figures.[63] Mainstream newspapers' ritualistic reliance on objectivity grants political figures, dissenting groups, and social movements the ability to use the media as a public relations arm.[64] Thus, we can expect racially coded messages in the media to become more implicit as the narrative progresses.

To complicate President Obama's first-term narrative even further, digital media emerged as a new way of life journalists could no longer ignore or discount as a fad. Few, if any, doubt digital media play an important role in the intersections of race, politics, media storytelling, and the processes of governing.[65] "The communication channels [and] the nature of a social system, such as its norms, and the degree to which the communication network structure is highly interconnected" affects how quickly ideas are adopted.[66] If dissenting deliberation contributes to a healthy democracy,[67] and mainstream media (political institutions) narrowly define issues to only two polemic perspectives due to the "strategic ritual of objectivity,"[68] then digital media ideally, at its best, should provide platforms for more diverse deliberation, contributing to a more liberal society. This ideal hasn't materialized to the extent many had hoped as digital media, like other platforms, are, for many individuals, echo chambers.

The construction of the tea party narrative, then, was especially crucial to a democracy hoping to escape its history of slavery and oppression.[69] After reelecting President Obama to a second term on November 6, 2012, scholarly questions remained about the role[s] digital media play in engendering black political representation at national levels. Did President Obama's two terms accidentally coincide with our storytellers' new media adoptions? What did digital news coverage of President Obama's white adversaries say about a changing media landscape and a possibly changing society?

NOTES

1. Tali Mendelberg, *The Race Card: Campaign Strategy, Implicit Messages, and the Norm of Equality* (Princeton, NJ: Princeton University Press, 2001).

2. *Chicago Defender,* "Sorry About the Birth Certificate." Accessed July 30, 2017. https://chicagodefender.com/2011/05/03/sorry-about-the-birth-certificate-i-rsquo-ve-been-hunting-osama/.

3. Teresa Mastin, Shelly Campo, and M. Somjen Frazer, "In Black and White: Coverage of U.S. Slave Reparations by the Mainstream and Black Press," *Howard Journal of Communications* 16, no. 3 (2005): 201–223.

4. Mark Dolan, John Sonnett, and Kirk Johnson, "Katrina Coverage in Black Newspapers Critical of Government, Mainstream Media,." *Newspaper Research Journal* 30 (2009): 34.

5. Dolan et al., "Katrina Coverage in Black Newspapers," 34.

6. Jinx Broussard, *African American Foreign Correspondents: A History* (Baton Rouge, LA: Louisiana State University Press, 2013). Jinx Broussard, *Giving a Voice to the Voiceless: Four Pioneering Black Women Journalists* (London, England: Psychology Press, 2004). Dolan et al., "Katrina Coverage in Black Newspapers." Rosalee Clawson, C. Harry, and Eric N. Waltenburg, "Framing Supreme Court Decisions: The Mainstream Versus the Black Press," *Journal of Black Studies* 33, no. 6 (2003): 784–800. Mastin et al., "In Black and White."

7. Dolan et al., "Katrina Coverage in Black Newspapers."

8. Mastin et al., "In Black and White."

9. Ibid.

10. Ibid., 216.

11. Dolan et al., "Katrina Coverage in Black Newspapers."

12. Clawson et al., "Framing Supreme Court Decisions."

13. Ibid., 794.

14. Ibid., 796.

15. Timothy Cook, *Governing With the News: The News Media as a Political Institution* (Chicago, IL: University of Chicago Press, 1998): 5.

16. Benjamin LaPoe, *Gender and Racial cues During the 2008 Democratic Party's Presidential Candidate Nomination Process: Social Responsibility in the 21st Century* (Ann Arbor, MI: ProQuest, 2008).

17. Charlton McIlwain, "Race for America 2008: Breaking Through on a Different Track," *Qualitative Sociology* 35, no. 2 (2012): 229–235.

18. Raphael Sonenshein, "Can Black Candidates Win Statewide Elections?" *Political Science Quarterly* 105, no. 2 (1990): 219–241.

19. Carol Swain, *Black Faces, Black Interests: The Representation of African Americans in Congress* (New York, NY: University Press of America, 2006). Lawrence Hanks, *The Struggle for Black Political Empowerment in Three Georgia Counties* (Knoxville, TN: University of Tennessee Press, 1987). Charlton McIlwain and Stephen M. Caliendo, *Race Appeal: How Candidates Invoke Race in U.S. Political Campaigns* (Philadelphia, PA: Temple University Press, 2011).

20. *Chicago Defender*, "Barack Obama sweeps to victory: First Black U.S. President," *Chicago Defender*, October 18, 2011. Accessed November 5, 2015. http://chicagodefender.com/2008/11/04/barack-obama-sweeps-to-victory-first-black-u-s-president/.

21. William Sloan, *The Media in America: A History* (Hammond, IN: Publishing Horizons, 1993). Enoch Waters, *American Diary: A Personal History of the Black Press* (Chicago, IL: Path Press, 1987). Steven Mintz, *African American Voices: A Documentary Reader* (Hoboken, NJ: Wiley-Blackwell, 2009). Carl Senna, *The Black Press and the Struggle for Civil Rights* (New York, NY: F. Watts, 1993).

22. Vanessa Williamson, Theda Skocpol, and John Coggin, *The Tea Party and the Remaking of Republican Conservatism* (New York, NY: Oxford University Press, 2011). Chris Karpowitz, J. Quin Monson, Kelly D. Patterson, and Jeremy C. Pope, "Tea Time in America? The Impact of the Tea Party Movement on the 2010 Midterm Elections," *Political Science and Politics* 44, no. 2 (2011): 303.

23. Lloyd Marcus, "Herman Cain: Runaway Slave," Tea Party Nation, October 18, 2011. Accessed January 5, 2012. http://www.teapartynation.com/profiles/blog/show?id=3355873%3A BlogPost%3A1568547&xgs=1&xg_source=msg_share_post.

24. "Fox News Flourishes in the Age of Obama," *Virginia-Pilot*, August 18, 2009, E-5.

25. "Better Ideas for Health Care Option," *Post and Courier*, August 18, 2009, A-10.

26. "Options are Public or Profit," *Palm Beach Post*, August 19, 2009, 10A.

27. Rich Lowry, "Obama's Option Play May be Too Little Too Late," *Contra Coast Times*, August 19, 2009, Opinion.

28. Dan Boyd, "Tea Party Protestors Stir Things Up," *Albuquerque Journal*, April 16, 2009, A1.

29. "Protests are About Obama, Not Health Care," the *State*, August 18, 2009, A-0.

30. "Lacking Facts and Reason, Health Care Foes Use Fear," *Kansas City Star*, August 18, 2009, A-11.

31. Neil Vigdor, "Rabble-Rousers Target Himes' Town Hall Meetings," *Connecticut Post*, August 18, 2009.

32. "GOP Wants to Attack, Not Help," *Lowell Sun*, August 23, 2009, Editorial.

33. Larry Mitchell, "TV Dust Up Could Cost Herger His Obscurity," *Chico-Enterprise Record*, August 26, 2009, Local.

34. Ibid.

35. Garance Franke-Ruta, "Carter Cites Racism Inclination in Animosity Toward Obama," *Washington Post*, September 16, 2009. Accessed May 15, 2010. http://voices.washingtonpost.com/44/2009/09/15/carter_cites_racism_inclinatio.html.

36. Swain, *Black Voices, Black Interests*. Hanks, *Black Political Empowerment*.

37. Ibid.

38. Keith Reeves, *Voting Hopes or Fears?: White Voters, Black Candidates & Racial Politics in America* (New York, NY: Oxford University Press, 1997). Jannette Dates and William Barlow, *Split Image: African Americans in the Mass Media* (Washington, DC: Howard University Press, 1993). Gail Dines and Jean M. Humez, *Gender, Race, and Class in Media: A Text-Reader* (Thousand Oaks, CA: Sage Publications, Incorporated, 2002). Beverly Keever, Carolyn Martindale, and Mary Ann Weston, *U.S. News Coverage of Racial Minorities: A Sourcebook, 1934–1996* (Westport, CT: Greenwood Press, 1997). Robert Entman and Andrew Rojecki, *The Black Image in the White Mind: Media and Race in America* (Chicago, IL: University of Chicago Press, 2001).

39. Ibid.

40. Ibid.

41. Black press research defines mainstream newspapers as those that are not minority media, regardless of their partisan and ideological leanings.

42. Ben LaPoe and Jinx Broussard, "Tea Party Trickster Resonates the 2010 Midterm Elections: Newspapers' Crafting of the Palin Myth." Paper presented at the 2012 Southern Political Science Association annual conference in New Orleans, Political Communication Division.

43. Ben LaPoe, "Crafting the Narrative of Tea Party Dissent: Unpacking Cultural Resonance, Myth, and Black Political Empowerment." Paper presented at the 2011 NCA annual conference in New Orleans, Political Communication Division.

44. Ibid.

45. Ben LaPoe, "Death in the American Family: Framing of Health Care Reform After Senator Edward Kennedy's Death." Paper presented at the 2010 AEJMC annual conference in Denver, Mass Communication and Society Division. LaPoe, "Crafting the Narrative of Tea Party Dissent."

46. "Reform as Intended," *Washington Times,* August 18, 2009. Accessed February 12, 2011. http://www.washingtontimes.com/news/2009/aug/18/reform-as-intended/.

47. George Bennett, "Coffee Party Debuts in West Palm Beach as Anti Tea Party," *Palm Beach Post,* March 13, 2010. Accessed May 24, 2010. http://www.palmbeachpost.com/news/news/state-regional/coffee-party-debuts-in-west-palm-beach-as-anti-tea/nL5Pr/.

48. Entman and Rojecki, *Black Image in the White Mind.* LaPoe, "Crafting the Narrative of Tea Party Dissent."

49. Williamson et al., *The Tea Party and the Remaking of Republican Conservatism.* Karpowitz et al, "Tea Time in America?"

50. LaPoe and Broussard, "Tea Party Trickster."

51. "Sarah Palin's Myth of America," *Time Magazine,* 2008. Accessed October 20, 2010. http://www.time.com/time/politics/article/0,8599,1840388,00.html.

52. "Tea Party Favorite Storms Castle in Delaware Primary; O'Donnell Latest 'Outsider' to Defeat GOP Establishment," *Washington Times,* September 15, 2010, A1.

53. "Who's Who in the Tea Party," *Ottawa Citizen,* November 3, 2010, A7.

54. LaPoe, "Crafting the Narrative of Tea Party Dissent."

55. Entman and Rojecki, *Black Image in the White Mind.* Stuart Hall, "Racist Ideologies and the Media," *Media Studies: A Reader* (2000): 271–282.

56. Entman and Rojecki, *Black Image in the White Mind.* Christopher Campbell, *Race and News: Critical Perspectives* (New York, NY: Routledge, 2012). Reeves, *Voting Hopes or Fears.* Dates and Barlow, *Split Image.*

57. Seth K. Goldman and Diana C. Mutz, *The Obama Effect: How the 2008 Campaign Changed White Racial Attitudes* (New York, NY: Russell Sage Foundation, 2014). Tali Mendelberg, *The Race Card: Campaign Strategy, Implicit Messages, and the Norm of Equality* (Princeton, NJ: Princeton University Press, 2001).

58. Fred Seaton Siebert, Theodore Peterson, and Wilbur Schramm, *Four Theories of the Press: The Authoritarian, Libertarian, Social Responsibility, and Soviet Communist Concepts of What the Press Should Be and Do* (Champaign, IL: University of Illinois Press, 1956).

59. Mendelberg, *The Race Card.*

60. Walter Reich, *Origins of Terrorism: Psychologies: Ideologies, Theologies, State of Mind* (Washington, DC: Woodrow Wilson Center Press, 1998).

61. Robert Benford and David A. Snow, "Framing Processes and Social Movements: An Overview and Assessment," *Annual Review of Sociology* (2000): 611.

62. Michael Schudson, *The Sociology of News* (New York, NY: Norton, 2003).

63. Benford and Snow, "Framing Processes." Jeroen Van Laer and Peter Van Aelst, "Cyber-Protest and Civil Society: The Internet and Action Repertoires in Social Movements," *Handbook of Internet Crime* (2009): 230–254. Mitch Berbrier, "Half the Battle": Cultural Resonance, Framing Processes, and Ethnic Affectations in Contemporary White Separatist Rhetoric," *Social Problems* (1998): 431–450. Lance Bennett, Regina Lawrence, and Steven Livingston, *When the Press Fails* (Chicago, IL: University of Chicago Press, 2007). Gaye Tuchman, *Making News: A Study in the Construction of Reality* (New York, NY: Free Press, 1978).

64. Cook, *Governing With the News*. Timothy Cook, "The News Media as a Political Institution: Looking Backward and Looking Forward," *Political Communication* 23, no. 2 (2006): 159–171.

65. Timothy Cook, *Governing With the News: The News Media as a Political Institution* (Chicago, IL: University of Chicago Press, 1998). George Rodman, *Mass Media in a Changing World* (New York, NY: McGraw-Hill, 2010). Evgeny Morozov, *The Net Delusion: The Dark Side of Internet Freedom* (New York, NY: PublicAffairs, 2012).

66. Everett Rogers, *Diffusion of Innovations* (New York, NY: Free Press, 2003), 222.

67. Diana Mutz, *Hearing the Other Side: Deliberative Versus Participatory Democracy* (Cambridge, England: Cambridge University Press, 2006).

68. Gaye Tuchman, *Making News: A Study in the Construction of Reality* (New York, NY: Free Press, 1978).

69. Beverly Keever, Carolyn Martindale, and Mary Ann Weston, *U.S. News Coverage of Racial Minorities: A Sourcebook, 1934–1996* (Westport, CT: Greenwood Press, 1997).

Chapter One

Black Press and Resonant Myths

Journalists, through storytelling, are part of an interpretative community that helps shape, build, and reflect cultural realities.[1] Diverse news like the black press are still needed and essential for a pluralistic democracy. "The press always takes on the form and coloration of the social and political structures within which it operates."[2] A variety of forces impact this process, such as indexing, ideology, sourcing, norms and routines, profit, government regulations, and technology, among others.[3] While all of these factors are significant, this book examines the storytelling process through a cultural lens. This book is significant because framing studies show thematic stories exhibit longer-lasting effects than episodic stories.[4] Thus, studying how journalists convert episodic events into thematic narratives is important. To our knowledge, little or no research exists investigating resonant myth and implicit racial frames in the digital black press.

Intellectual W. E. B. Du Bois wrote, "It is a peculiar sensation this double consciousness, this sense of always looking at one's self through the eyes of others, of measuring one's soul by the tape of a world that looks on in amused contempt and pity."[5] The double consciousness Du Bois described intuitively helps explain a driving force of the black press. Du Bois argued black newspapers were necessary because African Americans had a dual-identity whites could not understand. Blacks were (in no intended order): (A) Americans and (B) African Americans in a white America. Mainstream media, owned and controlled by whites, are not, nor have they ever been, prepared to interpret and represent black realities, experiences, stories, and issues with accurate perspectives because of dominant white ideologies.

Dominant white ideologies began appearing in the territory currently labeled the United States when the demographics began of the area shifted in the 1600s from Native American to predominantly White Anglo-Saxon Protestant Europeans (WASP).[6] Early in the twentieth century, southern and eastern European immigrants "challenged the nation's WASP identity . . . and led to the vision of the United States as a melting pot society in which newcomers became Anglo Americans by shedding the culture, language, foods, and identities of their homelands and ancestors."[7] During this time, assimilation wasn't as challenging for southern and eastern Europeans as it was for nonwhite groups because they could physically blend in, providing time and space for them to abandon their ancestors' traditions, norms, and values and acquire WASP customs.

Many nonwhites were not able or permitted to assimilate because of their "other," physical, characteristics. From this experience derived the "stew pot," or "salad bowl," experience. In this philosophy, each individual and group retains their identity while contributing nuanced diversity to society— an important principle driving the notion of pluralism, a concept more aligned with the individualistic nature of the Unites States' aspirations than the melting pot/assimilation model. The expectation of assimilation remained in many white ideologies and values supporting those perspective lenses.

Two religious beliefs helped form early whiteness:

> First was the Anglo-Saxon belief that the color white represented things that were pure, clean, good, and reflective of the spiritual light. The color black, on the other hand, represented impurity, filth, evil, and spiritual darkness. Both concepts persist to this day. Second, the Puritan concept of predestination relied upon observation to distinguish the "elect" from the "damned." Those who seemed relatively prosperous and self-sufficient were deemed superior to those who were enslaved. Against this religiously seated and strongly held attitude the posture of the English colonists towards Blacks in the New World is predictable even among inhabitants of the Northern seaboard. In fact, trading of slaves was the predominant commodity on New York's Wall Street into the 1700s partly because Puritan law was ambiguous on the subject.[8]

"Racism and the media touches directly the problem of ideology since the media's main sphere of operations is the production and transformation of ideologies."[9] Media's interventions and construction of race is a mediation of racial friction in the United States. By ideology, we mean "those images, concepts, and premises which provide the frameworks, through which we represent, interpret, understand, and make sense of some aspect of social existence."[10] Mediated communications are the primary medium where differing ideologies conflict. Collaborations of meaning define an ideology instead of secluded and segregated beliefs. While ideological statements may be voiced by individuals, ideologies are not produced by "individual consciousness or intention."[11] Instead, ideologies inform intent. "They pre-date individuals, and form part of the determinate, social formations and conditions in which individuals are born."[12]

Ideologies engender diverse styles of "social consciousness:"[13]

> Ideologies work by constructing for their subjects (individual and collective) positions of identification and knowledge which allow them to utter ideological truths as if they were their authentic authors. . . . In modern societies, the different media are especially important sites for the production, reproduction, and transformations of ideologies. . . . What they produce is, precisely, representations of the social world, images, descriptions, explanations, and frames for understanding . . . the media construct for us a definition of what race is, what meaning the imagery of race carries, and what the "problem of race" is understood to be. . . . Overt racism . . . mean those many occasions when open and favorable coverage is given to arguments, positions and spokespersons who are in the business of elaborating an openly racist argument or advancing a racist policy or view. . . . Inferential racism . . . mean those apparently naturalized representations of events and situations relating to race, whether "factual" or "fictional," which have racist premises and propositions inscribed in them as a set of unquestioned assumptions.[14]

One essential storytelling ingredient in the ideology expression and building calculus is resonant myth. Resonant myths, interpretive frameworks reliant on archetypal figures, endured countless changes in storytelling platforms, the most recent being the emergence of digital media. Therefore, as scholars struggle to accurately predict what media environment will emerge in the future as a result of new technologies and a changing field, it is intuitive to use resonant myth, one of the few narrative devices not fickle to emerging technologies, as a conceptual framework to analyze the texts created by journalists as they attempt to maintain their profession and distinguish themselves from citizens who have access to the same technologies.

Resonant myths culturally inform journalists, helping convert episodic events into truthful, thematic narratives. Journalists, as both societal members and shapers, instinctively use lasting explanatory models (myths) that resonate with them and their audiences in order to mediate reality. Resonant myths are not inaccurate descriptions or unfounded stereotypes; instead, myths are sacred stories, sustained by archetypical figures over geographic space, time, and societies, dating back at least to the days of Homer. Journalists apply resonant myths subconsciously as they build meaning in an increasingly eclectic world.[15] Media images and texts serve as a structure of knowledge participating in the ritual of crafting an "ordered world" for society. Ideally, journalists' contributions to this process provide accurate accounts of reality's occurrences for the public. But journalists, more often than not, don't operate in an ideal world. For instance, Dan Berkowitz wrote:

> Although the profession of journalism is founded upon an ideology of objectivity that believes in the discovery of existent truths, in practice, journalists learn to polarize an issue and define its parameters to facilitate their accom-

plishment of work. In essence, news is framed rather than reported freshly, so that information from news occurrences is quickly transposed onto a story framework known in advance—even before an occurrence has taken place. [16]

Resonant myth couples two qualitative concepts, cultural resonance and myth. Cultural resonance argues journalists produce texts echoing society's ideologies; research can gain insights into what audiences value by examining the products a for-profit media system produces for society. [17] Myth conceptually posits journalists instinctively use interpretative mythological templates reliant on archetypes, in existence in societies across space and time since the days of Homer, to mediate and make sense of a multifaceted, subjective, socially constructed reality. [18] Thus, resonant myth proposes journalists, in deciphering a complex reality, use interpretative templates (myth) reverberating with the society they are interpreting (resonance). "As both a part of their culture and as storytellers for that culture, journalists construct stories through narrative conventions [myth] that are culturally resonant for themselves and for their audiences." [19]

Resonant myth explains the embedded meanings and undercurrents of "communication-as-culture" texts. [20] Because scholars posit news aspires to reflect reality through frames [21] "that emphasize certain facts while suppressing others" and consequently "promote certain political and moral evaluations while hindering others," then, media frames "must *resonate* with what writers and readers take to be real and important." [22] Resonance symbolizes an artifact of significance evoking, or amplifying, a strong emotion or association. [23] Because media texts are part of an associated, sharing, fellowship among members of society whose voices participate in creating culture, resonant myth perspectives provide insights into what values and beliefs are supporting society's ideologies. [24] This is important because "ultimately, what is really at stake—for presidential candidates and protest groups . . . is what the news said" and "the language of news is what matters." [25] Exploring these cultural frames and the meaning tethered to the evoked symbols provides a nuanced perspective into the holographic pictures of society's race relations via politically oriented communication and the press. [26]

On resonant myth, Jack Lule wrote:

> Myth is not unreality. Myth is not a false belief. Myth is not an untrue tale . . . myth is . . . a sacred, societal story that draws from archetypal figures and forms to offer exemplary models for human life. . . . Myths . . . play crucial social roles. . . . It sees myth—and . . . news—as an important way a society expresses its prevailing ideals, ideologies, values and beliefs. [27]

Lule identified seven master myths: the victim, the scapegoat, the hero, the good mother, the trickster, the other world, and the flood. The victim sacrifices, usually without consent, a great deal and endures the tragedy in an almost heroic-like way. This myth is used most often when confronting death, extreme tragedies, and loss. The use of the scapegoat is normally used as an attempt to degrade a political leader, narrated as very combustible, who is perceived as extreme. The figure is used as an example of what happens to leaders and dissenters when they deviate too greatly from society's norms. On the scapegoat:

> If news is only a dispassionate observer and reporter of political events, coverage of radical groups . . . should be interesting but relatively straightforward. The political protest should provide some debatable issues for a story. The passion should contribute some provocative emotion. The conflict should make for dramatic narratives. Radical thinkers should make for thoughtful news. If news is myth [if a group is a scapegoat], however, coverage of radical groups should be much more combustible and complex.[28]

The hero is one of the more popular and enduring myths. The figure personifies culture's core values and beliefs, frequently in the face of overwhelming challenges normally causing other figures to abandon their values. The hero is humble, initiates a quest, wins battle decisively, and returns as triumphant.[29] The good mother is a figure of nurturing virtue, kindness, and generosity. This maternal figure is always willing to sacrifice for the good of her children as she "oversees the passage from this life to the next."[30]

The trickster is a complex figure, blatantly mocked and narrated as a "crude and lewd moralist" serving as a "model illustrating the necessity for societal rules."[31] This figure is similar to the scapegoat because it highlights why rules are necessary and what happens when those rules aren't obeyed. However, unlike the scapegoat, whose fall happens during a climatic event, the trickster's undoing is in a continual state of ruin.

The other-world myth shows how society views foreign lands. Two models exist, the land of delights and a land of barbarians. The land of delights narrates a distant society as a type of utopia; the utopic land is used as a way of expressing discontent with societal issues at home. The land of barbarians is a narrative of the distant society as immensely inferior to home, populated with savages out to devour "good" ideologies. This is a way to express relative peace at home. The flood is a myth of disaster. The story is one of devastation inflicted upon society by the universe. Society is helpless against forces crushing it for reasons unknown to them and out of their control.[32]

All of these myths have inverses as well. For every hero there is a villain; for every good mother there is a bad mother; for every scapegoat there is a model citizen; for every other world there is a familiar world; for every flood there is a drought. The myths Lule identified are not the only ones. For instance, Stuart Hall highlighted the restless native myth as a model typically used by mainstream journalists portraying nonwhites as a massive, hostile horde desiring to figuratively consume whites. Christopher Campbell discussed the myth of assimilation as a framework where the only way the "others," nonwhites, can function in society is to behave like whites even though they will never be treated as equals.[33] What myths resonate with journalists and audiences elaborate dominant ideologies; what myths they choose not to use, tells us what ideologies are interpreted as less important.[34] By examining what myths journalists use to narrate certain events, we can understand the language used to convert those events into broader cultural themes. "Whether we are experiencing the world through a lens of speech or the printed word or the television camera, our media metaphors classify the world for us, sequence it, frame it, enlarge it, reduce it, color it."[35] Digital news stories provide a unique environment to examine how journalists use resonant because digital platforms encourage journalists to harness collective resonance.

Digital media increase access to diverse views and communities typically ignored but digital media also encourage groups associated with aggressive white supremacy—hate groups.[36] White supremacists in post–Civil War eras "drew on discontent rooted in political fundamentalism and the fear of abdication of power to non-whites," comparable to today's "white nationalist" label.[37]

> Extremists and hate mongrels use the Internet to access a potential audience of millions and to create a breeding ground for hate. . . . White supremacist groups committed themselves to violent opposition to racial inclusion. They positioned themselves as guardians of law and order in order to protect traditional values during a period of rapid social change and geographic mobility. . . . White supremacist discourse . . . is part of a system of institutionalized whiteness. . . . White supremacy, rather than being the aberration, resonates with many themes or face, class, gender, and sexuality in mainstream politics, academia, and popular culture. . . . Since the advent of the Internet, [explicit] white supremacist organizations have increased membership.[38]

Academics debate the intensity and valence of the morphing relationships between digital media, traditional media, and society.[39] Conventionally, "audiences look to the news to set their political and economic agenda and to explain the news."[40] But, at times, the relationship is reversed. For-profits news looks to their audiences for the agenda. In some sense, this has been done in a variety of ways in the past, such as public opinion polls, focus groups, and market research. However, digital platforms now offer opportunistic tools, such as Search Engine Optimization (SEO), to systematically and quickly change media content.

Digital media writers use search engine analysis tools, such as Google Analytics or Google Keyword, to research what words people use when searching for a given topic. They then apply the resulting word clusters as frequently as possible in the first three hundred words. Why? Because they are trying to elevate their messages' appearance in the first two pages of a search; if they fail to do that, their content becomes invisible. This can change journalism's mediated content on the web. Not since the telegraph, one could argue, has a technological tool so noticeably changed the substantive content of mediated communication.

One concept explicating this relationship and furnishing conceptual mortar is collective intelligence, similar in many ways to the term echo chamber.[41] The construct proposes individual knowledge, through computer mediated communication, aggregate digitally and the resulting content acts as a single organism.[42] Technological determinism, technology influencing the content media produce, serves as a broad conceptual umbrella. Three basic views exist modern scholars adopt regarding this concept. First, they entirely accept it—technology has everything to do with what product is produced by the media. Second, they entirely reject it—societal environments create conditions under which certain technologies are allowed to percolate to the top, and it is the environments' use of technology determining the press content. Third, they admit it is a combination of the two previous stances. Different societal forces, at different times, under different conditions, influence the dissemination of mediated communication in different ways.[43]

One frequently cited example of technological determinism is the telegraph, arguing journalism crafted the inverted pyramid because of the telegraph. On the surface, this might seem like a clear case of technology molding media content. The Associated Press (AP) did not design inverted pyramid constructs until the Civil War. As a casualty of war, some telegraphs were destroyed. So, the AP began sending the most important information first, followed by the next most important information, followed by the next important information, and so on—anticipating the telegraph might be destroyed, at least the important information got through. Thus, journalism's inverted pyramid was born. Had the country not been at war with itself, at that time, under those conditions, would the inverted pyramid have emerged? While it is not easy to answer, it is clear the social environment, along with telegraph, of the time influenced the emergence of the inverted pyramid. In many ways, the digital platforms are similar. Yes, the technology changed the journalism industry; and yes, U.S. culture is changing as well.

"Journalism as it is, is coming to an end."[44] With digital media revolutionizing[45] the mass communication arena, researchers sometimes have difficulty applying old theories and frameworks to the new environment. Some scholars suggest a need for new theories and frameworks, possibly a paradigm shift towards "systems thinking."[46] One interpretative framework placed within the "systems thinking" paradigm assisting scholars better understand relationships between society and digital media is collective intelligence. This framework, originating from entomology, proposes computer-mediated collaboration contributes to a society functioning as a single organism—much like an ant colony.

"There is certainly a striking parallelism between the development of human and ant societies."[47] For instance, anthropologist Topinard suggested the development of human societies occurs in six separate stages: hunting, pastoral, agricultural, commercial, industrial, and intellectual. Ant colonies correspond with three of these stages: hunting, pastoral, and agricultural. Like human societies, some ant colonies are classified as "hunters" and inhabit wooded areas; they hunt alone; the focus of the society is on the individual. Battles within society are between individuals, resembling Homeric heroes.

However, differences do exist. First, ant societies are dominated by females. Few cultures in the world are led by women. Second, all ants are born with equal bodies. Third, ants live in anarchist socialism; each individual completes their duty for the betterment of the collective whole without an elite guiding them or instructing what task to encompass or how to accomplish the mission. Wheeler's work summarized "seemingly independent individuals can cooperate so closely as to become indistinguishable from a single organism . . . becoming a super organism."[48] This argument would later be the foundation for John B. Smith's work.

In 1994, Smith wrote *Collective Intelligence in Computer-Based Collaboration.* In his attempt to relate collective intelligence to new media and society, Smith wrote "a group of human beings can carry out a task as if the group, itself, were a coherent, intelligent organism working with one mind, rather than a collection of independent agents."[49] Smith and his research cohort were initially concerned with hypermedia computer systems and their application to technical and scientific writing. Smith believed if they could better comprehend the cognitive process of writing, then they could construct more efficient computer systems consistent with the writing process. "That is, if we could identify key mental activities that comprise expository writing, then we should be able to build corresponding features into our computer systems to support and, we hoped, enhance those same activities."[50] Smith outlined five major constructs in his attempt to a "reasonably well-defined" concept of collective intelligence: intelligence amplification, collective intelligence parameters, collaboration and cooperation, opinion leaders/experts, model of information flow, and artifact-based collaboration. Together, these concepts demonstrate how collective intelligence blossoms as a result of computer-based collaboration.

Intelligence amplification (IA) is a key assumption vital to the feasibility of computer-based collaboration. Smith wrote:

> The view of collective intelligence as a form of behavior made possible by
> some form of mediating computer system places it within the general tradition

of *intelligence amplification* (IA). This perspective takes the position that computer systems can be developed that partially mirror human mental functions; thus, by increasing the capacity or speed of operation of those functions, these systems can thereby increase or amplify the mental capacity of the human user working with them. As a result, quantitative increases in specific functions may produce qualitative differences in intellectual behavior, making the computer a necessary but not sufficient tool for enabling this mode of thinking.[51]

The key element in this assumption is because computer systems are built by humans to mirror "human mental functions," then those computer systems can "increase or amplify the mental capacity of the human user."[52]

Tying the concepts of resonant myth and collective intelligence together are digital tools like Search Engine Optimization. On the surface, SEO and collective intelligence might seem like disjointed concepts. The methods deployed to achieve high SEO are what combine these constructs. For instance, the first method, keyword analysis, is a key player in harnessing cultural resonance. Keyword analysis is "the process of mining keyword search data to find the best balance between the keywords you need and the best potential niche."[53] Writers for online mediated content use analysis tools, such Google Keyword Search. They type in the topic they are about to write about. Then, Google Keyword Search analysis Google's search engine to see what search terms people are typing in when searching for that topic. The tool then produces a word cluster, with values next to each word with each value being how many times those words were used in a search about that topic on Google during the past month. Journalists then use words from that cluster in their content so to elevate its visibility online. Resonance means constructing mediated content based on what the press believes is salient to the audience. Collective intelligence posits a group of anonymous contributors, through computer-mediated communication, can act as a single, conforming, status quo–upholding organism through their concerted efforts. SEO harnesses culturally resonant values through a collected, intelligent, connected network. Resonant myth, as a key ritual for ideological formation and articulation, is primarily concerned with maintaining social order and upholding the status quo.[54]

News is an important place where the elaborations and formations of racial ideology occur.[55] As Du Bois argued, mainstream news cannot fully comprehend what it is like to be black in the United States; if the black press didn't exist, the only elaboration on racial ideologies would contribute to white ideological hegemony without any black perspectives. The black press, historically, has resisted white supremacist ideologies by advocating, educating, filling holes of misinformation perpetuated by the mainstream press, providing spaces for communities, and bringing visibility to issues impacting African-American communities either entirely ignored by the mainstream press or vilified.[56] Diverse news are organizations owned by, run by, and intended for minorities, in this book's case, the black press.[57] Three criteria must be met for a newspaper to be considered part of the black press: (1) It must be owned and operated by African Americans (2) It must be intended for an African-American audience (3) It must champion causes for the African-American minority.[58] Similarly, one may ponder the definition of mainstream newspapers. In the diverse media area of study, mainstream newspapers are those not meeting the criteria for being an organ such as the black press. In other words, if the press is not part of diverse media, it is part of the mainstream media, regardless of political, partisan, or ideological leanings—white media, owned and managed by whites, and intended mostly for a white audience.

The first African-American newspaper, *Freedom's Journal*, edited by Samuel Cornish and John Russworm, concisely summarized this mission in the first issue in 1827 with the statement, "to plead our cause."[59] Historical context is probably salient for some questioning why African Americans felt the need to plead their cause. Nearly all, with maybe the exception of some students in states where the history books describe it as a worker program or immigration, are aware of the Transatlantic slave trade that helped found the nation currently known as the United States of America. Those frequently whitewashed stories in our modern history books, even in the textbooks using the term slavery, frequently omit the brutal, dehumanizing practices of the time period.[60]

Steven Mintz, in the very first paragraph of his historical book of primary sources, wrote:

> A woman listed in the census simply as Celia was just 14 years old in 1850, when a 60-year-old Missouri farmer named Robert Newsome purchased her. A widower with two grown daughters, the 60-year-old Newsome raped Celia before he had even brought her to his farm. For five years, he kept her as his sexual slave, forcing her to bear two illegitimate children. In 1855, pregnant a third time and ill, she struck back, knocking her abuser unconscious by hitting him in the head with a club and burning his body in her fireplace. During her murder trial, Celia's attorneys argued that a woman had a right to use deadly force to prevent rape. But the court ruled that in Missouri, as in other slave states, it was not a crime to rape a slave woman. Celia was found guilty and hanged.[61]

One of the first primary goals of the African-American press was to advocate against slavery, to gain equality, to be seen not as property but as humans with the same fundamental rights. *Freedom's Journal*, published about 130 years after *Publick Occurrences* (generally acknowledged by most historians as the first American newspaper even though it resembled more of a pamphlet due to its infrequent production) tried to dispel misperceptions and stereotypes disseminated by mainstream newspapers for more than a century.[62]

Freedom's Journal experienced internal conflict the African-American press would confront for its entire existence—how to advocate for equality and dispel misperceptions in a white supremacist culture quick to murder any black who dared challenge white hegemony or displayed non-assimilation tendencies.[63] *Freedom Journal*'s solution was to temper its enthusiastic condemnation of slavery and replace it with advice on how African Americans should behave, such as advice on manners and on how to dress.[64] Cornish was born free in Delaware in 1795. "He saw hope in journalism, for he knew that newspapers, along with pamphlets and tracts, had played a major role in developing a sense of unity and purpose among the colonies."[65] Russworm was born free in Jamaica in 1799. College educated, he settled in New York City. "Joining the select circle of abolitionists and activists there, he quickly won recognition as an articulate and dedicated leader in the antislavery crusade."[66] Blacks agreed equality and full integration into society was the ultimate goal; but they didn't agree on the means of achieving that goal.[67] One prominent African-American leader, Booker T. Washington, espoused what would come to be known by some as an accommodation stance. Washington believed African Americans should seek vocational training, start from the bottom and work their way up. He believed eventually, if they became valuable assets to society, there was no way being ostracized would continue.[68] History shows he overestimated white ideologies' acceptance of inclusivity, pluralism, and cultural synthesis.

Another influential figure, Du Bois, disagreed and labeled this "the Atlanta Compromise."[69] Du Bois recommended a more explicit protest, which was epitomized by the Niagara Movement, a group of African-American leaders who met annually in Niagara and discussed the best ways to achieve full equality and pluralistic integration.[70] The Niagara Movement openly challenged the U.S. government and American society in general, and promised that unless their demands for equality were met, they would continue protesting discriminatory legislation. Some scholars characterized this approach as "militant," which shouldn't be confused with espousing violence, but rather an explicit protest against inequality, an extremely dangerous endeavor given the context of the time.[71]

Freedom's Journal, and many other African-American newspapers, struggled financially for extended periods; making a profit was nearly unthinkable.[72] Financial problems existed for the African-American press primarily because the intended audience, African Americans, were slaves, freed slaves, or free people of color; they had limited finances to purchase the newspapers.[73] Financial conditions did not improve much for the African-American press after emancipation because, though their audience was no longer legal slaves, their financial resources were still severely limited, an issue still persisting to this day because, in part, the theft of those communities' wages was never reconciled. [74]

Unlike *Freedom's Journal*, some antebellum and Civil War African-American newspapers were more assertive in tone. [75] Fredrick Douglass, writing for the *North Star*, was fairly explicit in his tenor. [76] He encouraged African Americans to defend themselves at all costs. For instance, he told them to sleep with a revolver under their pillow to fight off current or former slave owners who tried retaining them. [77] Following the Civil War, though they were no longer "legal" slaves, African Americans still fought discrimination; little did they know the battle for equality was just beginning. [78] Especially in the south, African Americans fought legislation designed for continued oppression, known as Jim Crow laws. [79] The convict lease system is a prime example. This legislation stated any African American convicted of a crime could be "leased" to a farm where they were forced to work a time period equivalent to their convicted sentence. [80] Not surprisingly, after this legislation was drafted, substantially more African Americans were convicted of crimes, an uncanny parallel with modern for-profit prisons, disingenuous drug wars, and high incarceration rates among black communities. [81]

As World War I approached, many whites joined the military while African Americans were denied the right to serve, forced to take the jobs, temporarily, white males vacated. [82] Du Bois, initially, explicitly protested and demanded integration more quickly. [83] However, after the NAACP criticized him, and the U.S. government threatened to prosecute him for seditious acts, Du Bois tempered his protests. [84] In the *Crisis*, he advocated for the African-American community to "close ranks." This stance encouraged African Americans to unite with all of America to fight her enemies abroad; blacks would continue their civil rights battle once the war was won. While this might be perceived as lacking an open advocacy-oriented protest stance Du Bois once encouraged, it served another function—a call for the African-American community to aggregate, unite, and solidify—the genesis of racial solidarity and black political empowerment. [85]

Between World War I and World War II, the interwar years, material conditions did not improve much, if at all, for African Americans. [86] As World War II approached, African Americans were again denied the right to fight. [87] The *Crisis* said it would never again return to its "close ranks" philosophy because blacks' rights were not addressed effectively following World War I. [88] A letter to the editor would come to characterize the explicit protest nature of the African-American press during World War II. [89] James Thompson, an African-American cafeteria worker, wrote a letter to the editor in the black press stalwart, the *Pittsburgh Courier*, founded in 1910 by Edwin Nathanial Harleston, a security guard for a Heinz plant who also had a passion for writing poetry, initially and then later joined by Robert Lee Vann, an aspiring lawyer eventually persuaded to end his legal career for the newspaper. With his call for African Americans to fight for freedom at home and freedom abroad, the Double-V campaign was born. "We are Americans too . . . we have a stake in this fight," frequently accompanied this pulse. This period was the pinnacle of black press protest.[90]

African Americans were eventually permitted in the military but were frequently assigned menial roles.[91] A few combat divisions comprised of African Americans did exist. This became a major focal point of the black press during this time,[92] covering the black soldiers that did exist and then championing them—bringing to salience their more than capable abilities in combat.

Carl Senna noted, "World War II had revitalized a major theme of the black press, the civil rights struggle."[93] The practice of championing African Americans and African-American soldiers continued during Vietnam and civil rights. Mike Davis, one of three African-American foreign correspondents to cover the Vietnam War for the black press for an extended period of time,[94] went one step further beyond covering the soldiers' achievements, he focused on humanizing them by offering specifics, such as parents, siblings, education, and hometown. Black press journalists like Davis highlighted while the military was integrating, something even more insidious occurred: proportionally speaking, more African Americans died in battle; more were put in harm's way.[95] They had won the right to fight, then they fought for the right not to be sacrificed. This did not mean the black troops were afraid of fighting; instead, the black press hoped by highlighting this issue it would push the U.S. government and military towards more egalitarian policies. Again, the mainstream press ignored this cause.[96] During this period of Vietnam and civil rights battles, the black press assertively challenged white ideologies aligned with supremacy.[97] In 1964, the Civil Rights Act signaled a major step toward eradicating the institutionalized oppression of African Americans; the black press played a pivotal role in overcoming the major hurdle toward black political empowerment by debunking justifications for maintaining the separate but equal doctrine.[98]

Resisting institutionalized white supremacy frequently required an assertive advocacy tone, an issue journalism researchers sometimes struggle with regarding the African-American press and the perceived lack of objectivity resulting from this advocacy role.[99] From its inception, regardless of the degree of protest, the language used in the African-American press was considered emotional because it "bluntly and reliably ridicule[d] anyone perceived as standing in the way of black progress."[100] The emotional perception led some to argue the black press's language could not correlate with objectivity. However, it is important to remember mainstream newspapers didn't adopt objectivity until, relatively speaking, the emergence of radio when becoming the authority of facts and truth was believed to be the savior of mainstream newspapers.[101] The first newspapers in the colonies were highly partisan, often owned by political figures hoping to use the press to express their perspectives and persuade others to agree with them. The language used was emotionally charged, blunt, and often ridiculed opposing viewpoints. This trend continued until a new technology, radio, threatened newspapers' livelihood. To survive, and remain relevant, the industry hung its hat on accuracy and objectivity, achieved, in part, by removing some of the perceived emotional language.

For a large portion of mainstream newspapers' history, the tone was primarily sensational and emotional.[102] In this sense, African-American newspapers and mainstream newspapers are similar—during their origins, they struggled to stay afloat financially and their content was labeled sensational and partisan.[103] The practices characterizing the penny press and yellow journalism served as a blueprint for struggling black newspapers to emulate for profitability.[104] They used aggressively framed stories, in part, because their audience wanted it, because the practice helped sell newspapers, and because those types of messages were needed to counter the false images perpetuated by the mainstream press.[105]

The ultimate goal of objectivity is to report truth as accurately as possible.[106] Research has demonstrated, regarding African Americans and issues connected to race, mainstream news failed miserably on reporting truth.[107] One can reasonably argue the mainstream press, with the exception of the civil rights era and possibly the antebellum and Civil War eras, never objectively or truthfully covered African Americans and issues related to race. The black press served to fill this vacuum of substance and presented their communities more accurately. The black press's advocacy resulted in more truthfully narrated accounts.

"In a variety of ways across the diversity of genres and outlets, the mass media convey impressions that blacks and whites occupy different moral universes, that blacks are somehow fundamentally different from whites."[108] Though the struggle for black political empowerment is far from complete and the mainstream press still leaves much to be desired in terms of race coverage, combatting the portrayal of African Americans as "other" continues to be a focus. More recent black press research examines how the African-American press covered a Supreme Court ruling, *Adarand Constructors, Inc. v. Federico Pena, Secretary of Transportation*, regarding employment practices.[109] The case challenged a construction practice awarding contracts to certain companies promising to use some of the funds to hire smaller, African-American-owned companies for part of the work. Some whites cried fouled, labeled it reverse discrimination (a disingenuous term because African Americans have never acquired enough political representation capable of institutionalizing policies adversely affecting white communities on even a remotely comparable scale), and sued. The Supreme Court ruled the practice was not unconstitutional.[110] Proportionately speaking, the black press contributed more articles than did the mainstream press on this case.[111] The black press also interpreted the ruling more intricately than the mainstream press. The black press coverage included historical context pertinent to the legislation and shaped a thematic narrative; the mainstream press omitted the history and included only episodic coverage.

Black press reporting of Hurricane Katrina, compared to mainstream coverage, interpreted government response to the disaster as the continued diaspora of African Americans.[112] In other words, the black press interpreted the government's response as deliberately negligible, mishandling the crisis because it affected a large swath of blacks. Covering the issue of slave reparations, the black press thematically interpreted the issue, connecting it to the historical context of the African-American community and their plight in the United States; the mainstream press interpreted it episodically, focusing only on the case and its rulings, perpetuating an interpretation of African Americans as other.[113]

The desire, and the stakes, for equality have not diminished since civil rights, though that battle looks fundamentally different than it once did. African-American communities aren't fighting for emancipation, for the right to fight, or for the explicit right to vote (though they are still resisting voter suppression); instead, the struggle is now to overcome the perceived other stigma, to achieve full cultural pluralistic integration through black political empowerment, to dispel notions that institutional racism is a thing of the past, and to overcome continued systematic policies not offering equal opportunities to blacks—such as disproportionate deaths by police officers and barriers to education. Historically consistent, the African-American press faces many hurdles while it continues pleading its cause. For instance, the integration of African-American journalists into the mainstream press presents a different problem; many of the best African-American journalists, who used to count on the black press as the only employment venue, now work for mainstream news, making some attempts at diversifying their staff but engendering a talent drain.

This would seem to be, on the surface, a positive societal marker indicating accelerated integration. Research cautions optimism because black journalists who work in the mainstream press are not able to offer the same racial perspective they can in the black press because of mainstream press norms and routines.[114] White-owned mainstream newspapers regulate the black double conscience—reinforcing white hegemony and enabling white supremacist ideologies to flourish in some parts of the country. Black journalists in the mainstream press are forced to answer their white counterparts who ask whether they are a reporter first and then an African American or an African American first and then a reporter. In the "other" vein of thinking,[115] it seems some mainstream reporters do not believe one can be both at the same time. Though African-American reporters are obtaining success working in the mainstream press, a black press is still needed to plead their perspective.

Due to dwindling resources, the modern African-American press continues to struggle and frequently reprints mainstream newspaper wire stories, unless a racial issue is involved.[116] One potential tool for the African-American press to recapture its influence in its community is digital media.[117] Indeed, ethnic media editors see digital platforms as a space for resurgence and a renewed visibility.[118] Because digital media are a major focus and a major goal of the black press, and because this is a historic transitional phase for the black press, their digital content is the focus of this book.

NOTES

1. Sue Robinson, "SOMEONE'S GOTTA BE IN CONTROL HERE: The Institutionalization of Online News and the Creation of a Shared Journalistic Authority," *Journalism Practice* 1, no. 3 (2007): 305–321. Barbie Zelizer and Stuart Allan, *Journalism After September 11* (London, England: Taylor & Francis, 2011). Daniel Berkowitz, *Cultural Meanings of News: A Text-Reader* (Thousand Oaks, CA: Sage Publications, 2010). James W. Carey, *Communication as Culture, Revised Edition: Essays on Media and Society* (London: Routledge, 2008). Jack Lule, *Daily News, Eternal Stories: The Mythological Role of Journalism* (New York, NY: The Guilford Press, 2001).

2. Siebert, *Four Theories of the Press,* 1.

3. Tuchman, *Making News.* Schudson, *The Sociology of News.*

4. Ben Detenber, Melissa R. Gotlieb, Douglas M. McLeod, and Olga Malinkina, "Frame Intensity Effects of Television News Stories About a High-Visibility Protest Issue," *Mass Communication & Society* 10, no. 4 (2007): 439–460.

5. William Du Bois, *The Souls of Black Folk* (Mineola, NY: Dover Publications, 1994), 16.

6. Clint Wilson, Félix Gutiérrez, and Lena Chao, *Racism, Sexism, and the Media: The Rise of Class Communication in Multicultural America* (Los Angeles, CA: Sage Publications, Incorporated, 2013).

7. Ibid., 5.

8. Ibid., 58.

9. Hall, "Racist Ideologies," 89.

10. Ibid.

11. Ibid.

12. Ibid.

13. Ibid.

14. Ibid., 91.

15. Jack Lule, *Daily News, Eternal Stories: The Mythological Role of Journalism* (New York, NY: The Guilford Press, 2001). Dan Berkowitz, "Suicide Bombers as Women Warriors: Making News Through Mythical Archetypes," *Journalism & Mass Communication Quarterly* 82, no. 3 (2005): 607–622.

16. Berkowitz, "Suicide Bombers," 608.

17. James Ettema, "Crafting Cultural Resonance: Imaginative Power in Everyday Journalism," *Journalism* 6, no. 2 (2005): 131–152. LaPoe, "Crafting the Narrative of Tea Party Dissent."

18. Lule, *Daily News.* Berkowitz, *Social Meanings of News.* Victoria LaPoe, Ben LaPoe, and Dan Berkowitz, "*Nurse Jackie* and *HawthoRNE* Stick it to the Mother Myth: Gender and Resonance Online." Paper presented at 2012 ICA annual conference in Phoenix, Ethnicity and Race in Communication Division. Barbara Barnett, "Medea in the Media Narrative and Myth in Newspaper Coverage of Women Who Kill Their Children," *Journalism* 7, no. 4 (2006): 411–432.

19. Berkowitz, "Suicide Bombers," 608.

20. Ettema, "Crafting Cultural Resonance."

21. Robert Entman, "Framing: Toward Clarification of a Fractured Paradigm," *Journal of Communication* 43, no. 4 (1993): 51–58. Erving Goffman, *Frame Analysis: An essay on the Organization of Experience* (New York, NY: Harper & Row, 1974). Dietram Scheufele and David Tewksbury, "Framing, Agenda Setting, and Priming: The Evolution of Three Media Effects Models," *Journal of Communication* 57, no. 1 (2007): 9–20. Bertram Scheufele, and Dietram A. Scheufele, "Framing and Priming Effects," *The International Encyclopedia of Media Studies* (2013).

22. Ettema, "Crafting Cultural Resonance," 272, emphasis added.

23. Michael Schudson, "How Culture Works," *Theory and Society* 18, no. 2 (1989): 153–180.

24. Ibid.

25. Lule, *Daily News*, 5.

26. Ibid.

27. Ibid., 15.

28. Ibid., 62.

29. Ibid.

30. Ibid., 106.

31. Ibid., 124.

32. Ibid.

33. Hall, "Racist Ideologies." Campbell, *Race and News*.

34. Lule, *Daily News*. Berkowitz, *Social Meanings of News*.

35. Neil Postman, *Amusing Ourselves to Death: Public Discourse in the Age of Show Business* (New York, NY: Penguin Books, 1985), 10.

36. Christopher Brown, "WWW.HATE.COM: White Supremacist Discourse on the Internet and the Construction of Whiteness Ideology," *The Howard Journal of Communications* 20, (2009): 189–208.

37. Ibid.

38. Ibid., 189–192.

39. Clay Shirky, *Here Comes Everybody: Revolution Doesn't Happen When Society Adopts New Technology, It Happens When Society Adopts New Behaviors* (New York, NY: Penguin Books, 2008). Lawrence Lessig, *Remix: Making Art and Commerce Thrive in the Hybrid Economy* (New York, NY: Penguin Press, 2008). Danah Boyd, "Can Social Network Sites Enable Political Action?" *International Journal of Media & Cultural Politics* 4, no. 2 (2008): 241–244. James Curran, "What Democracy Requires of the Media," *The Institutions of American Democracy: The Press* (2005): 120–140. Kaye Trammell and Ana Keshelashvili, "Examining the New Influencers: A Self-Presentation Study of A-List Blogs," *Journalism & Mass Communication Quarterly* 82, no. 4 (2005): 968–982. Morozov, *The Net Delusion*.

40. Robinson, "Someone's Gotta Be In Control," 153.

41. John Smith, *Collective Intelligence in Computer-Based Collaboration* (Hillsdale, NJ: Lawrence Erlbaum Associates, 1994). Kathleen Jamieson and Joseph N. Cappella, *Echo Chamber: Rush Limbaugh and the Conservative Media Establishment* (New York, NY: Oxford University Press, 2008).

42. Ibid.

43. C. Valle, "Communication, Technology and Power," *Media Development* 4 (2009): 17–21.

44. M. Deuze, *Media Work – Digital Media and Society Series* (Cambridge: Polity Press, 2007), 141.

45. Andrea Miller and Amy Reynolds, *New Evolution or Revolution?: The Future of Print Journalism in the Digital Age* (New York, NY: Lang Publishers, 2014).

46. K. Portney, "Civic Engagement and Sustainable Cities in the United States," *Public Administration Review* 65, no. 5 (2005): 577–589.

47. Ibid., 5.

48. Ibid., 236.

49. Smith, *Collective Intelligence*, 1.

50. Ibid., ix.

51. Ibid., 5.

52. Ibid.

53. A.I. Business Solutions, "Search Engine Optimization: The Key Elements." Retrieved June 1, 2011, at www.ai-bs.com.

54. Lule, *Daily News*. Dan Berkowitz, *Cultural Meanings of News: A Text-Reader* (Los Angeles, CA: Sage Publications, 2010). James Ettema, "Crafting Cultural Resonance: Imaginative Power in Everyday Journalism," *Journalism* 6, no. 2 (2005): 131–152.

55. Hall, *Racist Ideologies*.

56. Roland Wolseley, *The Black Press U.S.A.* (Ames, IA: Iowa State University Press, 1971). Broussard, *African-American Foreign Correspondents*. Pat Washburn, *The African American Newspaper: Voice of Freedom* (Evanston, IL: Northwestern University Press, 2006).

57. Jinx Broussard, *Giving a Voice to the Voiceless: Four Pioneering Black Women Journalists* (London, England: Psychology Press, 2004). Maxwell Brooks, *The Negro Press Reexamined: Political Content of Leading Negro Newspapers* (Los Angeles, CA: Christopher Publishing House, 1959). Frederick Detweiler, *The Negro Press in the United States* (Chicago, IL: University of Chicago Press, 1922). Hayward Farrar, *The Baltimore Afro-American: 1892–1950* (Westport, CT: Greenwood Press, 1998). Frankie Hutton, *The Early Black Press in America: 1827 to 1860* (Westport, CT: Greenwood Press, 1993). Armistead Pride and Clint C. Wilson, *A History of the Black Press* (Washington, DC: Howard University Press, 1997). Senna, *The Black Press and the Struggle for Civil Rights*. Pat Washburn, *The African American Newspaper: Voice of Freedom* (Evanston, IL: Northwestern University Press, 2006). Roland Wolseley, *The Black Press U.S.A.* (Ames, IA: Iowa State University Press, 1971).

58. Wolseley, *The Black Press U.S.A.*

59. Ibid.

60. Mintz, *African-American Voices*.

61. Ibid., 1.

62. Sloan, *Media in America*.

63. Pride and Wilson, *A History of the Black Press*.

64. Ibid.

65. Pride and Wilson, 11.

66. Pride and Wilson, 13.

67. Washburn, *The African American Newspaper*. Wolseley, *The Black Press U.S.A.*

68. Ibid.

69. Ibid.

70. Ibid.

71. Broussard, *African-American Foreign Correspondents*.

72. Pride and Wilson, *A History of the Black Press*.

73. Ibid.

74. Ibid.

75. Ibid.

76. Washburn, *The African-American Newspaper*.

77. Senna, *The Black Press and the Struggle for Civil Rights*.

78. Ibid.

79. Ibid.

80. Ibid.

81. Ibid.

82. Ibid.

83. Washburn, *The African-American Newspaper*.

84. Ibid.

85. Ibid.

86. Senna, *The Black Press and the Struggle for Civil Rights*.

87. Ibid.

88. Washburn, *The African-American Newspaper*.

89. Ibid.

90. Ibid.

91. Broussard, *African-American Foreign Correspondents.*
92. Ibid.
93. Senna, *The Black Press and the Struggle for Civil Rights*, 131.
94. Broussard, *African-American Foreign Correspondents.*
95. Ibid.
96. Ibid.
97. Senna, *The Black Press and the Struggle for Civil Rights.*
98. Ibid.
99. Ibid.
100. Washburn, *The African-American Newspaper*, ix.
101. Sloan, *Media in America.*
102. Ibid.
103. Bernell Tripp, *Origins of the Black Press: New York: 1827–1847* (Vision Press, 1992).
104. Pride and Wilson, *A History of the Black Press.*
105. Tripp, *Origins of the Black Press.*
106. Sloan, *Media in America.*
107. Entman and Rojecki, *Black Image in the White Mind.* Dates and Barlow, *Split Image.*
108. Entman and Rojecki, *Black Image in the White Mind*, 6.
109. Clawson et al., "Framing Supreme Court Decisions: The Mainstream Versus the Black Press."
110. Ibid.
111. Ibid.
112. Dolan et al., "Katrina Coverage in Black Newspapers Critical of Government, Mainstream Media."
113. Mastin et al., "In Black and White: Coverage of U.S. Slave Reparations by the Mainstream and Black Press."
114. Nayda Terkildsen and David F. Damore, "The Dynamics of Racialized Media Coverage in Congressional Elections," *Journal of Politics* 61 (1999): 680–699.
115. Entman and Rojecki, *Black Image in the White Mind.*
116. Washburn, *The African-American Newspaper.*
117. Ibid.
118. Masadul Biswas and Ralph Izard, "Viability of Online Outlets for Ethnic Newspapers." AEJMC Convention in Denver, Colorado, August 4–7, 2010.

Chapter Two

Intersections of Race, Media, and Politics

Academics exploring the democratizing nature of the internet vigorously debate the relationships between digital media and society. [1] The interactions between governments, media, and public dissenting voices expressed via digital media are central to these debates. [2] If dissenting deliberation contributes to a healthy democracy [3] and mainstream media narrowly define issues to only two polemic perspectives due to the "strategic ritual of objectivity," [4] then the internet should provide platforms for more diverse deliberation—thus contributing to a more informed, democratic, and open-minded society. For instance, even in one of the more closed societies, China, in terms of dissent and challenges to cultural hegemony, the internet provides a space for ideology elaborations. [5] Thus, we can expect online content from the black press to challenge other hegemonic ideologies disseminated by the mainstream press.

For the most part, news outlets still disseminate similar content digitally as they do in their traditional spaces. [6] The speed and scale of the content is unprecedented, but the character of the content isn't significantly different. Interactivity is the major uniqueness of the internet. [7] Because interactivity is one of the internet's major contributions to the information age, and because minority groups use social media like Facebook and Twitter more than whites, [8] this book measures interactivity by coding a web story's reported Facebook likes and retweets. With black press editors viewing digital media as an important platform to express their voices and the unprecedented speed and scope of digital media's reach, this is an important opportunity for the black press. The historic press continues fulfilling its pluralistic roles via digital media, diminishing inaccurate portrayals repetitively distributed by the mainstream press, and amplifying ignored issues and perspectives.

The mainstream press, an institution supposedly dedicated to presenting an accurate picture of reality (or at least as close to truth as possible), historically portrayed African Americans and race one of two ways. Concisely put, the mainstream press has a long history of inaccurately vilifying blacks as threats to society or ignoring African-American communities and issues. The trend can be traced as far back as the colonial period.[9] Early communications frequently portrayed African-American slaves as inhuman barbaric creatures; most communications highlighted slave rebellions and were usually accompanied by white panic and retaliation.[10] It should be noted here during this time African Americans were not the only nonwhites to be covered this way; American Indians were portrayed as savages as well with extermination frequently posited as the solution for dealing with the "Indian problem."[11] Even at the very genesis of this country's founding, anyone who was not white was portrayed as other, with that other being much less desirable and often a threat to perceived civilization.[12]

The mistreatments of nonwhites always engendered justifications. "Like every other human being who takes gross advantage of a weaker person, they found justifications for their actions."[13] One justification for the slave trade was that the "heathen" Africans were pagans and forcing them to leave Africa and expose them to Christianity was in their best interest.[14] Some defended the slave trade by arguing Africans were primitive savages and saving them from their "brutish conditions" in Africa was a courtesy.[15] Another justification was Africans were the ones enslaving other Africans and then selling them to European countries. This justification ignored this practice was minimal at best prior to European presences and greatly amplified after the first African slaves were capture by the Portuguese for the Atlantic slave trade. Thus started the progression of stereotypes portraying African Americans first "as savages, then as property, later as enemies, and then as strangers,"[16] but nearly always as "other."

This trend continued up to and after the Civil War, when slavery was challenged and purportedly outlawed. Prior to this period, African Americans were either ignored or portrayed negatively as dangerous threats in the mainstream media.[17] Leading up to the Civil War, a period known as the antebellum period, some of the earliest abolitionists included Charles Osborn, Elihu Embree, William Swain, Benjamin Lundy, and William Lloyd Garrison.[18] Garrison, founding the *Liberator* newspaper on January 1, 1831, is probably the best-known early white abolitionist and advocated for immediate emancipation. Regarding African-American representation in the mainstream press, this period proved to be a deviation from the previous norm because it advocated for issues pertinent to the black community, unlike the majority of mainstream press coverage either ignoring blacks or casting them in a negative light.[19] Not all mainstream newspapers advocated for abolition. Some in the North and most in the South continued their oppressive coverage of black voices.

Mainstream newspapers routinely portray African Americans through a restless native framework.[20] This structure portrays African Americans as "restless natives" organized in a homogenous mass setting out to devour white ideologies. "Popular culture is still full today of countless savage and restless 'natives,' and sound-tracks constantly repeat the threatening sound of drumming in the night, the hint of primitive rites and cults."[21] This restless native framework emerged during President Obama's first term in coverage of the tea party.[22] "These 'natives' always move as an anonymous collective mass—in tribes or hordes. . . . And against them is always counter posed the isolated White figure, alone 'out there,' confronting his Destiny or shouldering his Burden in the 'heart of darkness.'"[23]

From one perspective, the use of the restless native framework for the tea party could be a positive social marker; instead of ignoring or vilifying African Americans, the mainstream press was, for the most part, negatively framing whites challenging black political representation. From another perspective, it could be a negative social marker; thousands, if not millions, of whites did aggregate to aggressively oppose the first African-American president with little substantive, logical, or intelligent rationale for their dissent. This could be a mainstream press aberration akin to the antebellum or civil rights period; even though the mainstream press returned to its routine of vilifying or ignoring race after those periods, those two moments in history were extremely important in trying to correct previous racial injustices, similar to the significance of President Obama's first term.

Even though mainstream newspapers continued misrepresenting African Americans, the struggle between President Obama and his adversaries marked a historical moment for black political representation in a digital age. The task, then, is examining the press's role in this conflict because "the media are not only a powerful source of ideas about race. They are also one place where these ideas are articulated, worked on, transformed and elaborated."[24] Typically, during moments of friction when race is a significant variable, mainstream news interpret the deliberation as a zero-sum contest, one side wins everything and the other side loses everything.[25] Interpret is a significant word in the deciphering calculus. With the exception of a few handful of moments in history, the mainstream press interpreted race and African Americans in an extremely insensitive and inaccurate fashion, suggesting, for some, journalists working for the mainstream press tend to lean away from the racial comity end of the spectrum. Have some overtly racist journalists existed? Probably. But the interpret variable should not be overlooked. While journalism's overarching goal is to mediate reality as objectively and as accurately as possible, truth can be relative; two journalists can mediate the same "facts," both truthfully, but framed differently with different meaning.[26] Thus, while objectivity is the desired goal, interpretation is frequently the practice.[27] Those interpretations are molded by society, norms, routines, government officials, indexing, technology, and the journalists' ideology, education, values, and goals. Mainstream journalists' interpretations, regardless of intent, traditionally focus on African Americans as violent and as criminals, informed, in part, by their WASP ideologies rooted in their duty to colonialize the world with assimilation.[28] "Blacks in the news tend to look different from and more dangerous than whites even when they commit similar crimes."[29]

Journalism is not the only U.S. institution disenfranchising black voices; U.S. politics have a sordid history as well. History, and a lacking knowledge of history, is one critical component undergirding language used to interpret race. "Even though it was abolished over a century ago, slavery has left a lasting legacy—a legacy evident in racism, economic inequality, and the social and economic underdevelopment of large parts of the United States."[30] Race-related events have been the most difficult stories for mainstream journalists to translate into thematic narratives in part because mainstream journalists typically ignore the political history tethered to issues they cover.

If the interpretative community known as journalism does take on the coloration of its society and government, and if mainstream journalism has failed to accurately cover race—instead upholding white ideologies and ignoring minorities or framing them negatively, explaining President Barack Obama's two terms may be challenging for some. In 1990, Raphael Sonenshein wrote: "While black office-holding has steadily increased at the local level, statewide successes have been few and far between."[31] He posed the question of whether blacks would ever proportionally represent their communities at state or national political levels more than two decades ago. With a few exceptions, not much has changed significantly. Given the difficulty blacks have faced attaining national political positions,[32] then, the significance of President Obama's 2008 and 2012 victories cannot be overstated. During the 2008 campaign, he tried to avoid running as a "race" candidate, at least explicitly in the presence of national audiences.[33] Yet, mainstream newspapers made race the most salient issue once he won the Iowa Primary.[34]

Political racial solidarity, uniformly voicing and representing a group's interests, is considered one of the most potent ways to fight discrimination and gain full equality in the United States.[35] When Sonenshein asked, "can black candidates win statewide elections," Edward Brooke of Massachusetts was the only African American elected to the Senate during that century; Douglas Wilder of Virginia became the first African-American governor in 1989.[36] Historically, countless barriers restricted African Americans' opportunities to represent themselves in the U.S. representative democracy, such as Jim Crow, continued voter suppression, and the gerrymandering of districts.[37] While African Americans were, and still are, underrepresented proportionally at the national and state levels, they have begun seeing some progress—most notably, the election of mayors in urban areas.[38] This may partially explain mainstream media's poor historical record of covering minorities. Because of indexing, the idea "that journalists tend to calibrate the range of viewpoints in the news to reflect the balance of power,"[39] it could be expected for the mainstream press to articulate white ideologies in political communication. President Obama's election to the most powerful political office in the world changed that dynamic. Coupling racial solidarity and indexing, we hypothesize the black press was more indexed to President Obama's administration than the mainstream press because his administration was the most aligned with the voices and ideologies expressed in the black press.

Indexing is connected to the notion news media are a political institution not only depending on the other three branches of the U.S. government for content, but are also a necessary establishment for the government to function efficiently.[40] An institution must encompass social patterns embodying procedures, assumptions, and routines occurring and enduring over space and time in a fashion to supervise a societal sector.[41] In order to be a political institution, news personify the following components: (1) an indirect approach where media seek to influence policy, (2) observable action that is (3) purposive and (4) unified.[42]

Editorials are one channel news media directly seek to influence policy; however, the majority of content is indirect and most easily observable through news's routine of objectivity.[43] Indexing posits official source citation doesn't lead to official source bias because the officials cited are not hegemonic in their persuasion.[44] News, adhering to the ritual of objectivity, condense complex policies into only two, often polemic, views, missing many of the other political views between the ends of the spectrum.[45] Unlike observable editorials, the norm of objectivity is an indirect venue of shaping political policy because only two views are presented.

"The publicity provided by the news media can offer key assistance to officials."[46] News media influence not only public opinion, but official opinion as well. David Price's 1978 study of the House Commerce Committee found a highly visible issue in the press resulted in a highly responsive legislature.[47] Press functioning as a political institution is an observable action. News influence opinions of not only the electorate, but of other political actors (namely government officials) as well.[48]

The notion of news media purposively seeking to influence public policy does not mean a "consciously intended" act. News media do not always consciously deliberate on how to influence public policy. Rather, purposive implies their influence derives from functional aspects—like the strategic ritual of objectivity. For instance, the Harvey Molotch and Marilyn Lester study of an oil spill in 1969 concluded, "one dimension of power can be construed as the ability to have one's account become the perceived reality of others."[49] The functional ability of news media to construct reality inadvertently attracts political actors who wish to not only use the press as a vehicle for transmitting their opinions, but also as a hub for collecting information to inform their own opinions. News media are purposive about their objectivity, presenting two sides due to journalistic norms of aspired neutrality.[50]

Media fragmentation and the emergence of digital platforms initially may imply no, media are far from unified. However, media fragmentation has actually produced condensed collaboration.[51] News media seek and report the same stories—thus, seeking the same officials and political actors. Fewer and fewer voices are actually heard in a fragmented environment.[52] The press can be viewed as a unified political institution because media fragmentation has led to a smaller variety of narratives and these stories are frequently told only through two viewpoints—implicating a unified voice—and because the press, with a few exceptions (notably entertainment outlets pretending to be news),[53] are unified in their mission to report truth.

In 1980, then Vice President Walter Mondale said he would rather hold the power to be on the nightly news than the power to exercise a veto.[54] Despite vast changes in the media environment, the press can still be viewed as a political institution. News media indirectly and purposively influence public policies through an inadvertent unified voice. Vast empirical evidence exists supporting the observability of media's role(s) in public policy authorship.[55] Because media political actions are indirect, observable, purposive, and unified, one can consider the press a political institution—thus, encompassing social patterns embodying procedures, assumptions, and routines occurring and enduring over space and time in a fashion to inform and serve society.

Academics frequently debate the root causes contributing to black representative struggles at state and national levels, the more powerful positions, and what social patterns engender such trends. Some scholars argue the answer is simple—demographics based on visual markers, most notably skin color.[56] In urban areas, African Americans comprise a more significant portion of the electorate. At state or national elections, the proportions aren't as favorable. A political axiom states a voting district needs to be at least comprised of 65 percent African Americans for a black candidate to even consider possibly winning an election.[57] Whites, historically reluctant to vote for African Americans, comprise larger portions of the electorate at national and state levels than they do in some local and urban areas.[58] Race seems to be highly correlated with the electability of African-American candidates.[59]

Of course, exceptions always exist. For instance, Kansas City, Missouri's fifth district was comprised of 20 percent African Americans when Alan Wheat became the district's first black representative in 1982. Katie Hall won in the first district of Indiana, a 71 percent white constituency, during that same year.[60] It does appear some progress occurs but, it still seems race is a key variable to black political representation.

Some scholars argue the solution to increasing African-American representation is racial gerrymandering districts. Carol Swain disagrees and asserts the end solution of that practice dictates African Americans will be regulated to contests between two, or more, African-American candidates only. They'll never attain the experience needed to run against a white candidate at state or national levels. This was highlighted during the reconstruction era when African-American officials weren't fully aware of all the policies and procedures—knowledge very pertinent for a politician to effectively represent his or her constituents.[61]

This lack of experience can negatively impact how a candidate runs for reelection—a critical period because when a black candidate is the first African American to run in that district, black constituencies vote in large numbers during the initial election but those numbers typically dwindle during the reelection campaign.[62] That is why building coalitions with white constituencies, or at lease appeasing fears of severe resource allocation away from those whites, is important during that first term. If African-American officials can and do build those coalitions, then their reelection campaigns become slightly more manageable because they aren't required to expend as much resources to appease fear.[63] Thus, Swain argues racial gerrymandering districts shouldn't exist so African Americans can run against white candidates at local levels, preparing them better at state and national levels.[64] President Obama's first term serves as an ideal opportunity to examine how the press covered coalition building and how, if at all, race was incorporated into that narrative.

An important question to percolate while studying the modern black press is whether President Obama is an exception to the rule or part of progress. If he is part of representative equalizing, the question is not, then, whether black candidates can win national or state elections, but *how* they win elections and reelections at those levels. On November 6, 2012, President Obama was reelected in a surprising fashion, at least from a political communication scholar's perspective. Most political pundits predicted a very tight electoral race. With an unemployment rate hovering around 9 percent during much of his presidency, dipping to 7.9 percent just before the election, President Obama was the first president since FDR to win reelection in that type of economic climate. Governor Romney won more than 61 percent of the white vote, a proportion historically always enough to win the presidency. Traditional political wisdom would not have predicted President Obama's reelection. Obviously, something changed. Part of the answer is an increasingly pluralistic, though oftentimes reluctantly coupled with reactionary backlash, society linked with reemerging diverse presses taking advantage of the tools offered by digital media.

As a rule, African-American representatives usually win reelection.[65] But, for the representatives who don't, white dissenting voices, such as the tea party, are significant variables correlated with their loss.[66] President Obama's reelection defied scholars arguing other variables, such as context and the nature of politics, are more highly correlated with the election of African-American candidates than race.[67] Given the context, President Obama should have been a one-term president. Research argues political environment was the more important variable during the 2008 election.[68] The pertinent context was the previous administration and the economy. Some scholars argue President Obama's race had little to do with his election. Instead, George W. Bush, President Obama's predecessor, had done such a poor job and angered the public so much the U.S. electorate would have voted for a Democrat, regardless of the candidate's color and/or gender.[69]

However, during the 2008 general campaign, the polling numbers leading up to the general election were relatively close. Maybe the public wasn't so livid with Republicans they were willing to vote for an African American named Barack Hussein Obama, a name opening many doors for islamophobic attacks. Then, the economy collapsed and McCain admitted financial knowledge wasn't his expertise. President Obama's lead widened and this context eventually contributed to his election.[70]

Other scholars disagree, in part.[71] They posit race, or at least President Obama's historic symbolic power in terms of racial representation, was a more significant variable. This position admits context is correlated with the electability of an African-American candidate. In Obama's case, they argue the campaign he ran and its relationship with media, one acutely aware of race and how to effectively and implicitly frame race, contributed more significantly to his election than the "rejecting-Republicans-economy" context.[72]

President Obama's campaign was highly cognizant of the nuanced layers of race and organized his campaign around appealing to African Americans while not priming white voters' fears.[73] Prior to McIlwain and Caliendo's study, the majority of the racial implicit framing literature focused on how white candidates appealed to race, implicitly, to motivate white voters away from black candidates or white candidates tied to issues associated with African-American communities.[74] Race appeals, made by white and black candidates alike, do prime voters and influence their voting behavior. Their findings were not consistent with previous literature.[75] Their experiments found when an African-American candidate deployed an appeal to race, it actually lowered support for that candidate among black voters and increased support among white voters. The researchers also found that race appeals by a white candidate had no significant impact on deterring white voters away from a black candidate.

These findings would seem, on the surface, to be evidence suggesting racial priming isn't strongly correlated with the electability of an African-American candidate—possibly inferring context is more salient. One significant finding contradicts the latter. In the control groups, where no implicit race appeals were made, the participants perceived the candidates appealed to race. African Americans perceived the white candidate made an implicit race appeal against the black candidate, increasing their support for the black candidate. White participants perceived the African-American candidate to make an implicit race appeal when there was none, increasing their support for the white candidate. More formally: (1) in the manipulation group, when a white candidate did make a race appeal, support among white and African-American voters for the white candidate dropped (2) when an African-American candidate in the manipulation group did use a race appeal, support among white and African Americans for the African-American candidate dropped (3) in the control group, when the white candidate did *not* use an appeal, the African-American candidates perceived that he did and their support for the African-American candidate rose (4) in the control group, when the African-American candidate did *not* use an appeal, the white voters perceived that he did, raising their support for the white candidate. They perceived racial appeals when there were none. This implies in a biracial contest, race is in the minds of the voters regardless of whether the candidates appeal to race, suggesting race ideologies are very deeply embedded and highly salient in individuals' minds when thinking about politics. [76]

Individuals have been evolutionarily engineered to stereotype. [77] They are programmed to immediately look at someone who appears different and judge whether the individual intends to inflict harm and whether the person possesses the ability to competently inflict harm. The world radiates with such an overwhelming amount of stimuli no one brain could ever attempt to entirely process all of it. Instead, our brains create shortcuts known as stereotypes in order to judge whether harm exists. [78] Our brains develop these shortcuts, schema when not associated with a group of people, about everything. We have a schema for a chair. While walking down a hall and upon seeing one chair leg and the back of a chair around a corner, our brain assumes something resembling an object for sitting with four legs and possibly a back for rest will be present. This is a key, and frequently scary, element to priming. Once the brain perceives and directs a cue towards a stereotype, the brain expects to process the other characteristics comprising that stereotype. If the individual does not endorse a negative stereotype, but is aware it has existed, or still exists in some corners of society currently, that negative, dormant stereotype can still be primed.

Brains process stimuli two ways, peripherally and centrally. Centrally is consciously thinking about specific stimuli and attempting to process it. For instance, you are probably (hopefully still) centrally processing the words and messages we are trying to communicate via this book. Our brains don't centrally process much of the stimuli in the world. Typically, our brains rely on peripheral processing—a cue is present in the stimuli signaling to the brain what schema, a mental box of characteristics for a single object, the stimuli align with. Over time, for a variety of reasons, different people construct mental boxes (stereotypes) for types of people and what characteristics align with them. Media are one of the central platforms for shaping what characteristics are placed in the mental boxes for groups of people.

Traditional media perpetuated and reinforced negative stereotypes of people of color.[79] Most Americans inform their mental shortcuts of out-group members based on what they learn in the media since they typically are not in contact with out-group members on a frequent basis.[80] If racism is placed on a continuum, with racial comity on one end and explicit racism on the other, most Americans are in the middle; they don't centrally process race on a day-to-day, frequent basis.[81] Thus, the images of African Americans in media are instrumental in forming racial stereotypes and ideologies[82] because (1) media are a central space where race stereotypes are developed and (2) media content triggers thoughts about race that would have not occurred if race had not been introduced. Presenting one word referencing race motivates whites to view African-American candidates negatively.[83] As soon as race is involved in the mainstream press, whites think negatively about African Americans.[84] Thus, the types of stories journalists tell and the words and pictures they use to tell them are extremely important for race relations.

Operationalizing implicit racial frames has been one of the more difficult tasks for scholars. First, academics theorized a racial frame must be implicit to prime white voters.[85] Priming is the theory hypothesizing an implicit message in the news activates previously dormant racial attitudes—usually triggering whites to negatively perceive political candidates, white and black alike.[86] Why must such messages be implicit? It was thought in a society perceived as desiring more equality for all, racially explicit messages opposing values aimed at full equality for everyone are easily identified and rejected.[87] Thus, for a message to activate racially prejudiced actions, it must not be identified as racial—it must be implicit.[88]

The Willie Horton advertisement is one of the first implicit racial frames scholars studied.[89] During the 1988 presidential election, George Bush, a Republican, disseminated an attack ad on Democrat Michael Dukakis believed to have motivated white voters to view Dukakis negatively on racial grounds.[90] This was accomplished by appealing to their racial stereotypes of African Americans as criminals, formed, in part, by the mainstream news frequently covering blacks disproportionately as criminals.[91] By tying Dukakis to an African-American criminal, Bush was successful in priming a racial stereotype.[92]

On implicit racial frames, Tali Mendelberg wrote:

> What exactly is the difference between implicit and explicit messages? First, consider what makes an appeal racial. By my definition, a racial appeal is explicit if it uses racial nouns or adjectives to endorse white prerogatives, to express anti-black sentiment, to represent racial stereotypes, or to portray a threat from African Americans. . . . Implicit racial appeals convey the same message as explicit racial appeals, but they replace the racial nouns and adjectives with more oblique references to race.[93]

This definition of implicitness was an exceedingly valuable contribution and starting point. Empirical examinations of implicit racial frames in media coverage followed and stated an implicit racial frame consisted of a picture of the candidate, a reference to his/her race, and a reference to the race of his/her constituents.[94] Experiments illustrated implicit racial frames do impact the electability of a candidate.[95] African-American candidates compelled to use counter-stereotypes can be successful in dampening the priming of racial stereotypes.[96]

Acknowledging race is a significant variable in the electability of African-American and, frequently, white Democrats, some scholars argue the nature of politics and how candidates use media, not connected to race, for their campaigns is still the driving force.[97] For instance, Kathleen Jamieson, citing numerous campaigns, argues even when race is not an issue, such as between two white candidates or between two Republican candidates, campaigns are intensely negative. Candidates constantly attack the other's character and prime voter behavior tied to issues, such as religion, political party, character, family values, and taxes.[98] Misinformation and destroying an opponent's credibility are the essential nature of politics.[99]

Some argue issues typically salient to African-American communities are what motivate some voters away from or toward candidates, not race in general.[100] It should be noted here when we refer to black interests we do not mean to imply African-American communities are monolithic. They are not. However, certain issues do exist disproportionately and negatively impacting African-American communities, such as crime, mass incarceration, poverty, lack of resources and/or access for education, unemployment, lack of resources for credible legal defense, and health care.[101] It is beyond the scope of this book to examine *why* these issues negatively impact African-American communities, but it is an important point to highlight.

Many Americans believe U.S. society was founded on the individualistic idea of meritocracy and everyone had equal access to opportunities. If individuals apply themselves and work hard they can succeed and what they have in life they earned. Government should not stand in the way or present barriers to success and everyone should have an equal opportunity.[102] The myth of meritocracy is an important value of ideologies leaning towards white supremacy as they conveniently forget the ramifications and ripple effects of the genocide of Native Americans and the enslavement of African Americans, benefiting their white ancestors who were able, unlike nonwhite communities, to pass on what they had "earned." Historically, concerning African Americans, the fundamental American principle of meritocracy was not true because too many institutional barriers prohibited them from approaching, let alone fulfilling, their American dreams.[103] Thus, when whites, unable or unwilling to empathize with a history of institutionalized obstruction, read information about programs designed to compensate for centuries of slavery and oppression, they view the beneficiaries unfairly as handouts, contradicting white ideology of the American dream, meritocracy, and hard work. They also misperceive an allegation of intent resulting in defensive postures.[104] These perceptions and issues hurt African-American communities, regardless of whether the policies are intentionally designed to negatively impact blacks. This, in part, explains why programs such as affirmative action and welfare and issues such as crime and poverty disproportionally impacting the African-American community tend to prime whites negatively.

Another argument posits the type of campaigns black candidates run influences their electability, not their race or the coverage of them.[105] A substantial amount of research examines media representations of race and how President Obama used appeals in his campaign.[106] How does an African-American candidate use a race appeal in a national election when the majority of the electorate is white and his opponent is white? The answer is connected to the term "racial solidarity."[107] The notion here is political empowerment is a way to combat oppression, gain equality, and solve issues confronting African-American communities. Historically, since whites have been reluctant to vote for African Americans, this meant African-American communities needed to act as a solidified unit and vote for African-American candidates overwhelmingly when they emerged because blacks best understood the issues facing their communities. Racial solidarity translated into a race authenticity appeal—the notion an African-American candidate appealed to his or her race to convince constituents the black candidate was "authentic" and campaigning to represent solidified causes.[108]

On a national stage, presenting oneself as an authentic African American can be tenuous territory in the United States. The fear is by using race authenticity appeals, black candidates will negatively prime white voters because highlighting race situates those candidates as "other."[109] President Obama effectively achieved this goal by his use of amplified first-person plural pronouns.[110] When in front of a national stage, such as on television, a debate, or in front of a group of mostly whites, he went one step beyond using the phrases "us" or "we," which are typically used to authenticate one to the in-group. He included phrases such as, "the entire nation is in this together . . . regardless of sex, class, or race" quite frequently. This served two purposes. It appealed to his African-American audience's solidarity, authenticity function, but it also dampened potential priming in his white audience by convincing them he was part of their group also.[111] In front of an audience comprised mostly of African Americans, President Obama used the phrases "us" and "we" more frequently than a "national we" phrase and discussed issues pertinent to black communities. When in front of a white audience, he avoided the African-American issues; he didn't want to be perceived as an African-American candidate to whites, but he did when in front of African Americans.[112] Within this knowledge structure we examine what mythological frameworks the African-American press used to interpret the tea party and compare those myths to the ones used by the mainstream press. We compare the use of implicit racial frames in the two press organs. Together, we examine how the myths progress and compare them to differing levels of racial implicitness. Our hypothesis is the African-American press will use implicit racial frames more than the mainstream press because the black press's main function is to bring salience to racial issues. Two implicit racial frames exist in this study: a tea party implicit frame and a President Obama implicit frame. Connected to racial solidarity and indexing, we expect the black press to have more President Obama implicit racial frames and more tea party implicit racial frames than the mainstream press. The black press will interpret the tea party more conclusively as a group opposing black political empowerment than the mainstream press.

The goal of our research is to understand the processes and character of social life. We decipher symbols constructing meaning created by culture within the contexts of their time.[113] To precisely comprehend the character of social life today, to understand why some symbols are crafted, and to disentangle their meanings, one of the more powerful research techniques in the social sciences is content analysis.[114] Because this book is interested in how resonant myths emerged in black and mainstream newspapers and testing predictions attempting to examine implicit racial frames in the arc of the tea party story, we conducted a mixed-method content analysis combining qualitative and quantitative techniques and philosophies. We seek to understand what meanings were created and sustained within news coverage; and how meaning may or may not change within an ethnic-media-focused press.

RESEARCH INSTRUMENT

We conducted a mixed-method content analysis incorporating both qualitative and quantitative techniques.[115] The multilayered aspects of race and the intersections of media and politics led us to some very interesting, yet complicated, questions and predictions. We chose this complimentary mixed-method approach realizing it is "the most challenging, and so far the least common, option."[116] We argue the topics and issues studied in this book demanded a nuanced methodological approach and design. Qualitative and quantitative techniques both have their advantages and shortcomings. Sometimes qualitative work is critiqued for lacking empirical evidence by those not familiar with the methods, reading as more opinion piece a research study. Sometimes quantitative work is critiqued for not providing social science meaning. Coupling the two into the instrument helps construct a thorough content analysis able to describe and interpret.

On this type of mixed-method content analysis, David Altheide provided guidance:

> It is suggested that an ethnographic perspective can help delineate patterns of human action when document analysis is conceptualized as fieldwork. Prior research and awareness of an activity involved in the production of documents can theoretically inform sampling procedures, whereas constant comparison and discovery may be used to further delineate specific categories, as well as narrative description. In general, this means that the situations, settings, styles, images, meanings, and nuances are key topics of attention. . . . I suggest that several aspects of an ethnographic research approach can be applied to content analysis to produce ethnographic content analysis, which may be defined as the reflexive analysis of documents.[117]

Key to Altheide's work is the reflexive nature of content analysis. The quantitative codebook in this research design was informed by previous research, and the qualitative analysis is heavily reliant on being reflexive and reflective.

This research design has two components: a qualitative textual analysis viewed through a resonant myth conceptual framework and a quantitative content analysis theoretically driven by implicit racial frames, racial solidarity, black press history, and indexing. Media scholars approach researching texts from two points of view: a transmission point of view and a ritualistic point of view.[118] A transmission point of view is interested in how media messages are sent over geographic space and time and with what effect; a ritualistic point of view is interested in extracting embedded symbolic meaning created by culture. The quantitative, implicit racial frames portion of this analysis is a transmission point of view and the qualitative, resonant myth portion of this analysis is a ritualistic point of view. Before we explain how those two elements of the design were executed, it is more intuitive to first explain how we collected our data.

DATA COLLECTION

The unit of analysis for this book is each online news story about the tea party written by a sample of African-American and mainstream newspapers published online. The time frame to gather the sampling units for this book is from the modern inception of the tea party until November 13, 2012. This encompasses available stories about the tea party during President Obama's first term. We chose November 13 because that is one week after the 2012 presidential election, allowing for discussions about the tea party's impact, if any, on President Obama's reelection.

First, we identified which African-American newspapers had websites; these websites were accessible, were not under construction, and had searchable capabilities. We started with a list of modern African-American newspapers examined in a similar study.[119] That list contained twenty-two newspapers. We manually searched that list and found thirteen of those newspapers owned websites authoring stories about the tea party. Then, we consulted the AANP (African-American News and Periodicals), the resource Ethnic Newswatch, and the NNPA (National Newspapers Publishers Association) for lists of current and prominent African-American newspapers.[120] From that list, we manually searched which prominent newspapers had websites. We then selected newspapers based on prominence in their region in relation to circulation, advertising revenue, and staff size; regions included the East Coast, the Southeast, the Midwest, the Southwest, and the Northwest. The final sample of African-American newspaper websites consists of seventeen sites, with relatively decent circulation, and are geographically representative (see the appendix for a list of those seventeen newspaper websites). We recognize the ephemeral nature of the internet may make future research on this topic hard to replicate. Some newspapers without websites at the time of this study may have websites in the future and websites examined in this study may not exist or change drastically in the future. However, because this is a sample, and not a census of the entire population of black newspapers, we argue replicating this research is feasible. Also, this is a snapshot of the black press during a moment in time. Even a cursory knowledge of media history shows media are always in a state of change.[121]

The next step was to organize a list of mainstream newspapers' websites correlating with the list of African-American newspapers' websites. We retrieved a list of the highest circulating newspapers in the country, according to the Audit Bureau of Circulations, and first added the top fifty newspapers to the list. We then attempted to match, based from that sample, mainstream newspapers' websites, geographically, to the African-American newspaper sample for valid comparisons, or at least as close as we could get. We narrowed that list to fifteen mainstream newspaper websites based on the same criteria for their region we used in selecting the black newspaper websites (see the appendix for a list of those newspaper websites).

After compiling our list, we visited each website, typed in the term "tea party" in the site's search function, and printed off hard copies of the articles. We then manually sorted which articles were relevant. By relevant, we mean articles discussing the modern tea party, a dissenting group forming weeks after President Obama's inauguration. Some people really do organize real tea parties, with real drinkable tea, and advertise the event via newspaper articles. These, along with articles discussing the historical tea party preceding the American Revolution, were excluded from the analysis. Some newspaper articles discussed events or celebrations for the tea party preceding the American Revolution and did not cover the topics in this study. From the African-American newspaper sample, after sorting for relevancy and eliminating redundant articles, we found 1,144 articles on the tea party. From the mainstream newspaper sample, after sorting for relevancy and eliminating redundant articles, we found 11,363 articles. We used a systematic random sample of the articles to make the mainstream data more manageable. For the mainstream newspaper sample, we analyzed every eleventh article—reducing the data set to 1,033. We used systematic sampling, a version of random sampling, because this is the most powerful and most representative way to analyze a population and enables us to draw representative generalizations.[122] The systematic random sampling was not without limitations. Because we did not systematically random sample the black press articles, which would have made the sample too small to analyze, some inferential statistical tests for the hypotheses would have been problematic.[123] To compensate for the disparity in populations and sampling procedure, we used a test of two proportions for many of our predictions.[124] A few predictions needed a slightly more nuanced statistical approach and for those, we used Anovas. We did not collect all of the tea party articles that all black press newspapers wrote; our list of seventeen black newspapers was itself a sample. Thus, using inferential tests such as an Anova is still justified if that is the only option.[125]

QUALITATIVE DATA ANALYSIS

Qualitative textual analysis is concerned with extracting meaning from the texts. "Textual analysis is a method that communication researchers use to describe, interpret, and evaluate the characteristics of a recorded message."[126] Unlike quantitative research with calculations of frequency and reliability, the qualitative researcher analyzes information through overall interpretation and repetition of themes. Because this section of the book is interested in how black and mainstream newspapers constructed the tea party narrative over time, a textual analysis is appropriate.[127] Textual analysis requires a careful reading by the researcher of the texts, multiple times. This type of analysis extracts meaning from symbols embedded in the text and connecting them to broader narratives. On textual analysis:

> First, find the theme of the artifact. This involves asking, "what is the preferred reading of the artifact? What does the artifact ask the audience to believe, understand, feel, or think about?" . . . Second, find the interests expressed in the article. What voices or interests are included and/or favored in the primary themes? Third, find rhetorical strategies in the article that "might advance one ideology over another." . . . The "operational indicator," then, of journalists' crafting of resonance, is "the recurrence of formal textual features."[128]

This form of textual analysis is a valuable technique because "narrative is the best way to understand the human experience because it is the way humans understand their own lives."[129]

We began this analysis by reading through the texts and sorting based on recurrent themes.

We then conducted the quantitative data coding. We separated the stories again based on what myth we thought the story articulated and by recurrent themes. We then reread the texts and color-coded the rhetorical strategies and symbols informed by the resonant myth conceptual framework.

QUANTITATIVE DATA ANALYSIS

Overall, the quantitative analysis portion of the design has forty-eight variables. The first section of coding is comprised of identification. Because modern African-American newspapers contain many wire stories, we included that as a variable, including the type of wire, whether it was a predominantly white wire service such as the Associated Press, AP, or a predominantly black wire service such as the NNPA. This section also includes variables indicating the origins of a black or mainstream newspaper, the story's identification numbers, title, date of the story, URL, and whether the content is identified as news, commentary, or an editorial.

The second section consists of coders choosing the primary focus of the article. Thirty options exist, including tea party, President Obama, economy, unemployment, national debt, government spending, taxes, health care, Iraq, Afghanistan, foreign relations, terrorism, welfare, affirmative action, entitlement programs, crime, drugs, education, 2010 midterm elections, 2012 general election, race, gender, tea party as authentic voice, tea party as racist voice, tea party as possibly racist but not conclusive, tea party as possibly authentic but not conclusive, abortion, and other. These focus options came from previous research on the tea party, on issues salient to the black community, on coverage of black political empowerment, and on issues discussed during modern presidential elections.[130]

We used two criteria to determine a story's focus. First, because journalists are taught to not bury the lead, the title and first paragraph informed the focus. If the story maintained this focus throughout the story, we used these criteria to determine the focus. If the first criteria included more than one focus or if the rest of the story deviated greatly from the initial focus, we used sentence frequency to determine the story's focus. These variables are concerned with counting how many times a theme or issue is mentioned. From the list of possible foci, we added ideology and history. We added ideology because research on the mainstream press's coverage of the tea party points to ideology, and research on the black press says historical context is a key distinguishing feature. This does not mean that we put every sentence we collected into a category, though, since our list is fairly inclusive, most of them did fit somewhere. We coded when a sentenced focused on an issue or theme in our codebook. When a sentence focused on more than one issue or theme, we chose one focus. If two or more issues or themes were equally weighted in the sentence then we picked the one that came first. We did this because journalists are taught emphasis points in sentence structure. Audiences typically remember what is at the beginning or the end of a sentence and remember less the content in the middle. So, journalists put the information they want to emphasize either at the beginning or end, with most preferring the beginning of the sentence to help avoid passive voice. Thus, the first focus or issue was the one the journalist perceived to be the most salient.

The next two variables are tone variables; one is interested in tone in regards to the tea party and one is interested, if applicable, in tone towards Obama. Tone is measured as either negative, neutral, or positive. To be either negative or positive, sentences must contain explicit negative or positive language. For instance, "The tea party is a group of racists" or "President Obama is not doing a good job trying to solve issues affecting the African-American community" are examples of possible negative sentences that, if they outweigh the neutral sentences, could make a story negative. The next three variables consist of quote frequency for government officials, tea party members, and non-official and non–tea party member individuals to examine indexing comparisons between the two presses.

Variables eight through fifteen focused on implicit racial frames. Because we analyze how journalists interpreted the tea party, a group of whites opposing a black president, we expected two implicit frames, an implicit racial frame regarding President Obama and a tea party implicit racial frame. A President Obama implicit racial frame is one that contains: (1) a picture of the candidate (2) a reference to the candidate's race in the text and (3) a reference to the race of his/her constituents. This definition came from Caliendo and McIlwain's research on President Obama's implicit racial frames in the mainstream press. A story must contain all three of these to be considered a President Obama implicit racial frame.[131] Using the same terminology, a tea party implicit racial frame must be a picture of the tea party and a reference to its racial composition. Because the tea party is a dissenting group and not an elected official, we felt the need to include a reference to their constituents was unnecessary. Research has also shown that media race coverage tends to be an "us versus them" frame. Thus, we included a variable where both the tea party's race was mentioned and President Obama's race was mentioned; this constitutes an implicit "us versus them" frame. Variables sixteen and seventeen count how many stories included a photo, and the race of the individual in the photo. If the photo included more than one person with separate races, we chose the race that was most represented. Variables eighteen and nineteen counted the Facebook likes and Twitter Retweets reported on the story's page at the time.

INTERCODER RELIABILITY

One coder analyzed 10 percent of the sample and the author coded the entire 100 percent. Holsti's formula is used for intercoder agreement. The overall intercoder reliability was .884; reliability for tone was .914; reliability for focus was .891; and reliability for sentence theme was .823.

NOTES

1. Clay Shirky, *Here Comes Everybody: Revolution Doesn't Happen When Society Adopts New Technology, It Happens When Society Adopts New Behaviors* (New York, NY: Penguin Books, 2008). Lawrence Lessig, *Remix: Making Art and Commerce Thrive in the Hybrid Economy* (New York, NY: Penguin Press, 2008). Danah Boyd, "Can Social Network Sites Enable Political Action?" *International Journal of Media & Cultural Politics* 4, no. 2 (2008): 241–244. James Curran, "What Democracy Requires of the Media," *The Institutions of American Democracy: The Press* (2005): 120–140. Kaye Trammell and Ana Keshelashvili, "Examining the New Influencers: A Self-Presentation Study of A-List Blogs," *Journalism & Mass Communication Quarterly* 82, no. 4 (2005): 968–982. Morozov, *The Net Delusion*.

2. Andrew Chadwick, *Internet Politics: States, Citizens, and New Communication Technologies* (New York, NY: Oxford University Press, 2006).

3. Curran, "What Democracy Requires of the Media." Jurgen Habermas, *The Structural Transformation of the Public Sphere: An Inquiry Into a Category of Bourgeois Society* (Cambridge, MA: MIT Press, 1991). Jurgen Habermas, "Political Communication in Media Society: Does Democracy Still Enjoy an Epistemic Dimension? The Impact of Normative Theory on Empirical Research," *Communication Theory* 16, no. 4 (2006): 411–426.

4. Gaye Tuchman, "Objectivity as Strategic Ritual: An Examination of Newsmen's Notions of Objectivity," *American Journal of Sociology* (1972): 660–679.

5. Ben LaPoe and Andrea Miller, "Supervising Public Opinion: Voices Diffusing Disaster Coverage of the Dalian Oil Spill in China." Paper presented at the 2012 SPSA annual conference in New Orleans, Internet, Technology, and Media Division.

6. Shirky, *Here Comes Everybody*. Morozov, *The Net Delusion*. Boyd, "Can Social Network Sites Enable Political Action?"

7. Ibid.

8. Lori Pennington-Gray, Kiki Kaplanidou, and Ashley Schroeder, "Drivers of Social Media Use Among African Americans in the Event of a Crisis," *Natural Hazards* 66, no. 1 (2013): 77–95. Wilson et al., *Racism, Sexism, and the Media*.

9. Sloan, *Media in America*.

10. Ibid.

11. Ibid.

12. Ibid.

13. Keever et al., *U.S. News Coverage of Racial Minorities*, 63.

14. Ibid.

15. Ibid.

16. Ibid., 65.

17. Broussard, *African-American Foreign Correspondents*.

18. Sloan, *Media in America*.

19. Pride and Wilson, *A History of the Black Press*.

20. Hall, "Racist Ideologies."

21. Ibid., 164.

22. LaPoe, "Crafting the Narrative of Tea Party Dissent."

23. Hall, "Racist Ideologies," 164.

24. Hall, "Racist Ideologies," 161.

25. Ibid. Entman and Rojecki, *Black Image in the White Mind*.

26. Entman, "Toward Clarification of a Fractured Paradigm." Scheufele, "Framing as a Theory of Media Effects."

27. Berkowitz, *Cultural Meanings of News*.

28. Entman and Rojecki, *Black Image in the White Mind*.

29. Ibid., 114.

30. Mintz, *African American Voices*, xiii.

31. Sonenshein, "Can Black Candidates Win," 219.

32. Ibid. Swain, *Black Faces, Black Interests*.

33. McIlwain and Caliendo, *Race Appeal*.

34. LaPoe, "Gender and Race Cues."

35. McIlwain and Caliendo, *Race Appeal*.

36. Sonenshein, "Can Black Candidates Win," 1.

37. Swain, *Black Faces, Black Interests*. Hanks, *Struggle for Black Political Empowerment*.

38. Sonenshein, "Can Black Candidates Win." Robert Smith, "Recent Elections and Black Politics: The Maturation or Death of Black Politics?" *Political Science and Politics* 23, no. 2 (1990): 160–162. Carol Sigelman, Lee Sigelman, Barbara J. Walkosz, and Michael Nitz, "Black Candidates, White Voters: Understanding Racial Bias in Political Perceptions," *American Journal of Political Science* (1995): 243–265. Christopher Stout and Katherine Tate, "The 2008 Presidential Election, Political Efficacy, and Group Empowerment," *Politics, Groups, and Identities* 1, no. 2 (2013): 143–163. Todd Shaw, Kasim Ortiz, James McCoy, and Athena King, "The Last Black Mayor of Atlanta?" *Research in Race and Ethnic Relations* 18 (2013): 201–230.

39. John Maxwell Hamilton, Regina G. Lawrence, and Raluca Cozma, "The Paradox of Respectability: The Limits of Indexing and Harrison Salisbury's Coverage of the Vietnam War," *The International Journal of Press/Politics* 15, no. 1 (2010): 78–79.

40. Cook, *Governing With the News*. Cook, "Media as a Political Institution." Benjamin Page, "The Mass Media as Political Actors," *Political Science and Politics* 29, no. 1 (1996): 20–24.

41. Cook, *Governing With the News*.

42. Page, "Media as Political Actors."

43. Cook, *Governing With the News*, 5.

44. Lance Bennett, "Toward a Theory of Press-State Relations in the United States," *Journal of Communication* 40, no. 2 (1990): 103–127.

45. Ibid.

46. Cook, *Governing With the News*, 126.

47. Ibid.

48. Ibid.

49. Cook, *Governing With the News*, 127.

50. Ibid.

51. Cook, "Media as Political Institutions."

52. Ibid.

53. Dannagal G. Young and Russell M. Tisinger, "Dispelling Late-night Myths: News Consumption among Late-night Comedy Viewers and the Predictors of Exposure to Various Late-night Shows," *Harvard International Journal of Press/Politics* 11, no. 3 (2006): 113–134.

54. Cook, *Governing With the News*.

55. Ibid.

56. Sonenshein, "Can Black Candidates Win."

57. Swain, *Black Faces, Black Interests*.

58. Ibid.

59. Sonenshein, "Can Black Candidates Win."

60. Swain, *Black Faces, Black Interests*.

61. Hanks, *Struggle for Black Political Empowerment*.

62. Swain, *Black Faces, Black Interests*.

63. Ibid.

64. Ibid.

65. Ibid.

66. Hanks, *Struggle for Black Political Empowerment*.

67. Paul Sniderman and Michael Gray Hagen, *Race and Inequality: A Study in American Values* (Chatham, NJ: Chatham House, 1985). Paul Sniderman and Thomas Leonard Piazza, *The Scar of Race* (Cambridge, MA: Belknap Press of Harvard University Press, 1993). Jon Hurwitz and Mark Peffley, *Perception and Prejudice: Race and Politics in the United States* (New Haven, CT: Yale University Press, 1998). Paul Sniderman and Edward G. Carmines, *Reaching Beyond Race* (Cambridge, MA: Harvard University Press, 1997). Steven Finkel and John G. Geer, "A Spot Check: Casting Doubt on the Demobilizing Effect of Attack Advertising," *American Journal of Political Science* (1998): 573–595. Murray Edelman, *The Politics of Misinformation* (Cambridge, England: Cambridge University Press, 2001).

68. Kate Kenski, Bruce W. Hardy, and Kathleen Hall Jamieson, *The Obama Victory: How Media, Money, and Message Shaped the 2008 Election* (New York, NY: Oxford University Press, 2010).

69. Kenski et al., *The Obama Victory*.

70. Ibid.

71. McIlwain and Caliendo, *Race Appeal*.

72. Ibid.

73. Ibid.

74. Mendelberg, *The Race Card*. Tali Mendelberg, "Racial Priming Revived," *Perspectives on Politics* 6, no. 01 (2008): 109–123. Nayda Terkildsen, "When White Voters Evaluate Black Candidates: The Processing Implications of Candidate Skin Color, Prejudice, and Self-Monitoring," *American Journal of Political Science* (1993): 1032–1053. Nayda Terkildsen and David F. Damore, "The Dynamics of Racialized Media Coverage in Congressional Elections," *Journal of Politics* 61 (1999): 680–699. Nichalos Valentino, Vincent L. Hutchings, and Ismail K. White, "Cues That Matter: How Political Ads Prime Racial Attitudes During Campaigns," *American Political Science Review* 96, no. 1 (2002): 75–90. Nicholas Valentino, Michael W. Traugott, and Vincent L. Hutching, "Group Cues and Ideological Constraint: A Replication of Political Advertising Effects Studies in the Lab and in the Field," *Political Communication* 19, no. 1 (2002): 29–48. Stephen Caliendo and Charlton McIlwain, "Minority Candidates, Media Framing, and Racial Cues in the 2004 Election," *The Harvard International Journal of Press/Politics* 11, no. 4 (2006): 45–69. Charlton McIlwain and Stephen Caliendo, "Racial Frames and Potential Effects of Minority Candidates in the 2008 Presidential Election." In Annual Meeting of the Midwest Political Science Association, Chicago, Illinois, 2008. Jack Citrin, Donald

Philip Green, and David O. Sears, "White Reactions to Black Candidates: When Does Race Matter?" *Public Opinion Quarterly* 54, no. 1 (1990): 74–96.

75. McIlwain and Caliendo, *Race Appeal*.

76. Ibid.

77. Peter Caprariello, Amy Cuddy, and Susan T. Fiske, "Social Structure Shapes Cultural Stereotypes and Emotions: A Causal Test of the Stereotype Content Model," *Group Processes & Intergroup Relations* 12, no. 2 (2009): 147–155. Susan Fiske, Amy Cuddy, and Peter Glick, "Universal Dimensions of Social Cognition: Warmth and Competence," *Trends in Cognitive Sciences* 11, no. 2 (2007): 77–83. Walter Lippmann, *Public Opinion* (Mineola, NY: Dover Publications, 2004).

78. Ibid.

79. Christopher Campbell, *Race, Myth and the News* (Thousand Oaks, CA: Sage Publications, 1995). Donald Bogle, *Blacks in American Films and Television: An Encyclopedia* (New York, NY: Simon & Schuster, 1989). Julia Bristor, Renee Gravois Lee, and Michelle R. Hunt, "Race and Ideology: African-American Images in Television Advertising," *Journal of Public Policy & Marketing* (1995): 48–59. Paul Hartmann and Charles Husband, *Racism and the Mass Media* (Lanham, MD: Rowman & Littlefield, 1974). Dates and Barlow, *Split Image*. Donald Kinder and Lynn M. Sanders, *Divided by Color: Racial Politics and Democratic Ideals* (Chicago, IL: University of Chicago Press, 1996). Clint Wilson, Félix Gutiérrez, and Lena Chao, *Racism, Sexism, and the Media: The Rise of Class Communication in Multicultural America* (Los Angeles, CA: Sage Publications, Incorporated, 2013). Dines and Humez, *Gender, Race, and Class in Media*.

80. Entman and Rojecki, *Black Image in the White Mind*.

81. Ibid. John Zaller, *The Nature and Origins of Mass Opinion* (Cambridge, England: Cambridge University Press, 1992).

82. Hall, "Racist Ideologies."

83. Reeves, *Voting Hopes or Fears*.

84. Ibid.

85. Mendelberg, *The Race Card*.

86. Ibid. Jas Sullivan, "Race, Identity, and Candidate Support: A Test of ImplicitPreference." In Tasha S. Philpot and Ismail K. White, eds., *African-American Political Psychology: Identity, Opinion, and Action in the Post-Civil Rights Era* (New York, NY: Palgrave Macmillan, 2010).

87. Mendelberg, *The Race Card*.

88. Ibid.

89. Ibid.

90. Ibid.

91. Ibid.

92. Ibid.

93. Ibid., 8–9.

94. McIlwain and Caliendo, "Racial Frames and Potential Effects." McIlwain and Caliendo, *Race Appeal*.

95. Valentino et al., "Cues That Matter."

96. Citrin et al., "White Reactions to Black Candidates." Terkildsen, "When White Voters Evaluate Black Candidates." Stephen Caliendo and Charlton D. McIlwain, "Minority Candidates, Media Framing, and Racial Cues in the 2004 Election," *The Harvard International Journal of Press/Politics* 11, no. 4 (2006): 45–69. Charlton McIlwain and Stephen Caliendo, "Racial Frames and Potential Effects of Minority Candidates in the 2008 Presidential Election." In Annual Meeting of the Midwest Political Science Association, Chicago, Illinois, 2008.

97. Kathleen Hall Jamieson, *Dirty Politics: Deception, Distraction, and Democracy* (New York, NY: Oxford University Press, 1993). Edelman, *Politics of Misinformation*.

98. Ibid.

99. Ibid.

100. David Sears, Colette Van Laar, Mary Carrillo, and Rick Kosterman, "Is It Really Racism?: The Origins of White Americans' Opposition to Race-Targeted Policies," *The Public Opinion Quarterly* 61, no. 1 (1997): 16–53. David Sears and Patrick J. Henry, "The Origins of

Symbolic Racism," *Journal of Personality and Social Psychology* 85, no. 2 (2003): 259–275. Tessa Ditonto, Richard R. Lau, and David O. Sears, "Amping Racial Attitudes: Comparing the Power of Explicit and Implicit Racism Measures in 2008," *Political Psychology* (2013).

101. Swain, *Black Faces, Black Interests.*

102. Smith, "Recent Elections and Black Politics." Jennifer Hochschild, *Facing Up to the American Dream: Race, Class, and the Soul of the Nation* (Princeton, NJ: Princeton University Press, 1996).

103. Ibid.

104. Ibid.

105. Swain, *Black Faces, Black Interests.*

106. McIlwain and Caliendo, *Race Appeal.*

107. Ibid.

108. Ibid.

109. Entman and Rojecki, *Black Image in the White Mind.*

110. McIlwain and Caliendo, *Race Appeal.*

111. Ibid.

112. Ibid.

113. David Altheide, *Qualitative Media Analysis* (Thousand Oaks, CA: Sage Publications, 1996).

114. Klaus Krippendorff, *Content Analysis: An Introduction to its Methodology* (Los Angeles, CA: SAGE Publications, 2012).

115. Altheide, *Qualitative Media Analysis.*

116. Klaus Bruhn Jensen, "The Complementarity of qualitative and quantitative methodologies in media and communication research," in *A Handbook of Media and Communication Research*, Klaus Bruhn Jensen, ed. (London: Routledge, 2002), 272.

117. Ibid., 13–14.

118. Carey, *Communication as Culture.*

119. Clawson, "Framing Supreme Court Decisions: The Mainstream Versus the Black Press."

120. Personal interview with Dr. Jinx Broussard.

121. Sloan, *Media in America.*

122. David Knoke, George Bohrnstedt, and Alisa Mee, *Statistics for Social Data Analysis* (New York, NY: Wadsworth, 2002).

123. Roger Wimmer and Joseph R. Dominick, *Mass Media Research: An Introduction* (New York, NY: Wadsworth Publishing Company, 2006).

124. Ibid.

125. Ibid.

126. John Jack Morris, "Textual Analysis in Journalism," in *Qualitative Research in Journalism*, Sharton Iorio, ed. (Mahwah, NJ: Lawrence Erlbaum, 2004), 163.

127. Lule, *Daily News.*

128. LaPoe, "Crafting the Narrative of Tea Party Dissent," 12.

129. Laurel Richardson, *Writing Strategies: Reaching Diverse Audiences* (Thousand Oaks, CA: SAGE Publications, Incorporated, 1990), 133.

130. Swain, *Black Faces, Black Interests.*

131. McIlwain and Caliendo, *Race Appeal.*

Chapter Three

Black Press Tea Party Narrative

Through a resonant myth qualitative conceptual lens, an examination critically and culturally based, this chapter details the tea party newspaper articles produced by digital black newspapers.

BLACK PRESS TEA PARTY NARRATIVE

The black press harnessed the villain myth, the inverse of the hero, to interpret the tea party. The hero is the most popular and enduring myth. The figure personifies culture's core values and beliefs, frequently in the face of overwhelming challenges normally causing a figure to abandon his or her values. The hero is humble, initiates a quest, wins battle decisively, and returns as triumphant.[1] Conversely, the villain personifies fringe beliefs and values, usually the face overwhelmingly challenging the hero. The villain attempts to rob the hero of his or her morals. The villain is arrogant and tries to thwart the hero's quest. Typically, the villain eventually fails, though the villain can have some victories during the quest serving as setbacks for the hero and questions his or her courage.[2]

The black press's narrative added a unique precursor to the villain myth—historically consistent. The black press did not interpret the tea party as a "new" conservative group but rather a group of whites consistently opposing equality and African Americans throughout history. Regardless of the tea party's intents or motivations, they were perceived and articulated as historically consistent threats, villains, to their communities. The tea party was an extreme clique in a group, Republicans, that have not historically represented minorities' interests. The historically consistent villain is a divider, a hijacker of ideology, an angry figure demanding a lower standard of discourse while promoting a retroactive culture; this figure preys on vulnerable voices, has no conscience, and camouflages his or her communication through code words and actions.

Tea Party Surfaces, Again: 2009

The tea party narrative in the black press sample for this book first appeared on April 15, 2009, with an Associated Press article appearing in the *Chicago Defender* titled "Obama: Get the dread out of tax deadline day."[3] The story began, "President Obama declared on tax-filing day that he aims to ease the dread of deadline day with a simpler tax code that rewards work and the pursuit of the American dream," adding, "his words were hardly met with universal applause."[4] The story explained that the president's tax goals were immediately met with dissent. "Across the country, protesters met at state-houses and town squares to oppose Obama's federal spending since he took office. Organizers said they wanted to channel the spirit of the Boston Tea Party's rebellion."[5] According to the AP story selected by the *Chicago Defender*, this was the beginning of the tea party.

A week later, the *Chicago Defender* published a columnist's analysis of the tea party's formation. "I applaud any Americans who want to peacefully but forcefully critique their government, but these tea parties aren't about making change as much as they are about citizen anger being used to promote a corporate agenda."[6] The author attended a tea party gathering and observed the meeting "was reflective of a wide swath of America. So long as that 'wide swath' was mostly over the age of 45 and Caucasian and didn't vote for the sitting president."[7] He then commented on the group's stated reason for forming, "this version of [their story] has a nice 'anti-government tax' spin to it, even though that is not the real motivation behind the tea party."[8] He concluded the group's motivations originated from a disdain for a black president, not concerns over government taxing.

On September 4, 2009, the *Washington Informer* published an AP story reporting on the tea party's scorn of President Obama's health care reform efforts. The article, titled "Health Care Lobbyists Target Returning Congress," indicated the tea party was "unleashing a torrent" of traditional lobbying techniques.[9] The tea party, a group insisting it was "grassroots," had partnered with the health insurance industry to oppose reforming health care, according to the article. The *Skanner*, in Portland, published a story describing tea party health care reform protests in D.C., offering the group was gaining momentum with dissent originating with bailouts, tax policies, and the economic stimulus. It described the protest where tea partiers carried slogans "Obamacare makes me sick" and posters of President Obama dressed as Hitler and the joker. One "black republican leader denounced African-American politicians that she said had an 'affinity' for socialism" because they supported President Obama's platform.[10]

The *Los Angeles Sentinel* published an opinion piece by Reverend Jesse Jackson, who wrote that federally run health care was "a proven success," not socialism as the tea party argued.[11] He criticized the tea party's attacks on President Obama because its members were, he argued, unwitting pawns for corporations. "The angry tea party protestors who feel they are getting shafted by the government are aligning themselves with the very folks who are selling them out."[12] He pointed to Medicare as an example of successful government-administered health care.

An NNPA article published by the *New Pittsburgh Courier* and titled, "Tea Party Marchers Far Right and White," offered: "Comments from the crowd, and certainly their signs and t-shirts, indicated that it was more than big government being protested. There were many people displaying signs against health care reform, President Obama's right to take office and calling his ideology and religion into question."[13] Representative Elijah Cummings, a Democrat from Maryland, said, "when you listen to their comments, many of them didn't know what they were protesting. So it makes you wonder what it's really about," adding that the tea party "would rather kill Obama's dream than give his constituents what they need."[14]

On September 24, 2009, the *Skanner*, in a columnist's article titled "President Carter Was Right to Raise Race Issue," disputed Republican National Committee Chairman Michael Steele's assertion, "this isn't about race. It's about policy."[15] Steele was responding to former President Jimmy Carter's opinion stating, "an overwhelming portion of the intensely demonstrated animosity toward President Barack Obama is based on the fact that he is a black man."[16] This came a day after South Carolina Republican Congressman Joe Wilson yelled "you lie!" while President Obama addressed Congress.[17] The article added some historical context defending the perception the tea party's anger was more about race than actual issues. For instance, "one of the major criticisms of civil rights leaders for years has been that too many decent whites choose to remain silent on the issue of race, ceding the spotlight to mean-spirited Caucasians who are insensitive to the suffering of African Americans."[18] This, according to the columnist, resulted in more whites speaking out about race issues, which in turn caused more opposition by "crazy" whites who believe they are somehow more oppressed than African Americans.[19]

On September 24, 2009, the *Los Angeles Sentinel* published a columnist's article titled "Obama's Agenda and Rights' Attacks Interconnected."[20] He wrote that tea partiers

> are attempting to annihilate president Obama who, at times, gives them additional ammunition. He is being hit from several fronts on a host of issues in addition to healthcare reform, including immigration, Iraq, Afghanistan, terrorism, missile deployment, LGBT and the financial bailouts. The motivation

for the current scurrilous campaign against Obama is, in significant measure, racially motivated. [21]

The author's evidence to back up his claim pointed to Representative Wilson's "you lie" remark, conservative pundits denigrating President Obama's infant policies given no time to actually take effect, and tea party assertions that President Obama is a Muslim and a socialist and not an American citizen. The article also listed President Obama as a culprit because he didn't confront the racial undercurrents, instead "skirting the race issue and not discernibly" representing black concerns or issues; in other words, the columnist said President Obama was allowing the villain to bully him. [22]

The *Bay State Banner*, on October 1, 2009, published a commentary arguing the United States has no desire to have a real conversation on race. The author wrote: "If we resided in a post-racial society, then the words William Faulkner wrote in the mid-twentieth century would not ring true today: 'The past is never dead. It's not even in the past.'"[23] The author pointed to the attacks on President Obama as reason to believe America is not post racial. For instance, signs of "Afro-Communist" and "Obama Ribs n Chicken" permeated tea party rallies where the members carried guns and argued President Obama was not a true American. The author quoted former President Jimmy Carter, who said racism "bubbled to the surface because of a belief among many white people—not just in the South, but around the country—that African Americans are not qualified to lead."[24]

As 2009 neared its end, black press newspapers reflected on President Obama's first year. The *Los Angeles Sentinel* argued blacks' high expectations of President Obama were unfair. [25] While black unemployment still remained double the national average, President Obama had, it seemed, stopped the economic free fall from getting worse and had made significant gains on health care reform. A major barrier, the article argued, President Obama faced was the tea party and its growing influence on the Republican Party. The article also opined those who voted for President Obama were to blame for not actively and openly disagreeing with the tea party. "The tea party crowd capitalizes on the silence of the white majority, many of whom apparently voted for Obama out of desperation and have reverted to a more comfortable, race-based reticence."[26]

Tea Party's Political Traction: 2010

In 2010, a year when the tea party posed serious threats to African-American issues, black political power, and racial solidarity during the midterms, the historically consistent villain gained more traction. In an article titled, "Former Congressman, Palin Blast Obama at Tea Party Gathering," the *Baltimore Afro-American* described a tea party gathering where the primary focus was to denigrate the president and make it harder for his constituency to vote. [27] After bashing President Obama's policies and calling him a socialist and proposing a poll tax and literacy tests in order to vote, Congressman Tom Tancredo "claimed that there was a 'cult of multiculturalism' at work in the country. He told CBS news there 'was a devotion to a multiculturalist agenda' which he believed could 'divide American up into these subgroups.'" [28]

On February 11, 2010, the *New Pittsburgh Courier* criticized the mainstream press for trying to "legitimize the tea party movement as a resurgent mobilization of the American people but when you listen to them say who they are, there are distinct traces of the Republican Party in their approval of limited, or small government, and national security." [29] The article, titled "Tea Party Racism," recounted historical accounts using the same language as the tea party. For instance, Mississippi governor George Wallace and Republican Barry Goldwater, who "were directly opposed to blacks and their interests," used the same platform of anti-taxes and anti–big government as a vehicle of oppression, even though their policies did not reflect their beliefs in less taxes and smaller government. [30] The tea party, according to this article, was using the same political devices as their predecessors because they could not stand the sight of a black president who, at that point, had not substantively governed much differently than his conservative white peers.

Early during President Obama's first term, health care reform was a major priority. This issue is especially salient to the black community because it is one of those issues where African Americans are disproportionately disfranchised. The *Baltimore Afro-American*, on March 7, 2010, published a story about the National Urban League categorizing health care reform as a modern civil rights issue. The journalist noted President Obama's primary opponent to this legislation, the tea party, citing possible reasons "for the decline in faith in civil rights" issues "is the misunderstanding of what improving civil rights actually entails." [31] This story's interpretation of the tea party's opposition to health care reform viewed them as a barrier to achieving equal opportunity, a villain trying to stop their quest.

The *Los Angeles Sentinel* published on article covering a Supreme Court case, *McDonald v. City of Chicago*, that the columnist feared would prohibit cities from regulating ownership of firearms. "We have become addicted to violence," because "at home, violence is glorified, depicted rapturously in movies and TV" and "African Americans and Latinos are constantly depicted on television shows as more violent than we are. Our news programs run on the theory that if it bleeds, it leads. Far too many of the tea party zealots flaunt their guns, threaten violence and specifically invoke the president's name in threats." [32] The image of tea parties, protesting President Obama, gathering with guns signaled not only a substantive threat to black issues, but to physical safety as well, echoing visions of the Civil War and Jim Crow; the villain threatened on more than one front.

The image of "ugly, menacing" zealots continued in a *New Pittsburgh Courier* article titled, "Tea Party, Coffee Party: Why Not a Black Party."[33] The journalist, after discussing the coffee party, a group organized to be an antithesis to the tea party, wrote he was horrified by the "anti-government spirit of the tea party crowd that emerged to disrupt the flow of civil discussion about important issues."[34] He suggested "a black party could enable the discussion about accountability to focus on the cabinet agencies where the federal budget exists to achieve some of the things needed by the black community."[35] As tea party candidates were emerging to challenge incumbents in the midterm elections, and still vehemently protesting health care reform with violence, sometimes,[36] the journalist offered an entirely different approach: a group of protestors would peacefully assemble, work within the structure of the system, and advocate for the interests of the black community the journalist thought, with the exception of health care, were still being ignored, even by a black president.[37]

A common theme emerged in the black press's coverage contributing to the use of the historically consistent villain myth—the Republican Party and the tea party were not viewed as separately distinct entities; instead, from the black press's perspective, they were the same group with a distaste for diversity and minority issues. The *Chicago Defender* published an article titled, "Right-wing Republicans Often Masquerade as Tea Baggers," on March 31, 2010.[38] The columnist wrote the "conjunction of a black president and a female speaker of the house—topped off by a wise Latina on the Supreme Court and a powerful gay congressional committee chairman—would sow fears of disenfranchisement among a dwindling and threatened minority in the country no matter what polices were in play."[39]

Another *Chicago Defender* article took it one step further, asserting the tea party was not only racist in nature, but were essentially terrorists. The article, titled "Tea Party Serving Terrorism," opined:

> I have always maintained that there is a grotesque racial element to many tea party rallies and that the anger directed towards the Obama administration cannot be legitimately chalked up to passionate voters. Let's be candid: there are a lot of Americans out there that just hate the idea that there is a black man in the White House . . . I have been to tea party events, I have seen how these groups encourage and foment a level of antipathy and racism towards immigrants and the president that is nothing short of a soft shoe Klan rally.[40]

A *New Pittsburgh Courier* column titled "Tea Party Terrorism" agreed, stating, "if Obama really wants to rile up the public with a strong anti-terrorism stand he can start by looking in our own backyard at the growing militancy and violence associated with the tea party patriots movement."[41] The article, calling the tea party a "growing militancy" prone to violence, touched on a hypocritical belief reverberating through white America—only nonwhites can be terrorists. [42] This columnist highlighted, statistically speaking, terrorist acts are committed by more whites than nonwhites. He equated the growing tea party as an emerging terrorist threat, not only in terms of physicality, but also in the policies they espoused and opposed, all policies in one way or another detrimental to the black community. The tea partiers were not only terrorists because they threatened physical violence, but they also threatened legislative destruction. As the tea party gained traction nationally and it became apparent they could obtain success during the midterms, this terrorist, villainous threat became more real every day for the black community in 2010.

Different than most terrorists, whose primary objective is to inflict terror and chaos, the tea party did have a goal—stop black political representation. The *Tri-State Defender* reported on tea party platforms opposing health care reform on the tried and true "states' rights argument." [43] The tea party argued health care reform infringed on states' rights, much like secessionists argued in favor of slavery during the civil war and Republican legislators argued during the civil rights movement, according to the article. The author wrote: "Segregationists used the same ideas in the 1950s to oppose the *Brown vs. Board of Education* decision. . . . In the 19th century those who believed they had a right to enslave black America advocated the same concept." [44]

On April 1, 2010, the *Michigan Chronicle* published an article titled "Public Radio, Ethnic Media Sound Alarm of Growing Right Wing Extremism." It announced an initiative sponsored by Wayne State University investigating conservative extremism. [45] The initiative was driven by the collaboration of the "region's most-read independent newspapers, the *Jewish News*, the *Arab American News*, the *Michigan Chronicle*, and *Latino Press*." [46] The diversity of the collaboration indicates the tea party was a villain not only to the black community, but to a large cluster of nonwhites. "The explosive growth of three distinct groups, the tea party movement, the patriot movement, with the militias as their paramilitary arms, and the nativist anti-immigration movement has been under way for the past year" and threatened minority cultures. [47]

The *Los Angeles Sentinel* argued these groups, specifically the tea party, should not be viewed as separate from the Republican Party. "The so-called tea party and Republican Party are essentially the same," and "they differ only in style. The tea party's big dust bowl rally last weekend . . . was led by Sarah Palin, who, script in hand, whipped up a cheering crowd. 'Don't tread on me' signs and ugly anger set the tone of the rally in the desert." [48] In an attempt to try and more fully understand the anger radiating from the tea party, the *New Pittsburgh Courier* published an article titled "Tea-ed Off." [49] The only answer the article could come up with, after highlighting the hypocritical nature of their alleged policy platform, concluded the only plausible reason they could attack so vehemently was race: "With so much news coverage surrounding the heated rhetoric coming from the tea party, I thought it would be instructive to dissect their anger to see if we can come away with some understanding of their issues."[50] However, "when they say, 'we want our country back,' who is the 'we?' Are they referring to white people, since that is what their group is comprised of? . . . Name me one freedom that Obama or the Democrats have taken away from you."[51]

The *Chicago Defender*, on April 28, 2010, echoed similar sentiments:

> They have created a mythology world in their heads that has no resemblance to our actual reality. They are so unsettled by a black president of the United States, not to mention the changes that are underway in the country—demographically speaking—that they are searching for answers wherever they may be found.[52]

The notoriously conservative broadcast station and frequent tea party champion was a target of criticism of a *New Pittsburgh Courier* column titled, "Bill O'Reilly's Obsession With Playing Race Card."[53] The piece reported on O'Reilly's fascination with chastising those who ever questioned the racial nature of politics; he frequently asserted those who did raise racial concerns were "playing the race card," in order to win an argument.[54] When Al Sharpton suggested some, not all, of the tea party's members probably have some racial resentment or fear, O'Reilly attacked him. The article responded, "though calling the tea party gang and their supporters such as O'Reilly racist," may be an overstatement, "calling them white supremacists is right on target."[55]

The Republican Party, tea partiers, and conservative talk show hosts were not the only figures reported on in the black press's tea party narrative. They also criticized President Obama. In a news article written by the NNPA and published in the *New Pittsburgh Courier* on May 11, 2010, titled "Despite Widespread Appeals, Obama Fails to Nominate Black Woman to Supreme Court" the reporter described President Obama's inability, or unwillingness, to increase diversity on the Supreme Court.[56] "Still, the letter was strong and clear, sending an 'end-of-honeymoon' type message that President Obama must begin to listen to those he credits for having put him in office with hopes for black progress."[57] The article criticized President Obama for compromising with the tea party and Republicans, urging the president to fight back against the tea party and fight for African-American interests. A villain needs a hero to fight, and President Obama filled the hero role; however, this hero was not without faults, according to the black press—with timidity and overcompromising with the villain his primary failing.

Though the tea party was/is comprised primarily of whites, some non-whites do fill their ranks. In a column titled "Black Tea Party Activists Say Don't Call Us Traitors," the author reported on an incident when representatives were spit on and called racial slurs following passage of health care reform. Black tea partiers questioned the authenticity of the claims:

> There was mild surprise when a small contingent of black tea party bloggers and writers screamed loudly that Georgia congressman John Lewis made up that he was spit on and called the n-word as he left the cannon building across from the capitol in the hours before the final vote on the health care reform bill. The black tea party activists demanded that democrats produce the tapes to prove that Lewis attacked.[58]

The article then went on to explain historical context concerning general discontent blacks have with the Republican Party. President Abraham Lincoln was a Republican, and it was southern democrats primarily opposing him during the civil war. However, during the civil rights movement, the two parties switched agendas and ideologies and Republicans became the party opposing equality.[59] This modern version of Republicans tried to thwart and halt civil rights; they did not want African Americans in schools with white children, they did not want African Americans in the same restaurants or same buses as whites, and they certainly did not want blacks to have the right to vote. The article explains the black community has not forgotten Republican hostility.[60] So, when they see tea partiers attacking a black president for policies his white predecessors pursued, while at the same time trying to dismantle programs designed to ameliorate prior institutional racism and making it harder to vote or secure education, it is clear why the black press interpreted the group as a historically consistent villain.

For example, an editorial in the *New Pittsburgh Courier* on June 8, 2010, began, "Rand Paul is on the wrong side of history."[61] The author wrote:

> Rand Paul, the tea party Republican Senate nominee from Kentucky, recently made it clear in a series of media interviews that he disagrees with the public accommodations provision in the Civil Rights Act on the grounds that it intrudes on the rights of private business owners. In other words, if he had been around to vote for the act, he would have joined openly racist Southern conservatives in arguing that hotel, restaurant and retail store owners should have the right to bar African Americans from their establishment. That is a bizarre and retrogressive view, more suited to a political campaign in 1910 than in 2010.[62]

The *Skanner* published an editorial written by the NNPA editor-in-chief. The piece began by referencing the epithets Congressman Lewis experienced following the passage of health care reform. The author then expressed, in a society supposedly moving towards post-racialism, it appeared explicit racism was becoming more commonplace. These messages, he argued, were emanating primarily from the tea party: "It is the Obama factor. It is a big factor" because "having an African American as president has brought out the worst in some white Americans."[63] While President Obama's emergence brought out the best in some, the tea party represented the worst, "extremists who" see President "Obama as a Marxist, a socialist, they question whether he was born in the United States."[64] According to the author, it is nearly impossible to reason with a villain of this sort, one who will find fault in anything and everything President Obama tried to accomplish.

Well-known conservative commentator and tea party champion Glenn Beck booked a rally at the Lincoln Memorial on August 28, 2010—preventing black civil rights leaders from organizing a march "to commemorate the forty-seventh anniversary of the historic march on Washington and Dr. Martin Luther King's famed 'I Have a Dream' speech" at the location where it took place.[65] This was interpreted as an attack on Dr. King's legacy, and the National Urban League president vowed not to "let Glenn Beck own the symbolism."[66]

On June 30, 2010, the *New Pittsburgh Courier* reported the assault on civil rights' legacies continued. The column suggested white tea party candidates for the midterms were making serious progress and gaining popularity by attacking Social Security and unemployment benefits, saying the programs "have spoiled people to the point that you don't want the jobs that are available."[67] Another column on July 7, 2010, began "there have been only six African-Americans in the United States Senate in history."[68] Black solidarity is seen as one solution to helping solve problems plaguing the black community, such as unemployment. The 2010 midterms, according to the story, posed a serious threat, primarily from the tea party, because the Senate could be all white. With no black voices at the table, the article asked how could policies designed to protect their community be preserved, especially when the possible incoming tea party candidates believed they shouldn't exist in the first place.[69]

In an editorial titled "Racism in the Tea Party Must End," the *New York Amsterdam News* wrote:

> Our nation is caught in the throes of a sundry of potentially divisive issues, and it would only exacerbate the problems we collectively face to entertain bitter exchanges with the tea party or any other group that would derail us from our objective of One Nation, One Dream: a nation working together, not combating those who often forget how much we have in common.[70]

As the elections neared, the black press focused on salient policy platforms. For instance, the *Arizona Informant*, on October 4, 2010, published an article titled "Jobs Top Priority for One Nation Marchers."[71] The story began by reporting on the One Nation Working Together rally held at the Lincoln Memorial, intended to be a protest against the tea party–led rally held at the same place in August. The article then cited many protestors who expressed concern over jobs, and how the platforms proposed by the tea party could make unemployment worse. "We came to show our support for President Obama and to stand up for jobs, justice, and education."[72] The tea party, according to this article, attacked all of those, President Obama, jobs, justice, and education. The article did not view the tea party as a grassroots movement; instead, they were interpreted as big government, corporate pawns.[73]

Beyond their substantive proposals, the tea partiers' social stances were also scrutinized in the black press. "One by one, tea party challengers have veered away from the issues of taxes and spending" because, "either by the media or by the Democrats," the tea party insurgents were portrayed "not as populist alternatives to the mainstream GOP but as Republican regulars."[74] The article cited Carl Paladino, who said, "children shouldn't be brainwashed into thinking homosexuality is acceptable," and Ken Buck, who "tried to deflect questions about his stance against abortion," and Christine O'Donnell, who was portrayed as a witch preaching against "the evils of masturbation," and Sharron Angle, the "faith-based politician" who "doesn't believe the Constitution requires separation of church and state."[75] The tea party "was born in anger over the recession and the Obama administration's bailouts, and built largely on a platform of lower taxes and smaller government. But some of its candidates are getting tripped up on social issues."[76]

On October 14, 2010, the *Los Angeles Sentinel* published an article titled "GOP Pledges Tea Party Lynching."[77] The journalist wrote:

> In a stunning display of bigotry and viciousness, powerful Republicans are raising millions of dollars to support an extreme crop of GOP candidates . . . called "tea party candidates," and they are being funding by the Super rich who have been promised $4 trillion in tax cuts for their support of the GOP. These tea party Republicans are directly attacking blacks, Latinos, women and gays—and they are winning votes in the process.[78]

With polling numbers suggesting incumbents were in serious trouble versus tea partiers, the *Baltimore Afro-American* cited a study suggesting the black vote could be crucial to a democratic win, and "the increasing traction of the tea party—including its racist elements" might "propel black voters to the polls and possibly deny the Republicans wins."[79] Black unemployment was double the national average during the recession; the black press gave President Obama credit for helping not make it worse. Losing key allies in Congress and the Senate was viewed as an attack on President Obama and the progress, though slower than hoped, he had made.[80] The *Skanner* wrote:

> In just a few weeks, we will face a critical turning point for our nation. On Tuesday, Nov. 2, your family's future, the strength of your community, and the direction of our country will be on the ballot. . . . So, to all my Republican colleagues and their new tea party friends . . . we're not taking one step back.[81]

To avert taking steps backwards, the *New Pittsburgh Courier* urged its audience to vote. In an editorial titled "We Must Vote," the writer offered:

> Now, less than two years later, as the country gradually recovers from the reign of George Bush and Dick Cheney and a Republican Congress, the same people who put us in this predicament are masquerading as the tea party in an effort to rid the country of President Barack Obama by placing do nothing obstructionists in the Senate, House and the governor's office throughout the country. . . . Many of us fought hard to get the first black man elected in 2008.[82]

The *Washington Informer* warned the tea party strategy to winning elections depended on low minority turnout.[83] The tea party won several elections during the 2010 midterms and several Democrat incumbents lost their jobs; black politicians who survived lost key leadership roles under the tea party–infused Congress. The villain, now strengthened by victory, did not waste any time attacking black interests.[84]

On November 10, 2010, the *Arizona Informant* addressed the extremism of tea party members and cited whites validating the characterization. "These boys are crazy, they're tea party people . . . I've had white people calling me up saying these guys are extremely conservative and so far out of the mainstream. Can you see them talking with Maxine Waters? I'd like to be a fly on the wall."[85] The *Florida Star* reported it took the tea party little time to fulfill campaign promises to attack minorities by cancelling unemployment extensions. According to the article, the villain organized and acted quickly.[86] The *Washington Informer* noted if the tea party successfully defeated President Obama, blacks would crash with him, "the GOP and the tea party may have captured the House and much of the governorships, but they have not captured the moral high ground or the battlefield of America where our civil rights martyrs spilled their blood to advance honorable causes."[87]

Tea Party Institutional Damage: 2011

After tea party successes during the 2010 midterms, online black newspapers reported on the damage the villain accomplished at an institutional level in 2011. On January 22, 2011, the *Baltimore Afro-American* reported a North Carolina "school board abolishes integration policy."[88] A tea party–controlled "school board in Raleigh, N.C. has abolished a school zoning policy intended to encourage racially—and economically—mixed schools."[89] The tea partiers said, "diversity should no longer be a priority for public schools."[90] The article quoted NAACP president Todd Jealous, "so far, for all the chatter we heard from tea partiers has not manifested in actually putting in place retrograde policies. But this is one place where they have literally attempted to turn back the clock."[91]

Michael Williams, a retired Texas Railroad commissioner, announced he would run for the Senate with tea party backing. The tea party favorite said, "he wants to bring his starkly conservative views—including no preferential treatment for blacks in higher education, acceleration of oil exploration in coastal areas and a reduced role for federal government in public policy."[92] On February 5, 2011, a Pennsylvania high school, heavily influenced by the tea party, abandoned "an education program built" to end "racial segregation" in public schools.[93] The proposed eradication of integration, according to the article, was similar to "one of the more prominent cases" in Raleigh, North Carolina, "where the tea party–backed Wake County School Board is advancing its agenda to end integration in the school system."[94]

While attacking one of civil rights' earliest issues, education, the tea party also sought to rewrite the history of race relations in America, according to a February 18, 2011, *New York Amsterdam News* article. The author wrote, "it is a good thing that the leaders within the tea party aren't in charge of running the nation's observances of Black History Month" because the tea party would tarnish and destroy the legacy of civil rights.[95]

> Recently, one of the movement's most high profile officials, Michele Bachmann, the ultra-conservative congresswoman from Minnesota, offered a total, well, whitewash, of the story of slavery . . . saying that the United States was founded by leaders with a tolerance for ethnic diversity and that the country's founders were responsible for abolishing slavery.[96]

The villain, once considered only a fringe group by many white newspapers, became part of the mainstream political culture in 2011—some tea party favorites, such as Michele Bachmann and possibly Sarah Palin, eyed the oval office.[97]

On February 14, 2011, President Obama released the 2012 budget. "Perhaps in reaction to Republican and tea party voters, the budget will cut $1.1 trillion from the federal deficit over the next ten years."[98] While few can argue that reducing the federal deficit is bad, the article expressed disappointment in where those cuts would occur. "Some unfortunate cuts such as the reduction for funding for Community Development Block Grants and the Low Income Energy Assistance Program" would hit African-American communities the hardest.[99] The *Chicago Defender* asked if the African-American community should bank on the recovery.[100] The columnist wrote:

> Good news—the unemployment rate is dropping, last month from 9 percent to 8.9 percent, a scant drop. Better news—the private sector is finally generating jobs, 192,000 to be exact, last month. . . . Even worst news is the intransigence of Washington tea party Republicans that want to cut budgets so drastically that they will minimize the future possibilities of our nation.[101]

A historically dependable tenet of the black press was reporting on issues affecting all nonwhites, not just African Americans.[102] The *Bay State Banner* noted how the tea party targeted all minority groups, not just blacks.[103] The news article reported on tea partiers arguing "illegal immigrants" were taking minorities' jobs. The articled quoted Representative Emanuel Cleaver II, Chairman of the Congressional Black Caucus, who said, "I am concerned by the majority's attempt to manufacture tension between African Americans and immigrant communities."[104]

Racial tensions continued to increase according to a *Philadelphia Tribune* article titled "Time Short, Tempers Flare in Budget Showdown" on March 28, 2011.[105] Regarding budget negotiations between the tea party, the GOP, and President Obama, the journalist quoted Senate Majority Leader Harry Reid, who said, "Republicans refuse to negotiate" because the tea party kept "our negotiating partner from the negotiating table. And it's pretty hard to negotiate with someone else on the other side of the table."[106] According to the article, Democrats and President Obama were not able to negotiate with Republicans.

Regardless of the tea party's desire to circumvent the president, and his allies, the black press still saw him as a powerful, symbolic figure. In a column titled "Obama Matters as a President and a Black Leader" the *New York Amsterdam News*, on April 7, 2011, noted President Obama's symbolic significance was impossible to ignore, no matter how much the tea party wanted to attack it and at the same time silent it.[107] The commenting professor wrote:

> The 2008 election of Barack Obama as president of the United States clearly represented another major step forward in the long struggle of African Americans for full equality. [Given] that the Bush administration's policies, [and the Republican party in general] were often hostile or indifferent to the black community, African Americans had every right to expect that the new president would substantively address their concerns. Therefore, it is most ironic that, as the black community's concerns to be largely taken for granted by the administration, those groups, [such as the tea party] who did not vote for him have used protest, media campaigns and the ballot box to compel Obama to deal with their concerns . . . In today's political climate, the right wing attacks on Obama by the tea party and others have clearly resulted in the black community's closing ranks to support the president even when they may disagree with his policies.[108]

The tea party narrative proved how strong black solidarity can be. While most black journalists or columnists were disappointed in their hero for not fully representing their interests, and at times, bowing to the interests of their villain, the tea party, the black press still supported him. The *Los Angeles*

Sentinel published a column titled "Obama's Twisting Blurs His Priorities" on April 21, 2001.[109] The author wrote:

> I support President Obama because he is unquestionably a positive alternative to George W. Bush. That said, however, like many others, blacks especially, I am very concerned about his propensity for accommodation and reversing himself on major issues. On certain domestic and foreign policy matters his position is indistinguishable from that of his predecessor.[110]

The author continued to argue the black communities' hero, President Obama, compromised with their villain, the tea party, too much.

President Obama compromised with the villain despite the tea party's propensity for disseminating explicit racism. For instance, on April 28, 2011, the *Skanner* published an article titled "Racism: The Monkey on the Tea Party's Back."[111] The NNPA correspondents wrote: "Another day. Another outrageous example of how deeply the election of a black American of mixed parentage has unhinged some conservative White Americans."[112] Marilyn Davenport, a tea party member on the Republican central committee in California, sent an email with a picture of Obama as a chimpanzee, "underneath the doctored photo, Davenport, who is 74, had typed the words: 'Now you know why—no birth certificate.'"[113]

When tea partiers contested raising the debt ceiling, a fairly normal procedure many presidents had executed prior to President Obama without much resistance, black press newspapers questioned their true motives. The *Tri-State Defender* published a column titled "Debt Ceiling, What's That? And Why Does It Need to Be Raised?"[114] The author wrote: "But, some approach the debt ceiling with a hidden agenda."[115] One prominent Republican, and at times tea party favorite, Newt Gingrich, criticized Ron Paul's debt ceiling stance and goal to "eviscerate the Medicare program."[116] According to the column, the tea party's backlash against Gingrich's opinion was so intense he reversed his position. "Those who believe the government" should protect minorities' interests "must advocate for it and reject the tea party arguments that the best government is a small one."[117]

While the tea party was dismantling education programs designed to give all children equal opportunity, and holding the debt ceiling hostage as a negotiating tool, the GOP field for the Republican nomination for president in 2012 began to emerge. The *Skanner* noted the GOP field, because of the tea party's influence, had shifted further to the right than it ever had in a presidential campaign.[118] The author wrote, "in the first presidential election since the tea party's emergence, Republican candidates are drifting rightward on a range of issues, even though a more centrist stand might play well in the 2012 general election"[119] One tea party figure driving the GOP platform further from the center was Michele Bachmann, the "John Wayne of political lies," according to one editorial.[120] "Whether making the round of Sunday morning talk shows, giving the tea party response to President Obama's State of the Union address, or announcing her own presidential campaign, Michele Bachmann does one thing consistently—lie."[121] The editorial included a transcript from a CBS *Face the Nation* episode on June 26 where Bachmann, referred to as "Sarah Palin with a brain" by the editorial, was constantly questioned about "facts" she cited. For instance, Bachmann said "Obamacare will cost the economy 800,000 jobs."[122] The host replied, "that is data that other people would question."[123] Bachmann retorted those numbers came from the Congressional Budget Office, not from her. The host clarified Fact-check.org produced those numbers, "the CBO didn't say that."[124] Instead, the CBO said labor workers would have more options than they currently did, receiving subsidies for insurance, "putting more money in their pockets," not losing money as Bachmann implied.[125]

The disagreements on policy issues and disingenuous statements may, on the surface, appear to be politics as usual. From the black press's perspective, however, the racial implications of the dialogue could not be ignored. For instance, the *Los Angeles Sentinel*, on July 15, 2011, published a column titled "Race Matters: Post-Racial Society a Hoax."[126] The author wrote: "Those with an iota of sophistication understand that race matters and that America is anything but a post-racial society. Unfortunately, that hoax, likely concocted by white-wing extremists, is embraced by a broad cross-section of the population, including so-called liberals and misguided blacks."[127] Why would tea partiers "concoct" a hoax about America being post racial? According to the author, to serve as camouflage for their policies designed to place economic and educational mobility barriers in front of minorities.

In August, when the tea party and Democrats avoided default by constructing a debt ceiling deal, the *New Pittsburgh Courier* called it, "a sugar-coated Satan sandwich."[128] While the deal avoided default for the time being, the author wrote: "As I write this, there may well be another monkey wrench thrown into the process of compromise, as tea party Republicans have been intransient and completely unwilling to compromise. President Obama and some Democrats, on the other hand, have been far too willing to compromise."[129] President Obama and Democrats, in an effort to appease their tea party villains, were "far too willing to compromise everything sacred—social security, Medicare, educational programs."[130] Any efforts to solve the debt issue possibly including sacrifices by wealthy white men were "off the table."[131]

On August 4, 2011, the *Chicago Defender* published an editorial titled "Americans Come Up Short in Debt Deal."[132] The author wrote:

> In a dog and pony show, you at least get to see a pony. In the political mess that unfolded in Washington, D.C. over the past few weeks regarding deficit

reduction and debt ceiling, all the American public got to witness was some really mangy dogs. . . . We saw naked and unrepentant hatred for the nation's first black president drive all decision making, to the point that nothing else mattered.[133]

The *Los Angeles Sentinel* published an article titled "Budget D-Day Avoided."[134] The articled cited President Obama, "It shouldn't take the risk of default, the risk of economic catastrophe, to get folks in this town to get together and do their jobs," adding, "our economy didn't need Washington to come along with a manufactured crisis to make things worse."[135]

The "manufactured crisis" designed to delegitimize President Obama and hurt the economy, intended to dampen his chances of reelection in 2012, did have consequences. Standard and Poor's, a global leader of financial intelligence, removed the United States of America from a list of "risk free borrowers," shortly after budget "D-Day" was avoided. According to the *New York Amsterdam News*, the firm's decision was "rightly dubbed by many as a 'tea party downgrade.'"[136] The columnist wrote:

The tea party has always been shrouded in a subtle cloak of racial insensitivity. They don't quite wear it on their sleeves, but they have mastered the wink-and-nod art of coded language. Their leaders and candidates regularly speak of the need to "take our country back," offering a message that is as clear as it is uncompromising. For them, it's troublesome that a Democrat is president of the United States—but it's horrifying that he's black. . . . Likewise, in the debt-ceiling debate, the tea party played its role to the hilt, blocking a comprehensive deal between Republican leaders and the president that might have prevented the downgrade. . . . The tea party is determined that Obama be vilified, humiliated, and, above all, defeated. Their passion is so strong, so rabid that they have determined that the country's historically stellar credit rating be damned, so long as their core objective is achieved.[137]

Tea Party and the Presidential Election: 2012

In 2012, the black press's coverage of the tea party was tied to the presidential election. Several tea party candidates emerged during the GOP primaries as potential threats to President Obama during the general election. The GOP candidate, however, ended up not being a tea party favorite. Mitt Romney was not admired by the tea party for his views, moderate compared to Bachmann, Perry, Santorum, and Cain, among others. Hoping to attract more tea party backing, he chose Wisconsin representative Paul Ryan, a tea party champion, as his vice presidential running mate. This decision signaled two meanings for the tea party villain. One, the group was beginning to lose some steam in terms of their political power since they didn't place a candidate at the top of the ticket. Second, though they were beginning to lose some momentum, the villain's platforms had become conventional enough to be placed on a presidential ticket, possibly one unfortunate incident away from the presidency.

On January 7, 2012, the *Chicago Defender* published a column titled "The Future of Black Political Power."[138] The author recalled the civil rights movement, when an "aroused, militant and insurgent black population used its political power for racial equality."[139] He interpreted the tea party as a "clear counter insurgent movement" designed to cripple the progress made during civil rights, a facet of the tea party that few, if any, white newspapers covered. "It is my view that the tea party and the right wing conservative movement are working every day to cripple the efforts of President Barack Obama" and the black community.[140]

The *New York Amsterdam News* reported on tea partiers playing "the race card for votes" in Iowa.[141] The journalist wrote:

> Santorum took great pains in the weeks leading up to the caucus to burnish in the minds of voters his staunchly conservative credentials. In doing so, he has chosen to make himself attractive to the far right, tea party–driven wing of the Republican Party. He emphasized his opposition to abortion, no matter the circumstance. He even took to making campaign appearances, rifle in hand, as Johnny-come-lately gun enthusiast, clearly pandering to the NRA vote. . . . [He] had displayed a puzzling pattern of seeking to leverage stereotypes of African Americans and public assistance to gain advantage in the election.[142]

A *New Pittsburgh Courier* article commented Santorum's attempts at using race to gain white voters was "just what the tea party and the other conservatives were looking for."[143]

On Super Bowl Sunday, former Michigan congressman Pete Hoekstra, a "tea party darling" challenging incumbent Democrat senator Debbie Stabenow, disseminated a "race-baiting" advertisement.[144] "Hoekstra's ad against Stabenow showing an Asian woman speaking in broken English and thanking the Democratic senator for claims that she helped send jobs to China, is not only racially insensitive," but also fairly common for many Republican candidates.[145] The journalist wrote "to understand the racist ad that former Michigan congressman Pete Hoekstra" had "used against incumbent Democratic senator Debbie Stabenow on Super Bowl day is to know that there is a long history in the GOP political playbook where the race card has always been used by extreme far-right candidates as a last resort to stoke the fears of white voters."[146]

The *Philadelphia Tribune*, on February 12, 2012, published an article titled "Culture Wars Imperil Obama."[147] The journalist began, "as far as conservatives are concerned, 2012 is the year of anger and authenticity."[148] The article reported on the Conservative Political Action Committee, known as CPAC. The journalist wrote:

What could be emerging is a moment where any White House success on the economy could take that issue off the national plate as a matter of urgency. That gives the grassroots on the right breathing space to mobilize around what then-candidate Obama called "guns and religion" in 2008. White social conservatives and their counterparts, mostly white progressives, may by preparing for a clash of the ideological titans over issues on the wedge. Where that leaves the unemployed and struggling is an open question that will find itself answered as the election approaches. [149]

To help advance their war on President Obama, tea party–backed legislation in some battleground states tried to make voting more difficult. Black newspapers covering the assault on voting rights pointed out laws like those cited in the article historically kept minorities from the polls. For instance, on March 18, 2012, the *Philadelphia Tribune* wrote, "while mostly Republicans and tea party members hailed Wednesday's signage of H.B. 934 by Pennsylvania Governor Tom Corbett, state Representative W. Curtis Thomas roundly slammed the measure as yet another attempt to stifle voter's rights."[150] The article, reflecting back on Jim Crow laws, quoted Representative Ron Waters, who said, "this is nothing more than an attempt by Republicans to keep seniors, minorities, and low-income citizens from their constitutional right to vote."[151] Given the tea party's "rabid passion" to defeat President Obama, it was not surprising "there is a correlation between Corbett's bill and the upcoming presidential and statewide elections."[152]

Fueled by tea party candidates, such as Michele Bachmann, the Supreme Court examined whether "Obamacare" was constitutional during this time also. In an article titled "Justices Signal Trouble for Health Care Law," the Cincinnati and Cleveland *Call and Post* wrote, "the fate of President Barack Obama's health care overhaul was cast into peril Tuesday as the Supreme Court's conservative justices sharply and repeatedly questioned its core requirement that virtually every American carry insurance."[153] A Supreme Court ruling saying one of the president's first major achievements was unconstitutional could provide the tea party with more momentum, ammunition, and traction as the election neared. [154]

Despite countless tea party–led attempts in Congress to repeal health care reform, the Supreme Court upheld the legislation's constitutionality. The *Washington Informer*, in an article titled "Obamacare Now Really Means Obama Cares," wrote:

> Who would have thunk [sic], back when the tea party faction of the Timothy McVeigh party (Republicans) coined the expression "Obamacare" as a pejorative reference to the Affordable Care Act which was signed into law by President Barack Obama, who would have thunk [sic] then that the derisive term would one day be the law of the land . . . who would have thunk [sic] that conservative judge Chief Justice John Roberts, who was so flustered looking into the eyes of the first black president that he would stumble over the words

of the oath of office . . . would be the decisive vote along with the court's four liberal justices?[155]

The somewhat surprising victory encouraged the black press and suggested maybe their villain was tiring, while their hero was just beginning to fight back. For instance, the *Philadelphia Tribune* wrote:

> President Barack Obama has entered re-election mode, and after nearly three years of taking it on the chin without counterpunching, the chief executive has finally, at long last, begun taking the fight to the GOP. And boy, are they upset about it. . . . Every one of these issues speaks to the decency, fairness, and compassion with which our government treats its most vulnerable citizens— and of the callous disregard for those citizens shown by today's tea-bagging GOP. The president was right to call out these hateful, greedy protectors of wealth for the few, and I'm glad he finally used some forceful language for a change.[156]

The *Skanner* asked, "three years later, what's become of the tea party?"[157] The article listed moments of success for the tea party during its first three years, most notably "when the tea party revolution sent new conservatives" to office in 2010; "but where has the tea party been since?"[158] According to the journalist, the lack of a tea party candidate at the top of the GOP presidential ticket reflected their diminishing influence, even though "tea party activists are still hard at work promoting" their ideology at all levels of government.[159]

The implementation of those ideologies, historically, failed blacks and other diverse communities.[160] "Over the last half century, GOP moderates, such as former Secretary of State Colin Powell have either been pushed out of the party or marginalized."[161] Those moderate voices in a party known for representing white elites "have been replaced by rabid tea party activists who have pushed an already conservative party to the extreme right."[162]

On June 21, 2012, the *Baltimore Afro-American* again reported on legislation designed to alter voting procedures.[163] "Tea party–backed Congressman Joe Walsh (R-Ill.) on June 19 introduced a bill he says will prevent voter fraud, but voting rights advocates are calling it another misleading and unnecessary piece of legislation."[164] The legislation would likely dampen minority voting, according to the article, and it was "interesting the way these bills are being coordinated or focused in certain states, such as the battleground states where Obama won" in 2008.[165]

When Romney addressed an annual meeting at the NAACP, he drew countless boos after he criticized President Obama and vowed to repeal health care reform.[166] The journalist wrote:

Republican presidential candidate Mitt Romney drew jeers from black voters
Wednesday as he criticized President Barack Obama and pledged to repeal the
Democrat's health care overhaul. . . . He acknowledged his Republican Party
doesn't have a perfect record on race relations, but pledged during a sometimes rocky speech that, if elected, he would work with black leaders to put the
country back to work.[167]

In a column titled "He's Got Guts, but Not Much Heart," the *Philadelphia
Tribune* opined: "I'll give Romney credit where credit is due. It took a lot of
gumption for him to stand in front of that audience," a black audience, "and
vow to repeal Obamacare, slash education, and set the cause of civil rights
back 75 years."[168] Adding to Romney's "rocky" speech, was "the fact that he
knows Republican outreach in minority communities ranges from nonexis-
tent to open hostility."[169] For instance, "the images of watermelons, bone-
through-the-nose witch doctors, and dressed up monkeys on their posters and
signs at rallies tells you all you need to know about how the tea party–dominated GOP feels about black people."[170] In a society supposedly
desiring more equality for all, the tea party shed any hopes of implicitness:
"Since Obama took office, the racists have shed any semblance of subtlety
they may have once had, and gone into full-tilt skinhead mode" and "now
that they've angered, alienated, disenfranchised and marginalized women,
blacks, browns, gays, the poor, the elderly, and anyone else who isn't a
Caucasian male millionaire, the GOP suddenly realizes the numbers they
have left won't win a national election."[171]

The answer to fight such racism was voting. The *Northfolk Journal and
Guide*, on July 11, 2012, urged African Americans to vote in a column titled
"The Necessity of the African American Vote."[172] The author noted: "We
also know that the Republican Party and the tea party activists are making
every effort to reclaim the white moderate and conservative voter as a means
of increasing votes against President Obama."[173] If President Obama lost it
wouldn't be the end of the world, "President Obama must understand that
black America can live with a Mitt Romney Presidency just as we did with
Ronald Reagan and both George Bushes; even though such an outcome
would almost permanently turn the clock of civil rights achievements back at
least 50 years."[174] The *Michigan Citizen* agreed: "The foundation of the
modern Republican Party is no longer rooted in Lincoln . . . its roots lie in the
racism of Thurmond, who did everything he could to block African
Americans from gaining expanded voting rights."[175]

From the black press's perspective, the tea party and the Republican Party
were nearly synonymous. Thus, as the election neared, the newspapers
viewed the entire Republican Party, not just the tea party, as the villain. The
historical nature of the Republican Party's "hostility" and lack of outreach to
minority communities informed their interpretation. When the tea party and

the GOP lost the presidential election, and President Obama secured a second term, the black press gasped in relief. Their villain had lost, for the moment, and their hero had prevailed. Not only did fear of setting civil rights back "at least 50 years" subside, but excitement grew because President Obama's reelection validated, according to the black press, the policies and initiatives he fought for during his first term. From the black press's perspective, despite President Obama's underwhelming purpose to represent black interests, his firmly cemented, and reapproved, symbolic representation signaled a shift away from their villain's ideologies.

The black press used the historically consistent villain myth as its primary interpretative template to construct the tea party narrative. Armed with history, tying the tea party to the Republican Party, and reminding its readers that a legal system built on precedent does not easily forget its past, the black press painted the tea party as a villainous threat to black political empowerment and black issues salient to their community.

NOTES

1. Lule, *Daily News*.
2. Ibid.
3. Liz Sidoti, "Obama: Get the Dread Out of Tax Deadline Day," *Chicago Defender*, April 15, 2009. Accessed June 1, 2012. http://www.chicagodefender.com/article-3899-obama-get-the-dread out-of-tax-deadline-day.html.
4. Ibid.
5. Ibid.
6. Jason Johnson, "Reflections in Tea Time," *Chicago Defender*, April 22, 2009. Accessed June 1, 2012. http://www.chicagodefender.com/article-4032-reflections-in-tea-time.html.
7. Ibid.
8. Ibid.
9. Alan Fram, "Health Care Lobbyists Target Returning Congress," *Washington Informer*, September 4, 2009. Accessed June 1, 2012. http://www.washingtoninformer.com/index.php/us/item/1594-health-care-lobbyists-target-returning-congress.
10. Associated Press, "Conservatives Protest Healthcare Reform in D.C.," *Skanner*, September 14, 2009. Accessed June 1, 2012. http://www.theskanner.com/article/Conservatives-Protest-Healthcare-Reform-in-DC-2009-09-14.
11. Jesse Jackson, "Fed-Run Health Care a Proven Success," *Los Angeles Sentinel*, September 17, 2009. Accessed June 1, 2012. http://www.lasentinel.net/index.php?option=com_content&view=article&id=5253:fed-run-health-care-a-proven-success&catid=90&Itemid=180.
12. Ibid.
13. Talibah Chikwen, "Tea Party Marchers Far Right and White," *New Pittsburgh Courier*, September 18, 2009. Accessed June 1, 2012. http://www.newpittsburghcourieronline.com/index.php/featured-news/national/359-tea-party-marchers-far-right-and-white.
14. Ibid.
15. George Curry, "President Carter Was Right to Raise Race Issue," *Skanner*, September 24, 2009. Accessed June 1, 2012. http://www.theskanner.com/index.php/article/President-Carter-Was -Right-To-Raise-Race-Issue-2009-09-24.
16. Ibid.
17. Ibid.
18. Ibid.

19. Ibid.

20. Larry Aubry, "Obama's Agenda and Rights' Attacks Interconnected," *Los Angeles Sentinel*, September 24, 2009. Accessed June 1, 2012. http://www.lasentinel.net/index.php?option=com_content&view=article&id=5200:obamaa-s-agenda-and-rights-attacks-interconnected&catid=95&Itemid=185.

21. Ibid.

22. Ibid.

23. Irene Monroe, "The Conversation America Won't Have on Race," *Bay State Banner*, October 1, 2009. Accessed June 1, 2012. http://www.baystatebanner.com/opinion58-2009-10-01.

24. Ibid.

25. Larry Aubry, "Obama: Promises, Ratings and Vicious Attacks," *Los Angeles Sentinel*, December 3, 2009. Accessed June 1, 2012. http://www.lasentinel.net/index.php?option=com_content
&view=article&id=4815:obama-promises-ratings-and-vicious-attacks&catid=95&Itemid=185.

26. Ibid.

27. "Former Congressman, Palin Blast Obama at Tea Party Gathering," *Baltimore Afro-American*, February 2, 2010. Accessed June 1, 2012. http://www.afro.com/sections/news/national/story.htm?storyid=67184.

28. Ibid.

29. Ron Walters, "Tea Party Racism," *New Pittsburgh Courier*, February 11, 2010. Accessed June 1, 2012. http://www.newpittsburghcourieronline.com/index.php/opinion/1398-tea-party-racism.

30. Ibid.

31. George Barnette, "National Urban League Supports Affordable Health Care as Today's Civil Rights Issue," *Baltimore Afro-American*, March 7, 2010. Accessed June 1, 2012. http://www.afro.com/sections/news/national/story.htm?storyid=67183.

32. Jesse Jackson, "Great Civilizations Aren't Ruled by Guns," *Los Angeles Sentinel*, March 11, 2010. Accessed June 1, 2012. http://www.lasentinel.net/index.php?option=com_content&view=article&id=4569:great-civilizations-aren-t-ruled-by-guns&catid=90&Itemid=180.

33. Ron Walters, "Tea Party, Coffee Party: Why Not a Black Party?" *New Pittsburgh Courier*, March 17, 2010. Accessed June 1, 2012. http://www.newpittsburghcourieronline.com/index.php/opinion/1642-tea-party-coffee-party-why-not-a-black-party.

34. Ibid.

35. Ibid.

36. Stephon Johnson, "Obama's 40-Yard Dash for Health Care Reform," *New Pittsburgh Courier*, March 17, 2010. Accessed June 1, 2012. http://www.newpittsburghcourieronline.com/index.php/featured-news/national/1652-obamas-40-yard-dash-for-health-care-reform-.

37. Walters, "Why Not a Black Party."

38. George Curry, "Right-Wing Republicans Often Masquerade as Tea Baggers," *Chicago Defender*, March 31, 2010. Accessed June 1, 2012. http://www.chicagodefender.com/article-7478-right-wing-republicans-often-masquerade -as-tea-baggers.html.

39. Ibid.

40. Jason Johnson, "Tea Party Serving Terrorism," *Chicago Defender*, March 31, 2010. Accessed June 1, 2012. http://www.chicagodender.com/article-7480-tea-party-serving-terrorism.html.

41. Jason Johnson, "Tea Party Terrorism," *New Pittsburgh Courier*, March 31, 2010. Accessed June 1, 2012. http://www.newpittsburghcourieronline.com/index.php/opinion/1742-tea-party-terrorism.

42. Wilson et al., *Racism, Sexism, and the Media*. Edward Said, *Covering Islam: How the media and the experts determine how we see the rest of the world* (New York, NY: Random House, 1997).

43. George Hardin, "Tea Party Invoking Stale States' Rights Argument," *Tri-State Defender*, March 31, 2010. Accessed June 1, 2012. http://www.tsdmemphis.com/index.php/archives/23-commentaries/5233-.

44. Ibid.

45. "Public Radio, Ethnic Media Sound Alarm of Growing Right Wing Extremism," *Michigan Chronicle*, April 1, 2010. Accessed June 1, 2012. http://www.michronicleonline.com/index.php/2011–08–04–18–06–26/rss-feeds/180-news-briefs/642-public-radio-ethnic-media-sound-alarm-of-growing-right-wing-extremism.

46. Ibid.

47. Ibid.

48. Larry Aubry, "President's Race Key Factor in New Forms of Racism," *Los Angeles Sentinel*, April 1, 2010. Accessed June 1, 2012. http://www.lasentinel.net/index.php?option=com_content&view=article&id=4390:presidenta-s-race-key-factor-in-new-forms-of-racism&catid=95&Itemid=185.

49. Raynard Jackson, "Tea-ed Off," *New Pittsburgh Courier*, April 7, 2010. Accessed June 1, 2012. http://www.newpittsburghcourieronline.com/index.php/opinion/1785-tea-ed-off.

50. Ibid.

51. Ibid.

52. Bill Fletcher Jr., "Black People With Guns?" *Chicago Defender*, April 28, 2010. Accessed June 1, 2012. http://www.chicagodefender.com/article-7691-black-people-with-guns.html.

53. A Peter Bailey, "Bill O'Reilly's Obsession With Playing Race Card," *New Pittsburgh Courier*, April 28, 2010. Accessed June 1, 2012. http://www.newpittsburghcourieronline.com/index.php/opinion/1946-bill-oreillys-obsession-with-playing-race-card.

54. Ibid.

55. Ibid.

56. Hazel Trice Edney, "Despite Widespread Appeals, Obama Fails to Nominate Black Woman to Supreme Court," *New Pittsburgh Courier*, May 11, 2010. Accessed June 1, 2012. http://www.newpittsburghcourieronline.com/index.php/featured-news/national/2011-despite-widespread-appeals-obama-fails-to-nominate-black-woman-to-supreme-court.

57. Ibid.

58. Earl Ofari Hutchinson, "Black Tea Party Activists Say Don't Call Us Traitors," *Chicago Defender*, May 12, 2010. Accessed June 1, 2012. http://www.chicagodefender.com/article-7756-black-tea-party-activists-say-dont-call-us-traitors.html.

59. Ibid.

60. Ibid.

61. Marc H. Morial, "Rand Paul Is On the Wrong Side of History," *New Pittsburgh Courier*, June 8, 2010. Accessed June 1, 2012. http://www.newpittsburghcourieronline.com/index.php/opinion/2263-rand-paul-is-on-the-wrong-side-of-history.

62. Ibid.

63. Hazel Trice Edney, "American Racial Temperature Rising," *Skanner*, June 14, 2010. Accessed June 1, 2012. http://www.theskanner.com/article/american-racial-temperature-rising-2010–06–14.

64. Ibid.

65. Pharch Martin, "Black Leaders Announce Move Against Conservative Attempt to Distort King's Dream," *New Pittsburgh Courier*, June 23, 2010. Accessed June 1, 2012. http://www.newpittsburghcourieronline.com/index.php/featured-news/national/2374-blacknleaders-announce-move-against-conservative-attempt-to-distort-kings-dream.

66. Ibid.

67. Ron Walters, "Republican Radicals Reject Unemployment Fund Extension," *New Pittsburgh Courier*, June 30, 2010. Accessed June 1, 2012. http://www.newpittsburghcourieronline.com/index.php/opinion/2414-republican-radicals-reject-unemployment-fund-extension.

68. Julianne Malveaux, "An All-White Senate," *New Pittsburgh Courier*, July 7, 2010. Accessed June 1, 2012. http://www.newpittsburghcourieronline.com/index.php/opinion/2470-an-all-white-senate.

69. Ibid.

70. Benjamin Todd Jealous, "Racism in the Tea Party Must End," *New York Amsterdam News*, July 14, 2010. Accessed June 1, 2012. http://www.amsterdamnews.com/opinion/editorials/racism-in-the-tea-party-must-end/article_1820eb14–5e40–591e-9454–6ef7a012924c.html.

71. James Wright, "Jobs Top Priority for One Nation Marchers," *Arizona Informant*, October 4, 2010. Accessed June 1, 2012. http://azinformant.com/index.php?option=com_content& view=article&id=255:jobs-top-priority-for-one-.

72. Ibid.

73. Ibid.

74. Michael Gormley, "Democrats Seize on Tea Party Candidates' Social Stances," *Skanner*, October 12, 2010. Accessed June 1, 2012. http://www.theskanner.com/article/democrats-seize-on-tea-party-candidates-social-stances-2010–10–12.

75. Ibid.

76. Ibid.

77. Isaac Abdul Haqq, "GOP Pledges Tea Party Lynching," *Los Angeles Sentinel*, October 14, 2010. Accessed June 1, 2012. http://www.lasentinel.net/index.php?option=com_content& view=article&id=3507:gop-pledges-tea-party-lynching&catid=81&Itemid=171.

78. Ibid.

79. Zenitha Prince, "Joint Center Report: Black Vote Possible Key to Democrat Victory," *Baltimore Afro-American*, October 16, 2010. Accessed June 1, 2012. http://www.afro.com/ sections/news/afro_briefs/story.htm?storyid=69025.

80. Ibid.

81. William Lacy Clay, "Republican Tea Party Out to Cripple Obama," *Skanner*, October 16, 2010. Accessed June 1, 2012. http://www.theskanner.com/article/republican-tea-party-out-to-cripple-obama-2010–10–16.

82. "We Must Vote," *New Pittsburgh Courier*, October 27, 2010. Accessed June 1, 2012. http://www.newpittsburghcourieronline.com/index.php/opinion/3270-we-must-vote.

83. "Republican Strategy Depends on Low Minority Turnout," *Washington Informer*, October 29, 2010. Accessed June 1, 2012. http://www.washingtoninformer.com/php/.../2786-republican-strategy-depends-on-low-minority-turnout.

84. Curtis Simmons, "Down But Not Out: Black Democrats Lose Committee and Subcommittee Chairmanships With House Loss," *New York Amsterdam News*, November 10, 2010. Accessed June 1, 2012. http://www.amsterdamnews.com/news/down-but-not-out-black-democrats-lose-committee-and-subcommittee/article_68b52e2a-8ee5–5689-a7ee-9be3d53d0262 .html.

85. Zenitha Prince, "Newly-Elected Black Republicans vs. CBC," *Arizona Informant*, November 10, 2010. Accessed June 1, 2012. http://www.azinformant.com/index.php?option=com_content&view=article&id=277%3anewly-elected-black.

86. "No Unemployment Extension," *Florida Star*, November 20, 2010. Accessed June 1, 2012. http://thefloridastar.com/?cat=6&paged=2.

87. "If GOP Beats Down President Obama Black American Crashes With Him," *Washington Informer*, November 25, 2010. Accessed June 1, 2012. http://washingtoninformer.com/ index.php/component/content/article/102-national-archive/1742-harvard-scholar-gates-arrested-charges-later-dropped/.

88. "N.C. School Board Abolishes Integration Policy," *Baltimore Afro-American*, January 22, 2011. Accessed June 1, 2012. http://www.afro.com/sections/news/afro_briefs/story.htm?storyid=70020.

89. Ibid.

90. Ibid.

91. Ibid.

92. "Michael Williams: Bow-Tied, Cowboy Boot-Shod Black Texan Carries Tea Party Backing in Run for Senate," *Baltimore Afro-American*, January 30, 2011. Accessed June 1, 2012. http://www.afro.com/sections/news/national/story.htm?storyid=70295.

93. "Pennsylvania's School's Racial Segregation Feared a Trend," *Baltimore Afro-American*, February 5, 2011. Accessed June 1, 2012. http://www.afro.com/sections/news/ afro_briefs/story.htm?storyid=70230.

94. Ibid.

95. Jonathan P. Hicks, "Tea party: Distorting American History," *New York Amsterdam News*, February 18, 2011. Accessed June 1, 2012. http://www.amsterdamnews.com/opinion/ tea-party-distorting-american-history/article_6e7b3b39-b224–50d8–9984–5d8e080c918c.html.

96. Ibid.

97. Ibid.

98. Rebecca Nuttall, "Obama Budget: First Cut Deepest," *New Pittsburgh Courier*, February 23, 2011. Accessed June 1, 2012. http://www.newpittsburghcourieronline.com/index.php/featured-news/national/3957-obama-budget-first-cut-deepest.

99. Ibid.

100. Julianne Malveaux, "Should We Bank on Recovery?" *Chicago Defender*, March 8, 2011. Accessed June 1, 2012. http://www.chicagodefender.com/article-10197-should-we-bank-on-the-recovery.html.

101. Ibid.

102. Broussard, *African-American Foreign Correspondents*.

103. Suzanne Gamboa, "GOP: Illegal Immigrants Taking Minorities' Jobs," *Bay State Banner*, March 10, 2011. Accessed June 1, 2012. http://www.baystatebanner.com/natl25–2011–03–10.

104. Ibid.

105. Andrew Taylor, "Time Short, Tempers Flare in Budget Showdown," *Philadelphia Tribune*, March 28, 2011. Accessed June 1, 2012. http://www.phillytrib.com/delawarecountrymetros/105-inthenews/inthenews/18309-time-short-tempers-flare-in-budget-showdown.html.

106. Ibid.

107. Anthony P. Browne, "Obama Matters as a President and a Black Leader," *New York Amsterdam News*, April 7, 2011. Accessed June 1, 2012. http://www.amsterdamnews.com/opinion/obama-matters-as-president-and-a-black-leader/article_47b92291-f8e4–5d7c-92c9–89c84c254742.html.

108. Ibid.

109. Larry Aubry, "Obama's Twisting Blurs His Priorities," *Los Angeles Sentinel*, April 21, 2011. Accessed June 1, 2012. http://www.lasentinel.net/index.php?option=com_content&view=article&id=2487:obama-s-twisting-blurs-his-priorities&catid=95&Itemid=185.

110. Ibid.

111. Lee A. Daniels and Stacey Patton, "Racism: The Monkey on the Tea Party's Back," *Skanner*, April 28, 2011. Accessed June 1, 2012. http://www.theskanner.com/article/racism-the-monkey-on-the-tea -partys-back-2011–04–28.

112. Ibid.

113. Ibid.

114. Julianne Malveaux, "Debt Ceiling, What's That? And Why Does It Need to Be Raised?" *Tri-State Defender*, May 26, 2011. Accessed June 1, 2012. http://www.tsdmemphis.com/index.php/opinion/6604-debt-ceiling-whats-that-and-why-does-it-need-to-be-raised.

115. Ibid.

116. Ibid.

117. Ibid.

118. Associated Press, "GOP Field Shifts Right in First Presidential Campaign Since Tea Party Emerged," *Skanner*, May 30, 2011. Accessed June 1, 2012. http://www.theskanner.com/article/GOP-Field-Shifts-Right-in-First-Presidential-Campaign-Since-Tea-Party-Emerged-2011–05–30.

119. Ibid.

120. George Curry, "Michele Bachmann: The John Wayne of Political Lies," *New Pittsburgh Courier*, July 8, 2011. Accessed June 1, 2012. http://www.newpittsburghcourieronline.com/index.php/opinion/4903-michele-bachmann-the-john-wayne-of-political-lies.

121. Ibid.

122. Ibid.

123. Ibid.

124. Ibid.

125. Ibid.

126. Larry Aubry, "Race Matters: Post-Racial Society a Hoax," *Los Angeles Sentinel*, July 15, 2011. Accessed June 1, 2012. http://www.lasentinel.net/index.php?option=com_content&view=article&id=1974:race-matters-post-racial-society-a-hoax&catid=95&Itemid=185.

127. Ibid.

128. Julianne Malveaux, "A Sugar-Coated Satan Sandwich," *New Pittsburgh Courier*, August 3, 2011. Accessed June 1, 2012. http://www.newpittsburghcourieronline.com/index.php/opinion/5058-a-sugar-coated-satan-sandwich.

129. Ibid.

130. Ibid.

131. Ibid.

132. "Americans Come Up Short in Debt Deal," *Chicago Defender*, August 4, 2011. Accessed June 1, 2012. http://www.chicagodefender.com/article-11486-americans-come-up-short-in-debt-deal.html.

133. Ibid.

134. Yussuf Simmonds, "Budget D-Day Avoided," *Los Angeles Sentinel*, August 4, 2011. Accessed June 1, 2012. http://www.lasentinel.net/index.php?option=com_content&view=article&id=1864:budget-d-day-avoided&catid=81&Itemid=171.

135. Ibid.

136. Jonathan Hicks, "The Tea Party Downgrade and What's Behind It," *New York Amsterdam News*, August 11, 2011. Accessed June 1, 2012. http://www.amsterdamnews.com/opinion/columnists/the-tea-party-downgrade-and-what-s-behind-it/article_671262fc-c37c-11e0-a4e7-001cc4c03286.html.

137. Ibid.

138. Leon Finney Jr., "The Future of Black Political Power?" *Chicago Defender*, January 7, 2012. Accessed November 15, 2012. http://www.chicagodefender.com/article-12324-the-future-of-black.html.

139. Ibid.

140. Ibid.

141. Jonathan Hicks, "In Iowa and Beyond, Candidates Play the Race Card for Votes," *New York Amsterdam News*, January 8, 2012. Accessed November 15, 2012. http://www.amsterdamnews.com/opinion/columnists/jonathan_hicks/in-iowa-and-beyond-candidates-play-the-race-card-for/article_1330d284-389a-11e1-9d0e-0019bb2963f4.html?mode=story.

142. Ibid.

143. Ulish Carter, "He's Back: Santorum Runs for President," *New Pittsburgh Courier*, January 13, 2012. Accessed November 15, 2012. http://www.newpittsburghcourieronline.com/index.php/opinion/6268-hes-back-santorum-runs-for-president.

144. Bankole Thompson, "Race-Baiting," *Michigan Chronicle*, February 8, 2012. Accessed November 15, 2012. http://www.michronicleonline.com/index.php/local/top-news/5455-race-baiting.

145. Ibid.

146. Ibid.

147. Charles Ellison, "Culture Wars Imperil Obama," *Philadelphia Tribune*, February 12, 2012. Accessed November 15, 2012. http://www.phillytrib.com/newsarticles/item/2732-culture-wars-imperil-obama.html.

148. Ibid.

149. Ibid.

150. Damon Williams, "State Reps. Decry Voter Id Law," *Philadelphia Tribune*, March 18, 2012. Accessed November 15, 2012. http://www.phillytrib.com/newsarticles/item/3527-state-reps-decry-voter-id-law.html.

151. Ibid.

152. Ibid.

153. "Justices Signal Trouble for Health Care Law," *Call and Post*, March 27, 2012. Accessed November 15, 2012. http://www.callandpost.com/index.php/news/national/1982-justices-signal-trouble-for-health-care-law.

154. Ibid.

155. Askia Muhammad, "Obamacare Now Really Means Obama Cares," *Washington Informer*, July 5, 2012. Accessed November 15, 2012. http://washingtoninformer.com/news/2012/jul/05/obamacare-now-really-means-obama-cares/.

156. Daryl Gale, "Respect the Man? You Lie!" *Philadelphia Tribune*, April 6, 2012. Accessed November 15, 2012. http://www.phillytrib.com/localopinion/item/3563-respect-the-man-you-lie.html.

157. Pauline Arrillaga, "Three Years Later, What's Become of the Tea Party?" *Skanner*, April 16, 2012. Accessed Novebmer 15, 2012. http://www.theskanner.com/article/three-years-later-whats-become-of-the-tea-party-2012–04–16.

158. Ibid.

159. Ibid.

160. George Curry, "Every Republican in Congress Fails Blacks," *Baltimore Afro-American*, May 4, 2012. Accessed November 15, 2012. http://www.afro.com/sections/news/national/story.htm?storyid=74903.

161. Ibid.

162. Ibid.

163. Zenitha Prince, "Federal Election Voter ID Sought by House Republican," *Baltimore Afro-American*, June 21, 2012. Accessed November 15, 2012. http://afro.com/sections/news/afro_briefs/story.htm?storyid=75364.

164. Ibid.

165. Ibid.

166. "Romney Draws Boos from NAACP Crowd," *Philadelphia Tribune*, July 11, 2012. Accessed November 15, 2012. http://www.phillytrib.com/newsarticles/itemlist/obama-care.html.

167. Ibid.

168. Daryl Gale, "He's Got Guts, but Not Much Heart," *Philadelphia Tribune*, July 13, 2012. Accessed November 15, 2012. http://www.phillytrib.com/localopinion/item/4879-he's-got-guts-but-not-much-heart.html.

169. Ibid.

170. Ibid.

171. Ibid.

172. John Warren, "The Necessity of the African American Vote in 2012," *Norfolk Journal and Guide*, July 11, 2012. Accessed November 15, 2012. http://www.thenewjournalandguide.com/commentary/item/1219-the-necessity-of-the-african-american-vote-in-2012.

173. Ibid.

174. Ibid.

175. Jess Jackson, "The GOP and the Vote: Return to Jim Crow," *Michigan Citizen*, August 5, 2012. Accessed November 15, 2012. http://www.michigancitizen.com/the-gop-and-the-vote-return-to-jim-crow.

Chapter Four

Mainstream Press Tea Party Narrative

Two resonant myths converged in the mainstream press's articulation of tea party dissent during President Obama's first term: the scapegoat and the trickster. The scapegoat first emerged in 2009, when the modern tea party was first noted by media. The trickster emerged in 2010, when the tea party experienced success during the midterm elections and continued through 2011. In 2012, the two myths were used together when tea partiers became conventional enough to possibly win the GOP nomination for a presidential run.

SCAPEGOAT AND DISSENTING VOICES: 2009

In 2009, mainstream newspapers used the scapegoat myth to interpret the tea party's narrative. On the scapegoat, Jack Lule wrote:

> If news is only a dispassionate observer and reporter of political events, coverage of radical groups . . . should be interesting but relatively straightforward. The political protest should provide some debatable issues for a story. The passion should contribute some provocative emotion. The conflict should make for dramatic narratives. Radical thinkers should make for thoughtful news. If news is myth [if a group is a scapegoat], however, coverage of radical groups should be much more combustible and complex.[1]

The scapegoat myth signifies a culture's prevailing ideology of the putative currency for dissenting voices. This myth is a critical caveat in a democratic society founded on principles of an open marketplace of ideas where disagreements frequently occur and, if voiced properly, contribute to democracy's progress. Sometimes, however, dissenting voices don't follow the established rules structuring democratic debate and, consequently, these voices are delegitimized in the press through the scapegoat myth.[2] The scapegoat isn't a figure posing a direct threat to the hegemonic order's way of life; instead, the scapegoat does not offer its perspective in an acceptable manner—not playing by society's agreed-upon rules.

Dissenting voices deviating from societal norms are symbolized as scapegoats when they "question basic values" of discourse and the scapegoat myth serves as a culture's attempt to "make an example of those who disagree too vigorously."[3] Mediated usage of the scapegoat myth to interpret the tea party unpacks mainstream resonant ideologies of white dissident voices aiming their oppositional tone towards black political empowerment.[4] In a society that professes its desire for equality, the context in which a political narrative is racially charged is as important as the actual resulting text; the myths not chosen for the narrative can be just as important as the myths used to tell the story. In this case, initially, the white press chose the scapegoat myth, not a villain.

In the tea party's case, these dissident voices were interpreted as scapegoats and partially delegitimized because they deviated from established discursive norms and questioned basic democratic values, but not the overall culture's way of life, according to the mainstream press. But, what norms and values did the mainstream press perceive the tea party broke? During that first year, mainstream newspapers weren't entirely convinced the tea party fractured any values, suggesting instead their protest was a pillar of American heritage.

For instance, an editorial in the *Arizona Republic* posited, "fed up with the economic stimulus, bailouts and big spending in general, conservatives have latched onto an unlikely occasion—tea parties."[5] The article highlighted not all press outlets criticized or delegitimized the tea party, initially; instead, they positioned the group as a legitimate discursive voice concerned about excessive government spending and overtaxation, saying the tea party "tapped into one of the nation's most enduring political protests."[6]

The *Atlanta Journal-Constitution* asserted President Obama's health care proposals relied on the premise of spending more money now would lower future costs; from the tea party perspective, this move could permanently destroy the federal budget.[7] The newspaper portrayed the tea party as composed of extremely mission-driven individuals with strong moral values and heady business tactics.[8] An emergent facet of mainstream newspaper stories was an attempt to rationally justify the group's existence because anti-spending and anti-tax dissent does not necessarily question American norms and values. According to the mainstream press, anti-tax and anti-spending values are sacred in American society, pervading the culture since, at least, the nation's founding.

However, some newspaper articles in 2009 did interpret the tea party as a horde of thousands gathering to disrupt, threaten, and intimidate. This narrative packaging inferred the tea party was not a legitimate dissenting voice, but a mob of angry, vocal, and passionate individuals. For instance, a *New York Times* article titled "Beyond Beltway, Healthcare Debate Turns Hostile" described tea party violence: "Bitter divisions over an overhaul of the health care system have exploded at town-hall-style meetings" where tea party "demonstrations have led to fistfights, arrests and hospitalizations."[9] Seen as vocal, angry, disruptive, and not concerned with providing constructive input into the debate, the tea party's dissenting narrative was constructed as a scapegoat because, in part, one norm of deliberative discourse in democratic societies is opposition designed at engineering a socially productive end. The tea party was delegitimized because the mainstream newspapers perceived them as not concerned with providing constructive alternatives; instead, the group was preoccupied with creating a "raucous," following a GOP mandate to thwart President Obama's policies and initiatives at all costs.[10]

Mainstream newspapers perceived the tea party as departing from another modern societal value fortifying the scapegoat label—suspicion of racial resentment. Evidence lies in the inception of the tea party's narrative and the subsequent distrust about the group's intent. Mainstream newspapers were not concerned with the "how" the tea party formed, but the "why" they formed. The tea party's formation was crafted as the result of a rant from a single individual, Rick Santelli. The *New York Times* described Santelli's "tirade" as a "televised rant" that encouraged "a Chicago tea party to protest the administration's housing plans."[11] Because this "rant" was narrated as the unintentional springboard for the group, the tea party's motivation for forming was directly linked with opposing Obama's presidency.

The tea party's complaint and/or fear of President Obama's "reckless spending" and "overtaxation" resonates with a historic white fear that views black officials as irresponsible leaders looking to provide handouts at any chance.[12] The exposition of this facet of the tea party narrative is connected, in part, to the dissent's explicit preoccupation with the financial aspects of President Obama's initiatives; the newspapers also noted how none of the tea party members seemed concerned when President Bush implemented similar financial policies. This was an important factor of the narrative. Given President Obama's nascent term, the tea party's formation after Republican presidents had spent more government money undermined the group's stated mission for opposition.

Some of the traditional press's crafting of the tea party narrative went one step further, from a movement of whites fearing a black leader funneling sources away from white communities towards black communities, to suspicions of racism founded by prejudice, not fear of losing the funding battle. This element of the narrative occurred shortly after the major bank bailouts legislation. Mainstream newspapers debated the tea party's stated concern of "reckless spending" and considered whether a concealed racial motivation existed. Some newspaper articles debated the authenticity of the tea party's anti-spending claims for forming because the spending began under the governing of a white Republican, a time period when those in the tea party did not feel a need to form. This was not a monolithic conclusion throughout the mainstream press; some articles stated the tea party's concerns were valid and that President Obama was, already, a reckless spender. [13]

The struggle of identifying motivations based on (1) racial prejudice or (2) fear of resource reallocation, shows how mainstream newspapers interpret the intersection of race and politics during a crucial debate on possibly historically significant social change. [14] The tea party, forming five weeks after President Obama's inauguration and supposedly fearful of economic policies emerging during the infancy stages of his administration without time to ferment, was interpreted as probably more afraid of black empowerment than genuine political dissent. But, this was never conclusively stated by mainstream newspapers; it was debated and discussed, but not mediated as fact. The scapegoat myth enabled journalists to take this route instead of conclusively stating one or the other. By devaluing the tea party's complaints, the reality described in the newspaper articles resonates with a modern value that agendas precipitated by racial prejudice are socially unacceptable.

TRICKSTER AND SOCIAL NORMS: 2010

In 2010, a year dominated by discussions about the midterm elections and the tea party's emerging power, mainstream newspapers shifted from the scapegoat myth to the trickster myth to tell the group's narrative. The trickster embodies traits displaying an unintelligent figure aiming to question social norms. [15] As a "subject of mockery, contempt, and ridicule," the "crude and lewd moralist" is a notorious rogue. [16] The "malicious spoiler" and "unconscious numbskull" illuminates the consequences of not adhering to social norms. [17] The formidable trickster confronts and battles the established social order. The trickster typically embodies an unintelligent figure motivated by rebelling against the status quo, eventually symbolizing the tragic tale of what occurs when established societal rules are not observed.

For the most part, mainstream press articles ignored the racial undercurrents of the tea party's success in 2010. For instance, a *Washington Post* column titled, "Tea Partiers More Wacky Mavericks Than Extremist Threat" ignored any racial legislative problems the groups posed; instead, the article opined the tea party was continued conservatism, even though it was slightly more extreme than modern society accepted. "Based on what I saw and heard, tea party members are not seething, ready-to-explode racists." [18] A column in the *Dallas Morning News* suggested: "the tea party just happens to be fired up during the first term of the nation's first black president," adding, "that makes it easy to suspect the tea party movement is racist, especially if you have an elastic definition of racism. But polls and conversations with tea partiers tend to confirm my sense that race brings no more than a teeny cup to this party."[19]

Instead of discussing the potential ramification the group posed to minorities, the mainstream press devoted a robust focus to the figures driving the group's traction during the midterms, rarely focusing on their actual policies and how those platforms could affect nonwhites. Some of those figures included Sarah Palin, Michele Bachmann, Joe Miller, and Christine O'Donnell. Palin, referred to as the "queen of the tea party," was an influential tea party figure in 2010 whose backing helped tea party candidates succeed during the midterms.

Newspaper coverage of Joe Miller and Christine O'Donnell, two of "Palin's picks," ignored the racial connotations of the tea party and its leader, Palin. Instead, journalists constructed Palin and the tea party as a trickster by attributing portions of the candidates' success to her "powerful" endorsements—symbolizing Palin's passion to be a Republican spoiler. For instance, the *Los Angeles Times* noted:

> Sen. Lisa Murkowski conceded the . . . primary . . . an outcome that illustrated voters' anger with the Washington establishment and the power of former Gov. Sarah Palin . . . [behind] in fundraising and in opinion polls, [it looked bleak for Miller]. . . . But he had Palin, who bucked state party leaders to endorse him.[20]

Mainstream news coverage frequently framed Palin as an unintelligent numbskull. The narratives constructed in the case of Palin's endorsements symbolized tea party intent to be a "malicious spoiler," to revolt against the Republican establishment, not American society in general.

Not all tea partiers won during the midterm elections. Some, like Sharon Angle and Christine O'Donnell, lost. Even the tea party losers signaled to the mainstream press the group contained legislative potency. For instance, on Sharon Angle, the *New York Times* wrote: "Ms. Angle's primary victory was a testimony to the power of the tea party."[21] The *Oregonian* opined: "Sometimes it's not clear who loves them the most: their supporters or their opponents. Supporters love their strict-constitutional zeal, their unwillingness to back down from the pure-capitalist convictions. Opponents love their gaffes—they're all novice big-race candidates—and the craziness that goes on around them."[22] The unwillingness to compromise was interpreted, later, by mainstream newspapers as a major discursive norm the tea party violated.

Both presses noted competent governing requires compromise—a value the tea party despised.

Mainstream newspapers also noted, at times, the tea party wasn't really a grassroots movement; instead, it was a group funded primarily by well-known and established conservative figures, such as the Koch brothers. The *New York Times* wrote:

> Tea party supporters and their candidates like to imagine themselves as insurgents, crashing the barricades of Washington to establish a new order of clean and frugal government. In earthbound reality, many of the people pulling the tea party's strings are establishment Republican operatives and lobbyists. Some have made money off the party for years. [23]

A disingenuous nature haunted the tea party in the mainstream press. The *Philadelphia Inquirer*, in a column titled "Facts Crash the Tea Parties," highlighted that the ideas allegedly driving the tea party's anger were not based on truth. [24]

SCAPEGOAT AND TRICKSTER SUCCESS: 2011

Following success in the midterm elections, mainstream newspapers used a blend of the scapegoat and trickster myths to interpret the tea party. They used a blend because, now with elected officials holding office, the tea party wasn't an outside rogue anymore; they had become part of the system in order to advance their agenda. However, their agenda was now questioned and interpreted as rogue. For instance, on February 11, 2011, the *New York Times* published a column on "the tea party and U.S. Foreign Policy." [25] "The tea party movement taps deep roots in U.S. history" and is "best understood as a contemporary revolt of Jacksonian common sense—the idea that moral, scientific, political and religious truths can be ascertained by the average person" and not only reserved for elites. [26] The *Philadelphia Inquirer* questioned the tea party's historical knowledge: "I spent a year watching the rise of the tea party movement," and the journalist believed he did "a decent job in understanding its roots causes, I have to confess I'm still baffled at how willing conservatives—and not just southerners—are now to argue that the war was about 57 other things besides slavery." [27]

One piece of legislation tea party officials pursued in 2011 was "Birther" bills, "a measure requiring presidential candidates to provide documents they are natural-born citizens." [28] The bill, sprouting from the belief President Obama wasn't an American citizen, had legs for three years. "The legislature has tried to pass a so-called Birther bill for three years. Supporters attribute this latest effort's success to some compromise, strong Republican support, recent media coverage and tea party influence."[29] The *Los Angeles Times*, in a column titled "Birther Blather Lives On," wrote:

> The new, of course, is the way in which the alternate realities of the Internet's fringes and brutally partisan talk radio empower the political culture of assertion and denial to which the birthers belong. It's a characteristic they share with a significant slice of the tea party movement, which advances not just its own version of contemporary America but a willed, faith-based version of our history as well.[30]

The mainstream press interpreted the proposed legislation as baseless, but stopped short of dissecting any racial undercurrents fueling the unwillingness to accept President Obama was American. Other baseless legislative proposals were also highlighted. For instance, in Florida, the tea party proposed to cut funding to a refuge for manatees. "Just when you thought politics and public policy could get no weirder around here, local tea party members are protesting a plan to protect manatees—because it would be against God and country."[31]

On August 1, 2011, the *Washington Post* reported on comments made by Vice President Joe Biden, who "made a deeply unfortunate comment. In response to the remarks of Rep. Mike Doyle (D-Penn.) about the tea party and fiscal conservatives that 'we have negotiated with terrorists.' Biden reportedly agreed that 'they have acted like terrorists.'"[32] The article criticized Vice President Biden for equating the tea party with terrorists and demanded an apology. Another article gave the tea party credit for trimming the deficit without raising taxes. "The tea party movement is getting credit for a debt extension bill that will trim the deficit without new taxes, although many of its members opposed the final legislation as insufficient."[33]

On August 12, 2011, the *New York Times* returned to the tea party's uncompromising nature. The columnist wrote: "Good governance in a democratic society is about the art of the deal, not fiats and dictum."[34] The absolute, uncompromising nature of the tea party broke a major democratic norm. "What we are witnessing is an extension and acceleration of the G.O.P's obscene genuflection to tea party tenets: give no ground; take no prisoners; accept no deal."[35]

No matter how hard the tea party tried, though, racial undercurrents could not be entirely ignored. For instance, when "Texas Gov. Rick Perry enter[ed] GOP race for president" on August 13, 2011, he was interpreted as a tea party favorite poised as a serious competitor for Mitt Romney and President Obama.[36] However, journalists would later learn of a Perry hunting camp containing a rock with the term "Niggerhead" painted on it; his hopes for the White House ended then.

As 2011 neared its end, it appeared the tea party was losing momentum, according to the mainstream press. "For the first time, it seems, more than half of the American electorate now holds a negative view of the tea party movement."[37] Another news article by the *Washington Post* wrote: "A leading member of the Congressional Black Caucus is standing by incendiary language he used at a recent town hall when he charged that tea party aligned members of Congress view African Americans as second class citizens and would like to see them hanging on a tree."[38] Even though the article suggested the black perspective was too sensitive and the congressman needed to apologize, it was becoming clear, coupled with their unacceptable negotiating practices and repeated racial flare-ups, the mainstream press was shifting away from the trickster myth and back towards the scapegoat.

Despite being interpreted as less powerful, the tea party did manage to place several tea party–backed candidates into the presidential race. The group even partnered with CNN for a GOP debate. "The fact that they're broadcasting and partnering with the tea party shows that they understand it's a broad-based political movement and that it isn't fractured and narrow" or extreme.[39] The trickster wasn't quite ready to yield the narrative to the scapegoat entirely, showing the two myths were used by the mainstream press in a complimentary fashion at the same time in some of the coverage.

On December 8, 2011, the *Atlanta Journal-Constitution*, in an article titled "Tea Party Turns Up the Heat on GOP," wrote: "Tea party groups around Georgia are mobilizing to challenge state elected officials they've deemed RINOS—Republicans in Name Only."[40] The article continued:

> The upstarts, who say it's time to clean up the party, are most upset about Republican support for next year's regional transportation tax referendums, but say a general lack of fiscal responsibility is reason enough to challenge incumbents. But those who have drawn tea party ire say their fellow Republicans have the wrong targets.[41]

Instead, the Republicans argued the tea party should be focusing on their villain, President Obama.[42] However, when the tea party did focus on President Obama, racial friction surfaced. For instance, a *Detroit Free Press* article reported on a Kansas tea party group portraying President Obama as a skunk. "A tea party group in Kansas said its depiction of President Barack Obama as a skunk is a satire, not racism."[43]

PRESIDENTIAL CAMPAIGN INFLUENCE: 2012

Comparable to the black press, the mainstream press coverage of the tea party in 2012 focused on the presidential election. Unlike the black press, though, race rarely emerged in the stories; instead, the coverage reported on the amount of influence the tea party may, or may not, have on the election. The mainstream newspapers barely mentioned the tea party candidate's platforms, instead relying on a "horse race" narrative, a tradition of the mainstream press. The lack of racial discussions in the mainstream press indicates the mainstream press did not perceive the tea party as a threat to the "American" way of life—a stark difference compared to the black press's coverage of the tea party.

On January 9, 2012, the *Dallas Morning News* reported on front-runner Mitt Romney's lack of appeal to the tea party. "Something happened to the tea party on the way to the election. After smashing success in congressional races two years ago and promises of transforming the political landscape, tea party activists can't agree on a presidential candidate."[44] The tea party activists interviewed in the article said defeating President Obama wasn't enough to advance their stated agenda; they needed to beat him with a candidate representing their interests. This was a change in attitude for some tea party members who previously believed beating President Obama was all that mattered, regardless of the instrument used to execute the victory. They viewed Romney as too moderate and too willing to work with Democrats.[45]

Part of the tea party's dilemma during the primaries was they had too many tea party candidates to choose from, none of which could gain enough support to beat Romney. In a sense, they were a victim of their own success; so many tea party favorites splintered the vote so "neither candidate has an edge in tea party support."[46] A *Detroit Free Press* column, reporting on how the heated rhetoric during President Obama's first term affected the political races, wrote:

> One seeks to destroy an enemy. And it makes you wonder: Is that really the way we the people see ourselves? The evidence of recent years suggests that it is. The so-called culture wars—a battle of ideas and ideals concerning abortion, faith, gay rights, gun rights, Muslim rights, global warming, health care, immigration—are fought with splenetic bile that would have been unthinkable not too very long ago. But that was before a congressman heckled a president, before guns were brought to presidential appearances, before a radio host called a college woman a "slut," before someone set a fire at the construction site of a Tennessee mosque, before "I want my country back" became a rallying cry. It was before there grew this gnawing sense that we do not need each other anymore, that the extremes are pulling the center apart.[47]

The author argued the tea party's tactics, the angry mob mentality contributing to their success in 2010, were now the reason they were struggling to solidify around a candidate for president and losing influence in the political process.

Despite trailing politically, according to the mainstream press, because of their unwillingness to abide by democratic desires for civil discourse (or at least somewhat toned-down rhetoric), the tea party's fiery language marched on. For instance, the *Tampa Bay Times*, on April 13, 2012 reported on Representative Allen West's McCarthy-like crusade against socialism. "The grand inquisitor of the tea party was holding forth at a town hall meeting in Jensen Beach this week when one of the pitchfork attendees asked him to estimate how many fellow members of Congress are card-carrying Marxists or International Socialists, as opposed to domestic Socialists."[48] Instead of dismissing the baseless question, West, in McCarthy fashion, stated he believed "78 to 81 members of the Democratic Party" are "members of the Communist Party."[49] Georgia governor Nathan Deal "vetoed a bill that could have eliminated state agencies, calling it redundant and costly," and in the process "angered tea party activists."[50]

On May 19, 2012, the *Philadelphia Inquirer* published a column titled "Dick Lugar's Departure a Sign of Washington Paralysis."[51] Lugar, a "six-term Republican senator from Indiana," was defeated in a primary "at the hands of a tea party insurgent."[52] The author wrote Lugar lost because "he occasionally had the temerity to work with Democrats."[53] His willingness to compromise and work with others outside of his own beliefs offended tea partiers' ideology and led to them organizing and defeating him. James Holmes, the Aurora Colorado theater shooter, was, initially, identified by ABC News as a member of the tea party.[54] The *Washington Post* condemned the inaccurate reporting; however, the rush to judgment by ABC News can, in part, be explained by the volatile behavior the tea party expressed for the past four years.

An Associated Press article in the *Dallas Morning News* asked: "Have race relations improved in the Obama era?"[55] After asking numerous citizens for their opinion, most saying relations have improved but by no means is America "Post Racial," the article pointed to the tea party as an area where possible racism still exists. The story wrote: "Obama dealt with fallout from the Gates affair during the summer of 2009, the tea party coalesced out of opposition to Obama's stimulus and health care proposals. The vast majority of tea partyers were white. A small number of them displayed racist signs or were connected to white supremacist groups."[56] The author argued the amount of racism in the tea party was small, initially, and, by 2012, had all but been eradicated from the group; it failed to mention the legislation the black press highlighted the tea party pursued after 2010 hurting minority groups, such as education, segregation, health care, and voting prohibitions.

Eventually, Romney became the GOP candidate for president and chose Paul Ryan as his running mate. However, as the election progressed, Romney still had trouble connecting with the base, according to the *New York Times*.[57] One citizen, who had supported tea party favorite Santorum, said about Romney, in the article: "He just doesn't seem to connect well, and I'm not sure he's a strong enough candidate, to be very, very honest . . . I'm probably going to hold my nose and vote for him."[58] The Romney campaign dismissed the lack of enthusiasm and believed the tea partiers would show up to vote for him regardless. One Romney pollster interviewed in the article said: "Intensity drives turnout. Every measure shows Republicans and conservatives are more intense in their opposition to President Obama than Democrats are in support of him."[59] The campaign disputed assertions the tea party wasn't excited about him enough, "arguing that dislike for Mr. Obama" would be enough to secure victory. In hindsight, it is clear the campaign overestimated the level of that intensity.[60]

As the election neared, voting rights surfaced in the mainstream press's tea party narrative. The *Los Angeles Times* published an article titled "Barbara Boxer Calls for Enforcement of Voting Rights Laws."[61] The article "described efforts by tea party members to remove at least 2,100 names from voter rolls in the swing state."[62] The *New York Times* wrote "redrawn districts test favorites of tea party."[63] The *Orlando Sentinel* wrote: "Despite a lack of evidence of voter fraud," a group, True the Vote, had partnered with the tea party "to launch efforts to challenge citizens at the polls."[64] Those attempts to either intimidate voters or explicitly repel them from the voting booths were the tea party's last grasps of hope for the 2012 presidential election. Following President Obama's reelection, the mainstream newspapers barely mentioned the tea party—indicating the scapegoat/trickster had possibly met its end, serving as an example of what happens if democratic principles aren't followed.

On November 13, 2012, the *Seattle Times* published an editorial providing recommendations for President Obama moving forward. Barely mentioning the tea party, the author did note they probably weren't entirely going away, though, their incentives now had to change.

> This is not the Republican Party of 2010. Today's Republicans no longer have an incentive to deny Obama victories. He's never running again. Most of today's Republicans understand that they need to decontaminate their brand. They're more open to compromise, more likely to be won over with deal making than browbeating. . . . But the point is the only way to get things done in a divided polarized country is side by side—an acceptable Democratic project paired with an acceptable Republican one.[65]

The mainstream press used two myths, the scapegoat and the trickster, to interpret the tea party narrative during President Obama's first term. The scapegoat emerged in 2009, when the tea party, through volatile rhetoric and suspected racial motivations, was viewed as attacking democratic values and beliefs. In 2010, when the tea party became mainstream enough to hold office, the group was narrated an unintelligent rogue. In 2011 and 2012 the two myths converged as the tea party lost momentum but continued trying to defeat President Obama.

NOTES

1. Lule, *Daily News*, 62.
2. Ibid.
3. Ibid., 63.
4. Ibid. Mendelberg, *The Race Card*.
5. Ronald Hansen, "Gop Holds Tea Party Stimulus Protest in Valley," *Arizona Republic*, April 3, 2009. Accessed June 2, 2012. http://www.azcentral.com/arizonarepublic/news/articles/2009/04/03/20090403teaparty0403.html?wired.
6. Ibid.
7. Sheila Poole, Craig Schneider, and Jim Tharpe, "Health Care Rallies Attract Lively Crowds," *Atlanta Journal-Constitution*, August 17, 2009. Accessed June 2, 2012. http://www.ajc.com/news/news/local/health-care-rallies-attract-lively-crowds/nQLZy/.
8. Ibid.
9. Ian Urbina, "Beyond Beltway, Health Care Debate Turns Hostile," *New York Times*, August 7, 2009. Accessed June 2, 2012. http://www.nytimes.com/2009/08/08/us/politics/08townhall.html.
10. Ibid.
11. Brian Stelter, "CNBC Replays its Reporter's Tirade," *New York Times*, February 22, 2009. Accessed June 2, 2012. http://www.nytimes.com/2009/02/23/business/media/23cnbc.html.
12. Hanks, *The Struggle for Black Political Empowerment*.
13. Nick Perry and Susan Gilmore, "Protestors, Supporters Greet Glenn Beck as He Visits Seattle, Mount Vernon," *Seattle Times*, September 27, 2009. Accessed June 2, 2012. http://seattletimes.com/html/localnews/2009950835_beck27m.html.
14. Mendelberg, *The Race Card*. McIlwain and Caliendo, *Race Appeal*.
15. Lule, *Daily News*. Berkowitz, *Cultural Meanings of News*.
16. Lule, *Daily News*, 124.
17. Thomas Murray and Carmin D. Ross-Murray, *Mythical Trickster Figures: Contours, Contexts, and Criticisms* (Tuscaloosa: University of Alabama Press, 1996), 34.
18. Robert McCartney, "Tea Partiers More Wacky Mavericks Than Extremist Threat," *Washington Post*, April 18, 2010. Accessed June 2, 2012. http://www.washingtonpost.com/wp-dyn/content/article/2010/04/17/AR2010041702652.html.
19. Clarence Page, "Tea Party Myths and Mistaken Views," *Dallas Morning News*. April 19, 2010, Accessed June 2, 2012. http://www.dallasnews.com/opinion/latest-columns/20100419-Clarence-Page-Tea-Party-myths-8600.ece.
20. Mark Thiessen, "Palin Endorses GOP Challenger in Alaska Senate," *Seattle Times*, August 24, 2010. Accessed June 2, 2012. http://seattletimes.com/html/politics/2012011400_apusalaskasenatepalinendorsement.html/.
21. Adam Nagourney, "Tea Party Choice Scrambles in Taking on Reid in Nevada," *New York Times*, August 17, 2010. Accessed June 2, 2012. http://www.nytimes.com/2010/08/18/us/politics/18vegas.html.
22. Douglas Perry, "The Kings and Queens of the Tea Party," *Oregonian*, November 2, 2010, Accessed June 2, 2012. http://blog.oregonlive.com/elections/2010/11/the_kings_and_queens_of_the_te.html.
23. "Tea Party's Big Money," *New York Times*, September 23, 2010. Accessed June 2, 2012. http://www.nytimes.com/2010/09/24/opinion/24fri2.html.
24. E. J. Dionne, "Facts Crash the Tea Parties," *Philadelphia Inquirer*, December 22, 2010. Accessed June 2, 2012. http://www.philly.com/philly/news/year-in-review/20100420_E_j_dionne_facts_crash_the_tea_parties.html.
25. Walter Russell Mead, "The Tea Party and U.S. Foreign Policy," *New York Times*, February 11, 2011. Accessed June 2, 2012. http://www.nytimes.com/2011/02/22/opinion/22iht-edrusselmead22.html.
26. Ibid.

27. Will Bunch, "The South's Gonna Do It Again," *Philadelphia Inquirer*, April 12, 2011. Accessed June 2, 2012. http://www.philly.com/philly/blogs/attytood/the-souths-gonna-do-it-again.html.

28. Alla Beard Rau, "Arizona's 'Birther' Bill Faces Legal Challenges," *Arizona Republic*, April 16, 2011. Accessed June 2, 2012. http://www.azcentral.com/arizonarepublic/news/articles/20110416arizona-birther-bill-legal-challenges.html.

29. Ibid.

30. Tom Rutten, "Birther Blather Lives On," *Los Angeles Times*, April 30, 2011. Accessed June 2, 2012. http://www.latimes.com/news/opinion/commentary/la-oe-0430-rutten-20110430,0,6735231.column.

31. Sue Carlton, "Pass the Tea and Stop the Manatee Insanity," *Tampa Bay Times*, July 15, 2011. Accessed June 2, 2012. http://www.tampabay.com/news.

32. Alexandra Petri, "Biden's Terrorist Gaffe," *Washington Post*, August 1, 2011. Accessed June 2, 2012. http://www.washingtonpost.com/blogs/compost/post/bidens-terrorist-gaffe/2011/08/01/glqakmtgol_blog.html.

33. Bruce Alpert, "Debt Limit Deal Struck Mostly on Tea Party's Terms," *Times Picayune*, August 2, 2011. Accessed June 2, 2012. http://www.nola.com/politics/index.ssf/2011/08/debt_limit_deal_struck_mostly.html.

34. Charles Blow, "Genuflecting to the Tea Party," *New York Times*, August 12, 2011. Accessed June 12, 2012. http://www.nytimes.com/2011/08/13/opinion/blow-genuflecting-to-the-tea-party.html.

35. Ibid.

36. Associated Press, "Texas Gov. Rick Perry Enters GOP Race for President," *Oregonian*, August 13, 2011. Accessed June 12, 2012. http://www.oregonlive.com/today/index.ssf/2011/08/texas_gov_rick_perry_enters_gop_race_for_president.html.

37. Leonard Pitts Jr., "Hooray for Common Sense: Tea Party in Decline," *Detroit Free Press*, August 16, 2011. Accessed June 12, 2012. http://www.freep.com/apps/pbcs.dll/article?aid=2011108160307.

38. Felicia Sonmez, "Rep. Carson: Tea party Wants to See African Americans 'Hanging on a Tree,'" *Washington Post*, August 30, 2011. Accessed June 2, 2012. http://www.washingtonpost.com/blogs/2chambers/post/.../glqafztmqj_blog.html.

39. Jeremy Peters and Brian Stetler, "For Debate Partners, An Unusual Pairing," *New York Times*, September 12, 2011. Accessed June 2, 2012. http://www.nytimes.com/2011/09/13/us/politics/13cnn.html.

40. Aaron Gould Sheinin, "Tea Party Turns Up the Heat on GOP," *Atlanta Journal-Constitution*, December 8, 2011. Accessed June 2, 2012. http://www.ajc.com/news/news/local-govt-politics/tea-party-turns-up-the-heat-on-gop/nqpmd.

41. Ibid.

42. Ibid.

43. "Protestor's Anger Could Lead to Probe," *Detroit Free Press*, December 12, 2011. Accessed June 2, 2012. http:www.freep.com/apps/pbcs.dll/article?aid=2011112120400.

44. Wayne Slater, "Front-Runner Romney Hardly a Tea Party Favorite," *Dallas Morning News*, January 9, 2012. Accessed November 16, 2012. http://www.dallasnews.com/news/politics/perry-watch/headlines/20120109-front-runner-romney-hardly-a-tea-party-favorite.ece.

45. Ibid.

46. Associated Press, "2012 Super Tuesday: Ohio Voters Torn Between Hearts, Wallets," *Oregonian*, March 6, 2012. Accessed November 16, 2012. http://www.oregonlive.com/politics/index.ssf/2012/03/2012_super_tuesday_ohio_voters.html.

47. Leonard Pitts Jr., "Candidate Says Good-Bye to Enmity, and the GOP," *Detroit Free Press*, April 10, 2012. Accessed November 16, 2012. http://www.freep.com/apps/pbcs.dll/article?aid=2012204100323.

48. Daniel Ruth, "West Channels His Inner Joe McCarthy," *Tampa Bay Times*, April 13, 2012. Accessed November 16, 2012. http://tampabay.com/opinion/columns/article1223719.ece.

49. Ibid.

50. Aaron Gould Sheinin and Kristina Torres, "Governor Vetoes Sunset Bill, Angering Tea Party Activists," *Atlanta Journal-Constitution*, May 4, 2012. Accessed November 16, 2012. http://www.ajc.com/news/news/local-govt-politics/governor-vetoes-sunset-bill-angering-tea-party-act/nqtz9.

51. Dick Polman, "Dick Lugar's Departure a Sign of Washington Paralysis," *Philadelphia Inquirer*, May 19, 2012. Accessed November 16, 2012. http://www.philly.com/philly/columnists/20120518_Dick_Lugar_rsquo_s_departure_a_sign_of_Washington_paralysis.html.

52. Ibid.

53. Ibid.

54. Erik Wemple, "Vetting Errors: ABC News and the Rush to Get it Wrong," *Washington Post*, July 25, 2012. Accessed November 16, 2012. http://www.washingtonpost.com/blogs/erik-wemple/post/.../gjqayuqp9w_blog.html.

55. Associated Press, "Have Race Relations Improved in the Obama Era," *Dallas Morning News*, July 29, 2012. Accessed November 16, 2012. http://www.dallasnews.com/incoming/20120729-have-race-relations-improved-in-the-obama-era.ece.

56. Ibid.

57. Trip Gabriel, "In Tight Iowa Race, Romney Struggles to Excite GOP Base," *New York Times*, August 3, 2012. Accessed November 16, 2012. http://www.nytimes.com/2012/08/04/us/politics/in-iowa-grass-roots-republicans-are-still-not-sold-on-romney.hmtl.

58. Ibid.

59. Ibid.

60. Ibid.

61. Alana Semuels, "Barbara Boxer Calls for Enforcement of Voting Rights Laws," *Los Angeles Times*, September 27, 2012. Accessed November 16, 2012. http://articles.latimes.com/2012/sep/27/news/la-pn-barbara-boxer-doj-voting-rights-20120927.

62. Ibid.

63. Jennifer Steinhauer, "In Iowa and Beyond, Redrawn Districts Test Favorites of Tea Party," *New York Times*, October 4, 2012. Accessed November 16, 2012. http://www.nytimes.com/2012/10/05/us/politics/tough-tests-for-steve-king-and-other-tea-party-favorites.html.

64. "False Protection," *Orlando Sentinel*, October 19, 2012. Accessed November 16, 2012. http://www.orlandosentinel.com/news/nationworld/sns-mct-editorial-false-protection-20121019,0,4057539.story

65. David Brooks, "In Search of Deal Making, Not Partisan Warfare," *Seattle Times*, November 13, 2012. Accessed November 16, 2012. http://www.seattletimes.com/html/opinion/2019676450_brookscolumnpoliticsxml.html.

Chapter Five

Racial Implicitness in the Black and Mainstream Press

We collected, read, and analyzed 1,144 black press and 1,033 mainstream press news articles, for a total of 2,177 online news stories. Table 5.1 shows how many digital articles we analyzed from each newspaper. For the black press, the *Philadelphia Tribune*, the *Portland Skanner*, and the *New Pittsburgh Courier* contributed the most tea party stories. For the mainstream press, the *Seattle Times*, the *Los Angeles Times*, and the *New York Times* contributed the most tea party stories.

Table 5.2 shows the regional breakdown of tea party coverage in the black and mainstream presses.

A two-tailed test of two proportions illustrates significant differences in the amount of tea party coverage in the presses by region. The black press's proportional tea party coverage in the Northeast and the Midwest was significantly more than the white press's proportional coverage in those regions. The white press's proportional tea party coverage in the Southeast, Southwest, and Pacific Northwest was significantly more than the black press's proportional coverage. The amount of coverage disseminated by the black press in the Northeast and the Midwest reflects the fact that most of the prestige black newspapers reside in those regions. These findings do not correlate with swing states during the 2012 presidential elections. For instance, two of the black press's largest contributors came from Pennsylvania, an important state in terms of electoral votes but not a state considered a swing state during the election. The other newspaper, the *Skanner*, in Portland, Oregon, resides in a typically liberal blue state during presidential elections. Because President Obama was never really concerned about losing these states, we can't attribute the amount of coverage from those newspapers with a perceived need of advocating for President Obama. However,

Table 5.1.   News Distribution

	Newspaper	Articles	%
Black Press	Arizona Informant	17	0.8
	Baltimore Afro-American	119	5.5
	Bay State Banner	70	3.2
	Chicago Defender	114	5.2
	Cincinnati and Cleveland Call & Post	9	0.4
	Florida Star	5	0.2
	LA Sentinel	47	2.2
	New Pittsburgh Courier	140	6.4
	Norfolk Journal and Guide	20	0.9
	Philadelphia Tribune	158	7.3
	Portland Skanner	143	6.6
	Sacramento Observer	4	0.2
	Tri-State Defender	61	2.8
	Washington Informer	55	2.5
	Michigan Citizen	19	0.9
	Michigan Chronicle	53	2.4
	New York Amsterdam News	110	5.1
Mainstream Press	Arizona Republic	43	2
	Atlanta Journal-Constitution	53	2.4
	Chicago Tribune	47	2.2
	Dallas Morning News	48	2.2
	Houston Chronicle	58	2.7
	LA Times	115	5.3
	New York Times	99	4.5
	Oregonian	51	2.3
	Orlando Sentinel	76	3.5
	Philadelphia Inquirer	57	2.6
	St. Petersburg Times	57	2.6
	Times-Picayune	37	1.7
	Seattle Times	154	7.1
	Washington Post	54	2.5
	Detroit Free Press	84	3.9
	Total	2177	100

Table 5.2. Test of Two Proportions for Region

	Black Press		White Press		Total	
Region	N	%	N	%	N	%
Northeast***	652	57	210	20.3	862	39.6
Southeast***	129	11.3	223	21.6	352	16.2
Midwest***	195	17	131	12.7	326	15
Southwest***	24	2.1	264	25.6	288	13.2
Pacific Northwest***	144	12.6	205	19.8	349	16
Total	1144	100	1033	100	2177	100

Two-tailed test of two proportions

***p< .01, **p<.05, * p<.1

the Midwest region, containing a few battleground states such as Ohio, Wisconsin, and Iowa, as a whole did contribute more black press tea party coverage than the mainstream press. One can reasonably argue this coverage was possibly correlated with President Obama's need to win those states.

All three mainstream press newspapers contributing the most tea party coverage also resided in states considered safe for President Obama in 2012. However, the Southwest region, containing significantly more mainstream press tea party coverage, did have two states, Colorado and Nevada, considered pivotal for President Obama's reelection. The Southeast also contained states, Florida and Virginia, considered battleground areas. While the most productive newspapers did not reside in swing states, the overall regions did. It is reasonable to argue the election, perceived as a contest between President Obama and tea party values, played a role, though probably minor, in how much the newspapers for both presses covered the tea party.

Significant differences in the types of article the presses disseminated also exist. Table 5.3 shows the breakdown of news, commentary, and editorial stories.

A two-tailed test of two proportions shows significant differences in the amount of news, commentary, and editorial stories about the tea party between the two presses. The black press sample published 469 commentaries and 33 editorial stories. The mainstream press sample published 295 commentaries and 17 editorial stories. Both of these differences were statistically significant. The mainstream press published 721 news stories and the black press published 642 news stories; this difference was statistically significant. This finding is not particularly surprising because, as newspapers driven by an advocacy goal, the black press historically has used commentary and editorials as a vehicle for combatting oppressive mainstream news coverage.

Table 5.3.   Test of Two Proportions for Story Type

	Black Press		White Press		Total	
Story Type	N	%	N	%	N	%
News***	642	56.1	721	69.8	1363	62.6
Commentary***	469	41	295	28.6	764	35.1
Editorial*	33	2.9	17	1.6	50	2.3
Total	1144	100	1033	100	2177	100

Two-tailed test of two proportions

***p< .01, **p<.05, * p<.1

The difference in usage of wires stories was significantly different. Table 5.4 shows the proportions of wire and non-wire stories used by the black and white presses.

The white press used significantly more non-wire stories. The black press used significantly more black wire stories. There was no significant difference in usage of white wire stories. The first finding was not unanticipated because mainstream newspapers have more resources to employ their own reporters to cover stories. The second finding was not unanticipated either because the mainstream press rarely, if ever, includes black press wire stories in their coverage. The third finding was somewhat surprising. Due to declining resources, the black press has recently incorporated a great deal of white wire stories, unless the story was racial in nature. The finding of no significant difference in usage of white wire stories suggests the black press, without hesitation, viewed the tea party narrative as one with serious racial undertones.

Our first prediction expected more implicit racial frames would exist in the black press than in the white press because it is the black press's mission to more accurately and inclusively cover their communities. This prediction also expected the black press to use a direct President Obama versus the tea party racial frame than the mainstream press. The prediction was supported by the data.

Even though the black press explicitly states it will focus on race when needed, we expected implicit racial frames to exist as a byproduct of that mission. In the black press, of the 1,144 stories analyzed, 18 (1.6 percent) included a President Obama implicit racial frame. In the white press, of the 1033 analyzed, 4 (0.4 percent) included a President Obama implicit racial frame. A one-tailed test of two proportions test showed that this difference is statistically significant, $p< .01$. Table 5.5 shows where these implicit racial frames occurred based on region, story type, and wire type. For the most part, the black press's implicit racial frames for President Obama originated from

Table 5.4.   **Test of Two Proportions for Wire Stories**

Story Type	Black Press N	%	White Press N	%	Total N	%
Non Wire***	745	65.1	849	82.2	1594	73.2
White Wire	231	20.2	182	17.6	413	19
Black Wire***	168	14.7	2	0.2	170	7.8
Total	1144	100	1033	100	2177	100

Two-tailed test of two proportions

***p< .01, **p<.05, * p<.1

the Northeast, where most of the prestige black newspapers reside, in news and commentary stories that were not from a wire service. For the mainstream press, the Southeast is the only region where no implicit racial frames for President Obama were found. This is somewhat surprising given the region's history. However, one can argue most of the states in that region were safe for Romney during the 2012 election so it is probable the usage of an implicit racial frame was not perceived as needed by the mainstream newspapers.

In the black press, 14 (1.2 percent) stories included a tea party implicit racial frame. In the white press, 6 (0.6 percent) included a tea party implicit racial frame. A one-tailed test of two proportions showed this difference to be statistically significant, though at a lesser level of significance, $p< .1$. Table 5.6 shows where these implicit racial frames occurred based on region, story type, and wire type. For the black press, the Northeast and the Midwest regions contained the most tea party implicit racial frames. For the most part, these were news stories that were either non-wire or white wire stories. For the mainstream press, the Northeast and the Southwest were the only two regions containing tea party implicit racial frames. These were all non-wire stories labeled either news or commentary.

In the black press, 37 (3.2 percent) stories referenced both President Obama's race and the tea party's overall racial composition in the same story. In the mainstream press, 5 (0.5 percent) referenced both. A one-tailed test of two proportions showed this difference to be significant, $p< .01$. The black press positioned the tea party narrative as a conflict between races significantly more than the mainstream press. Table 5.7 shows where these direct racial contrasts occurred based on region, story type, and wire type. The Northeast disseminated the racial conflict frame the most for the black press while the Southwest distributed the racial conflict frame the most for the mainstream press. Non-wire commentaries were the largest source of the racial conflict frame for both presses.

Table 5.5. Obama Implicit Racial Frames

		Black Press	White Press	Total
Region				
	Northeast	11	1	12
	Southeast	1	0	1
	Midwest	6	1	7
	Southwest	0	1	1
	Pacific Northwest	0	1	1
Story Type				
	News	12	3	15
	Commentary	5	0	5
	Editorial	1	1	2
Wire				
	Non-Wire	12	1	13
	White Wire	4	3	7
	Black Wire	2	0	2

We also expected the black press would reference President Obama's race more than the white press due to their mission to cover race and due to racial solidarity. In the black press, 209 (18.3 percent) stories referenced President Obama's race. In the white press, 17 (1.6 percent) stories referenced President Obama's race. A one-tailed test of two proportions showed that this difference was significant, $p < .01$. Based on priming research, one can argue this difference benefited President Obama during his first term. Mentioning his race in the black press, even though most of their audience—or any audience for that matter—arguably already knew his race, probably primed readers positively. In the mainstream press, the absence of racial cues probably lessened the dampening effect that mentioning a candidate's race can have on potential white voters. In this sense, both newspapers probably helped President Obama achieve reelection.

Table 5.8 shows where these race references occurred based on region, story type, and wire type. For the black press, the stories containing a reference to President Obama's race occurred mostly in the Northeast and were non-wire commentary. For the mainstream press, the stories containing a reference to President Obama's race occurred mostly in the Northeast and Southwest. These stories were mostly non-wire news and commentary pieces.

Table 5.6.   Tea Party Implicit Racial Frames

		Black Press	White Press	Total
Region				
	Northeast	6	4	10
	Southeast	3	0	3
	Midwest	4	0	4
	Southwest	0	2	2
	Pacific Northwest	1	0	1
Story Type				
	News	11	4	15
	Commentary	3	2	5
	Editorial	0	0	0
Wire				
	Non-Wire	7	6	13
	White Wire	7	0	7
	Black Wire	0	0	0

We expected the black press would reference the tea party's overall racial composition more than the mainstream press due to their mission to cover race, racial solidarity, and a cultural history consisting of whites oppressing blacks and attacking African-American officials. In the black press, 85 (7.4 percent) stories referenced the tea party's racial composition. In the white press, 15 (1.5 percent) stories referenced the tea party's racial composition. A one-tailed test of two proportions showed this difference to be statistically significant, $p < .01$.

Table 5.9 shows where these racial references occurred based on region, story type, and wire type. For the first time in the analysis, the Southeast emerged as a significant contributor of black press tea party coverage with 12 articles mentioning the tea party's overall racial composition. Not surprisingly, the Southeast region contributed 0 articles for the mainstream press mentioning the tea party's overall racial composition. For the black and mainstream press, commentaries and non-wire stories mentioned the tea party's overall racial composition the most among these two categories.

These findings all support our first prediction expecting the black press would contain more implicit racial frames about the tea party, President Obama, and usage of race conflict frames.

Our second prediction expected the black press would cover President Obama more positively and the tea party more negatively than the main-

Table 5.7.   Referencing Both Races

		Black Press	White Press	Total
Region				
	Northeast	22	1	23
	Southeast	7	0	7
	Midwest	5	0	5
	Southwest	0	4	4
	Pacific Northwest	3	0	3
Story Type				
	News	10	2	12
	Commentary	27	3	30
	Editorial	9	0	9
Wire				
	Non-Wire	30	4	34
	White Wire	0	1	1
	Black Wire	7	0	7

stream press based on racial solidarity. We created a scale for tone, with 1 being positive, 0 being neutral, and -1 being negative. To be positive or negative, the stories had to contain explicit language either supporting or condemning President Obama. For example, a story that explicitly stated, "President Obama's health care reform is good for our community," was considered positive if that type of sentence occurred more than neutral or negative sentences in the story. The same is true to be considered negative. The overall tone towards President Obama in the black press was 0.09. The overall tone towards President Obama in the mainstream press was -0.22. A one-way Anova comparing these two means showed the difference to be significant, $p < .001$. The black press, in stories mentioning the tea party, covered President Obama more positively than the mainstream press. However, the degree of positivity was not as high as expected, barely over neutral. As the previous chapter noted, this dampened enthusiasm for President Obama stemmed from a perception President Obama was not representing black interests enough and compromising with the tea party and Republicans too much.

We expected the black press would cover the tea party more negatively than the mainstream press. We used the same type of scale to measure tea party tone. In the black press, the overall tone towards the tea party was -0.31. In the mainstream press, the overall tone towards the tea party was

Table 5.8.   Referencing President Obama's Race

		Black Press	White Press	Total
Region				
	Northeast	123	6	129
	Southeast	25	2	27
	Midwest	40	3	43
	Southwest	6	4	10
	Pacific Northwest	15	2	17
Story Type				
	News	89	8	97
	Commentary	112	8	120
	Editorial	8	1	9
Wire				
	Non-Wire	154	13	167
	White Wire	24	4	28
	Black Wire	31	0	31

-0.01. A one-way Anova comparing these means showed the difference to be significant, $p < .001$. The black press did narrate the tea party more negatively than the mainstream press. Tea party tone in the mainstream press barely dipped below neutral. Compared to the black press, the mainstream press was very neutral in their tea party coverage, contradicting popular conservative figures constantly painting media as an anti-conservative institution. If mainstream media were, in fact, as liberal as many conservative figures claim, the tone for the tea party in the mainstream press would have been much more negative. In fact, mainstream press stories in this sample covered the tea party more positively than they did President Obama. These findings strongly support our second prediction.

Our third prediction expected the black press would focus on the tea party as racist more than the mainstream press and the mainstream press would focus on the tea party as an authentic deliberating voice more than the black press. This prediction was supported by the data. In the black press 42 (3.7 percent) stories focused on the tea party as racist. In the white press 5 (0.5 percent) stories focused on the tea party as racist. A one-tailed test of two proportions showed this difference is significant, $p < .01$. Table 5.10 shows where these stories occurred based on region, story type, and wire type. For the black press, the Northeast contained the majority of the racist tea party stories. Most of these stories were either news or commentary. Few, 5, origi-

Table 5.9.   Referencing Tea Party's Race

		Black Press	White Press	Total
Region				
	Northeast	55	4	59
	Southeast	12	0	12
	Midwest	10	2	12
	Southwest	3	7	10
	Pacific Northwest	5	2	7
Story Type				
	News	38	6	44
	Commentary	46	8	54
	Editorial	1	1	2
Wire				
	Non-Wire	65	13	78
	White Wire	9	2	11
	Black Wire	11	0	11

nated from white wire stories. For the mainstream press, the Southeast and Midwest both contained 0 tea party racist stories. The stories focusing on the tea party as racist were all non-wire stories and nearly evenly distributed by type.

We anticipated the mainstream white press would focus on the tea party as an authentic deliberating voice more than the black press. The black press contained only one story (0.1 percent) focused on the tea party as authentically constructed. The mainstream press contained 25 (2.4 percent) stories focusing on the tea party as an authentic deliberating group. A one-tailed test of two proportions showed this difference is significant, $p < .01$. Based on these findings, one can reasonably argue the relatively positive mainstream press coverage of the tea party contributed to the group's rise and influence. Had the mainstream press covered the tea party like the black press, it is doubtful the tea party would have experienced as much success as they did during the 2010 midterm elections and placed a tea partier on the 2012 presidential ticket as vice president. Priming research shows when mainstream press does highlight possible racism, the group or individual's popularity tends to drop due to our society's desire for equality. Had the mainstream press focused on the tea party as racist and not as an authentic deliberating voice, it is quite probable many readers would have dampened their support for the group.

Table 5.10.   Tea Party as Racist Focus

		Black Press	White Press	Total
Region				
	Northeast	19	2	21
	Southeast	8	0	8
	Midwest	5	0	5
	Southwest	1	2	3
	Pacific Northwest	9	1	10
Story Type				
	News	23	2	25
	Commentary	17	2	19
	Editorial	2	1	3
Wire				
	Non-Wire	25	5	30
	White Wire	5	0	5
	Black Wire	12	0	12

Instead, the mainstream press focused on the tea party more as an authentic voice than as a group motivated by racial prejudice.

Table 5.11 shows the distribution of these stories based on region, story type, and wire type. In the black press, the only story focusing on the tea party an authentic deliberating voice came from the Northeast and was a black wire commentary piece. In the mainstream press, the Southwest contributed the most stories stating the tea party was an authentic deliberating voice devoid of racial prejudice. These stories were mostly non-wire news and commentary pieces.

Our fourth prediction expected the black press would focus on the racial undercurrents of the tea party narrative more than the white press. This prediction was supported by the data. This expectation is different than explicitly claiming that the tea party is a racist group. Instead, these stories did not explicitly say the tea party is racist but focused on how the tea party's platform affected diverse communities, regardless of the group's intent. The black press disseminated 247 (21.6 percent) stories focusing on race. The mainstream press contained 5 (0.5 percent). A one-tailed test of two proportions showed this difference is significant, $p < .01$. Historically, media coverage of racial negotiations can be categorized into one of five developmental stages.[1] The first is exclusionary, where media ignore the racial undercurrents of a narrative. The second is the threatening-issue phase, where media

Table 5.11.   Tea Party as Authentic Focus

		Black Press	White Press	Total
Region				
	Northeast	1	7	8
	Southeast	0	3	3
	Midwest	0	3	3
	Southwest	0	12	12
	Pacific Northwest	0	0	0
Story Type				
	News	0	13	13
	Commentary	1	11	12
	Editorial	0	1	1
Wire				
	Non-Wire	0	23	23
	White Wire	0	2	2
	Black Wire	1	0	1

portray minorities "as a threat to the existing social well-being."[2] The third is the confrontation phrase where, after posing a threat to the hegemonic order, minorities are confronted and the response is constructed in violent ways. The fourth is the stereotypical selection phase, after the confrontation with minorities, "the social order must be restored, and transition must be made into a post-conflict period."[3] This is typically done by covering minority "success" stories. By "success," the mainstream media mean a successful assimilation into white society. The fifth and final phase is the multicultural phase, "the antithesis of exclusion."[4] Nonwhites are not always portrayed as threats, or as "successes." Instead, an increased sensitivity to issues affecting nonwhites is portrayed in the coverage.

The finding on the mainstream press virtually ignoring how the tea party's platforms and beliefs negatively affect African Americans suggests, in this case, the mainstream press coverage of the tea party fits into the exclusionary phase. One can reasonably argue, given President Obama's negative valence in the mainstream press stories, the coverage fits into the confrontation phase because President Obama was portrayed as the "other" presenting a threat to the American way of life, not the tea party. The inverse can be said of the black press's tea party coverage. President Obama symbolized black interests and the tea party's formation presented a tangible threat to those issues.

There were significant differences in other story foci as well. Table 5.12 compares focus proportions between the two presses that were not hypothesized. A two-tailed test of two proportions analyzes the significance.

Table 5.12 supports the argument regarding the exclusionary and confrontational phases of the tea party narrative. First, the mainstream press focused exclusively on the tea party more than the black press. Second, the black press, in stories mentioning the tea party, focused exclusively on Presi-

Table 5.12. Test of Two Proportions for Story Focus

Focus	Black Press N	Black Press %	White Press N	White Press %	Total N	Total %
Tea party***	96	6.8	236	22.8	332	15.3
President Obama***	139	12.2	40	3.9	179	8.2
Economy	44	3.8	33	3.2	77	3.5
Unemployment***	35	3.1	6	0.6	41	1.9
National Debt***	2	0.2	18	1.7	20	0.9
Government Spending	66	5.8	64	6.2	130	6
Taxes**	16	1.4	27	2.6	43	2
Health Care	40	3.5	34	3.3	74	3.4
Foreign Policy*	3	0.3	8	0.8	11	0.5
Terrorism	6	0.5	3	0.3	9	0.4
Welfare*	3	0.3	0	0	3	0.1
Crime	4	0.3	8	0.8	12	0.6
Drugs	1	0.1	2	0.2	3	0.1
Education	5	0.4	10	1	15	0.7
Occupy Wall Street	21	1.8	12	1.2	33	1.5
Midterm Elections*	65	5.7	79	7.6	144	6.6
2012 General Election***	135	11.8	226	21.9	361	16.6
2012 GOP Primaries	85	7.4	86	8.3	171	7.9
Gender	6	0.5	4	0.4	10	0.5
Tea party Possibly Racist	4	0.3	9	0.5	13	0.6
Tea party Possibly Authentic*	0	0	3	0.3	3	0.1
Total	1144	100	1033	100	2177	100

Two-tailed test of two proportions

***$p < .01$, **$p < .05$, * $p < .1$

dent Obama more than the mainstream press. The black press focused on unemployment, an issue disproportionately affecting black communities more than white communities, more than the mainstream press. This is an issue where many tea partiers argued unemployment services should be abolished; they viewed unemployment assistance to blacks as handouts and an unnecessary waste of taxpayers' money. Conversely, the mainstream press focused on taxes, a major tea party platform, more than the black press. The tea party's platform alleged President Obama would significantly raise taxes on everyone and the mainstream press served as a platform for the tea party to make that claim. The same can be said for the national debt. The tea party expressed a view President Obama was a reckless spender, a historical stereotype usually emerging in mainstream press coverage of nonwhite elected officials. The mainstream press made this a salient point of view.

Coupling racial solidarity and indexing, our fifth prediction expected the black press would be indexed to government sources more than the mainstream press while the mainstream press would be more indexed to the tea party than the black press. The data support this prediction. Overall, the black press used, on average, 2.2 government quotes per story. The mainstream press used 1.5 government quotes per story. A one-way Anova found this difference to be significant at $p < 0.001$. To our knowledge, no research exists on indexing in the black press. This is the only study we've found comparing indexing in the black press to the mainstream press. The finding of the black press being more indexed to a government with a nonwhite in the most powerful position poses several interesting propositions. American society is expected to increasingly become more diverse and, likely, see increased diversity reflected in government representation. If the mainstream press continues to avoid racial discourse and the substance of why some policies disenfranchise diverse communities, not citing those nonwhite officials as much as minority media, then one can expect the mainstream press to lose even more credibility among the electorate. This may change mainstream media's mission as well. At this point, the mainstream press is charged with being objective, reporting truth, and serving as a government watchdog. Mediating racial discourse is not explicitly stated as a role of the mainstream press. One can reasonably argue this explains our findings the mainstream press largely ignored the racial undercurrents of the tea party narrative and why the stories covered President Obama more negatively than the tea party; from the mainstream press's perspective, it is clear the substance and connection of political policies and their effects on diverse communities is not seen as relevant or objective. However, if demographic trends continue, we expect racial negotiations to increase in our pluralistic society. The mainstream press will have no choice but to move beyond the exclusionary phase and add reporting on race objectively and accurately to their mission.

We also anticipated the white press would use more tea party sources than the black press. Overall, the white press used 1.77 tea party quotes per story. The black press used 1 tea party quote per story. A one-way Anova found this difference to be significant at p< .001. The mainstream press used more tea party sources than the black press. The mainstream press included more tea party sources than they did official sources, meaning the mainstream press was more indexed to the tea party than they were to official sources. This adds an interesting dynamic to the indexing hypothesis. Either the mainstream press was more indexed to the tea party due to their governmental watchdog role or because the group is primarily white, which correlates with the mainstream press's primary audience. Regardless of the reason, this finding poses significant hurdles for the mainstream press if it hopes to break into the multicultural phase of coverage. It is highly probable both reasons contributed to the mainstream press's tea party indexing.

CONCLUSION

All five predictions were supported by the data and statistically significant. Given the mainstream press's awareness of its issues covering race, the public's perception about mainstream media discussing race too much and constantly "playing the race card," and some questioning whether newspapers like the black press are still needed today, these findings are not only, from one perspective disappointing, but important if American society is ever going to escape its anti-equality history. The black press used more implicit racial frames than the mainstream press in coverage of the tea party. The black press referenced President Obama's race and the tea party's overall racial composition more than the mainstream press. The black press used a direct race confrontational frame (mentioning President Obama's race and the tea party's race in the same story) more than the mainstream press. The black press covered President Obama more positively and the tea party more negatively than the mainstream press. One would expect, especially from the mainstream press, coverage like this to exist pre–civil rights, when only whites voted without institutional barriers. It is clear, despite some progress, black newspapers are still very much needed to express black voices and they are using digital media to fill that role.

Forty-two black press stories focused on the tea party as a group comprised of racists; this accounted for 3.7 percent of the black press sample. In contrast, five stories, 0.5 percent, of that nature occurred in the mainstream press. The mainstream press authored 25 stories focusing on the tea party as an authentic democratic deliberating voice—refuting the racist claim; this accounted for 2.4 percent of the mainstream press sample. In contrast, the black press authored only one story explicitly stating the tea party was not racist but an authentic discursive voice with legitimate concerns. The largest portion of focus for the black press's tea party stories was race—247 (21.65 percent). These stories didn't necessarily explicitly say the tea party was racist, but did focus on the racial undercurrents driving the tea party narrative. A key theme emerged in the black press race stories, "historically consistent."

The mainstream press contained five stories (0.5 percent) focusing on race. Instead, the mainstream press's two largest foci were the tea party (22.8 percent) and the 2012 general elections (21.9 percent). A key theme emerged in these stories—"ideology." In both cases, the mainstream press used these foci significantly more than the black press. The use of ideology as a way to interpret the tea party justified their existence as an authentic deliberating voice oblivious to their policies' effects on diverse communities.

The mainstream press's indexing to a group perceived by most nonwhites as a group hostile to minorities presents a significant challenge for mainstream newspapers. One could argue the mainstream press rewarded the tea party for being fairly antagonistic. What does this say about citizen deliberation? In regards to citizen engagement and deliberation, Diana Mutz wrote:

> We want the democratic citizen to be enthusiastically politically active and strongly partisan, yet not to be surrounded by like-minded others. We want this citizen to be aware of all of the rationales for opposing sides of an issue, yet not to be paralyzed by all of this conflicting information and the cross-pressures it brings to bear. We want tight-knit networks of mutual trust, but we want them to be among people who frequently disagree. And we want frequent conversations involving political disagreement that have no repercussions for people's personal relationships. At the very least this is a difficult bill to fill.[5]

Circumstances do exist when politics are so extreme even the most timid join in the discourse. During these moments, it is easy to view the "good citizen."[6] Health care reform was one of those instances where the debate was so intense it seemed everyone harbored opinions and were not afraid to share them. During these moments, it is understandable if media struggle to mediate the events. News routines dictate mainstream media would rely on previously established routines and techniques to cover unique events.[7]

"In the specific context of media coverage of social protests, past studies have demonstrated that differences in the way news stories are constructed can lead to particular audience effects."[8] The thematic structure of social protest stories frequently focus on crime, riot scenes, and the resulting chaos.[9] Media coverage tends to cast protestors as adversaries and accentuates violent acts and confrontation. These frames highlight the violent actions of a few while disregarding peaceful actions of the majority. However, those few violent protestors can and do engage in violent acts in order to attract media attention, thus altering the frame of the discourse from one of issues to one of clash.[10]

The mainstream press ignored race and elevated the tea party. The black press condemned the tea party and focused on race a great deal. Historically, the mainstream press portrays nonwhite protest groups as villains, as threats to society. However, as these findings show, the tea party, a white protest group, was not portrayed as villains or as a threat to society, suggesting the mainstream press tea party narrative contributed to white hegemony. Because of this, one can reasonably argue mainstream press's coverage of the tea party was socially irresponsible. On social responsibility, Dennis McQuail wrote, "In response to widespread criticism of the American newspaper press, especially because of its sensationalism and commercialism, but also its political imbalance and monopoly tendencies, a private commission of inquiry was set up in 1942 and reported in 1947."[11] This commission was extremely critical of the press for limiting minority voices.[12] Thus, social responsibility and the subsequent concept became a prevalent priority for the press.

After the formation of the United States of America, the press was characterized by partisanship. Frank Luther Mott called this period "the Dark Age of Partisan Journalism." Criticisms of the press included: (1) the press had wielded its enormous power for its own gain (2) the press had been controlled by big business (3) the press had resisted social change (4) the press covered superficial and sensational instead of important issues (5) the press had threatened morals (6) the press invaded personal privacy (7) the press is controlled by the business class.[13] It was in response to these dangerous faults that the Commission on Freedom of the Press formed shortly after World War II.

The subsequent concept—which desired a self-corrective, responsible press with no (or at the worst very little) government regulation that allowed an open marketplace of ideas and did not restrict the free flow of messages—outlined six tasks for the press:

> (1) servicing the political system by providing information, discussion, and debate on public affairs; (2) enlightening the public so as to make it capable of self-government; (3) safeguarding the rights of the individual by serving as a watchdog against government; (4) servicing the economic and services through the medium of advertising; (5) providing entertainment; (6) maintaining its own financial self-sufficiency so as to be free from the pressures of special interest.[14]

Peterson wrote that social responsibility "has this major premise: Freedom carries concomitant obligations; and the press, which enjoys a privileged position under our government, is obliged to be responsible to society for carrying out certain essential functions of mass communication in contemporary society."[15]

Social responsibility was born of several circumstances and is still an aggregate of ideas. The Industrial Revolution changed the world's landscape forever, and subsequently, the power and ability of the press changed. Also, journalism became "professional." Schools of journalism sprouted up across the nation which, in turn, brought educated individuals of principle. They wished to set high standards for their craft. Joseph Pulitzer stated in 1904: "Nothing less than the highest ideals, the most scrupulous anxiety to do right, the most accurate knowledge of the problems it has to meet, and a sincere sense of moral responsibility will save journalism from a subservience to business interests, seeking selfish ends, antagonistic to public welfare."[16] John Nerone stated: "Taken at its most benign, who could oppose the goal of an honest, industrious, conscientious press committed to the free flow of all information necessary to self-government?"[17]

From a social responsibility perspective, then, these findings show the mainstream press still struggles because distinctly different tea party narratives emerged between the black and mainstream online newspapers.

NOTES

1. Wilson et al., *Racism, Sexism, and the Media.*
2. Ibid., 130.
3. Ibid., 134.
4. Ibid., 136.
5. Mutz, *Hearing the Other Side*, 125
6. Mutz, *Hearing the Other Side.*
7. Tuchman, *Making News.*
8. Detenber et al.,"Frame Intensity Effects," 439.
9. Zhongdang Pan and Gerald M. Kosicki, "Framing analysis: An approach to news discourse," *Political Communication* 10, no. 1 (1993): 55–75.
10. Ibid.
11. Denis McQuail, *McQuail's Mass Communication Theory* (London: Sage Publications Inc., 2005).
12. R. Hutchings, *A Free and Responsible Press* (Chicago: University of Chicago Press, 1947).
13. John Nerone, "Social Responsibility Theory," *Last Rites: Revisiting Four Theories of the Press* (University of Illinois Press, 1995): 77–100.
14. Ibid.
15. Ibid.
16. Ibid.
17. Ibid.

Chapter Six

Advocating Resistance to Oppressive Ideologies

Resonant myths and implicit frames play a significant role in race and political communication. Black press coverage of the tea party interpreted overt racism, a platform aligned with prior policies effectively marginalizing black communities. During President Obama's first term, the black press continued advocating for resistance to white ideologies aligned with institutionalized white supremacy via the villain myth supported by implicit frames and tried resisting the white reactionary ethnocentricity by indexing to diverse executive branch officials more than the mainstream press. Mainstream news coverage of the tea party interpreted some inferential racism, at times. Given what academia knows about agenda setting and framing, the mainstream press's indecision and focus on intent rather than substance helped enable the tea party to move from a fringe group, driven ideologically by whiteness, into a perceived normalized state. Inclusion in mainstream politics began regressing backwards culturally and nurturing the political climate for the 2016 presidential campaign.

The absence of black perspective in the mainstream narrative of the tea party continues a history of investing in white possessiveness.[1] "As the unmarked category which difference is constructed, whiteness never has to speak its name, never has to acknowledge its role as an organizing principle in social and cultural relations. The possessive investment of whiteness . . . surreptitiously shapes so much of our public and private lives. Desire for slave labor encouraged European settlers in North American to view [non-whites] as racially inferior people suited 'by nature' for the [dehumanizing] subordination of involuntary servitude."[2] After colonial investment in whiteness, successive immigrants entered a racialized society. Whiteness became institutional, encouraging the extermination of Native Americans, the theft of

105

land, slavery, limiting citizenship to whites, restrictions of voting, exploita-
tion of labor, snatching nonwhites' property, and using law enforcement to
keep nonwhite communities "in check" usually through brutal means.[3]

"Although reproduced in new form in every era, the possessive investment in whiteness has always been influenced by its origins in the racialized
history of the United States—by its legacy of slavery and segregation, of
[Native American] extermination and immigrant restriction, of conquest and
colonialism. . . . Antiracist mobilizations during the Civil War and civil
rights eras meaningfully curtailed the reach and scope of white supremacy,
but in each case reactionary forces engineered a renewal of racism, albeit in
new forms."[4] The institutional adaptions, aided by the federal government
and mainstream media, of the possessive investment in whiteness always
widens resource gaps between whites and diverse communities. Many
whites, enabled by their privilege, fail to acknowledge the devastating effects
institutionalized white ideologies have on diverse communities. The United
States is still segregated in many ways and what is perceived as "normal" is
white, making it very challenging for many whites to comprehend whiteness.
For these individuals, unless a racial slur is used, race is almost never tied to
the issues being discussed and when race is mentioned, it is perceived as a
device to excuse failure.[5]

"The typical white person in . . . American situates racism in the past;
embraces formal equality; believes that America has done so much for blacks
and yet blacks never seem to think that it is enough; walks on eggshells
around blacks for fear of saying something offensive; believes in interracial
dating so long as it is not their son or daughter who is marrying black; does
not see themselves as racialized, but basks in white privilege; believes . . .
that blacks who are successful are the exceptions; believes that pretending
that race does not matter makes it true; and still harbors and makes decisions
based on the powerful marker of races that is embedded in American racial
reality. They do not recognize that often times black failure is not due to lack
of ability, but vast inequalities that still exist for many in this country because
of a combination of racial discrimination and socioeconomic status."[6] The
voices, perspectives, experiences, and ideologies expressed in the black press
are still critically necessary to enlighten the desolate wasteland devoid of
diversity substance known as traditional legacy news. Modern mainstream
journalism's concept of objectivity is not conducive to completely, and subsequently accurately, reporting on race and the issues disenfranchising diverse communities. Reading stories from both presses provides readers with
more lucid and nuanced understandings. Reading just one press is not sufficient in today's digital media environment. No excuse, other than not know-
ing about the black press, exists to not digest as many perspectives as possible. While many elements of society may change over time, such as technology, education, and opinions, we've shown both presses aren't changing

the way they cover racial issues digitally. The only change, it appears, is accessibility—more people are a click, thumb swipe, or retweet away from a black perspective than ever before and black newspapers expressing these voices will continue being needed for the foreseeable future for they are muted in mainstream coverage.

Speculation about intent is not constructive. Recall Entman's research showing the vast majority of white Americans do not hold racist views, but media cues can prime towards un-egalitarian assessments. Some research suggests how the story is framed may not be solely responsible for priming these views, but rather the substance of the story itself. Thus, it would be more constructive to not speculate about intent. Highlighting the substance of the issue and why it negatively impacts diverse communities would be more constructive than speculating about intent. Using conflict frames and the villain myth, the black press advocated resistance to a destructive ideology antithetical to the values of an alleged individualistic, pluralistic democracy. Not opposing the tea party's platform helped re-normalize white supremacist ideologies.

We compared how digital black newspapers, an institution dedicated to covering race more extensively than mainstream digital newspapers, interpreted dissent during President Obama's first term. Compared to the black press's coverage of the tea party, the mainstream press barely delegitimized and virtually ignored the diversity components undergirding the substance of the perspectives supported by the tea party. The black press used the villain framework, consistently highlighting parallels reminding their communities of past historical policies instituted by white supremacist ideologies, to cover the tea party and focused on the racial ramifications. The mainstream press used a mix of the scapegoat and trickster frameworks but ignored the consequence of the tea party's proposed platform to diverse communities. Without this comparison, one may view mainstream coverage representing the tea party as extremist hooligans, suspected but not "confirmed" of racial motivations, with no purposive agenda other than opposing the first black president. Given the mainstream press's history of covering race in our multicultural society, the tea party coverage would appear to be an aberration on the surface. Or, it could signal a changing mainstream media environment more sensitive to minority interests. Comparing this coverage to the black press's coverage helped because we were able to see how little the mainstream press connected the dots: the dots being, why the policies promoted by the tea party were invasive to black communities. From the black press's perspective, the mainstream media did not investigate nearly enough—being more a racial lapdog than watchdog.

Black newspapers immediately viewed the tea party as a villain out to destroy African-American communities. For instance, consider a 2009 black press story:

With the election of Barack Obama as this nation's first African-American president, many us had hoped we could finally close the door on America's original sin—slavery. But the vestiges of that institution linger, not only in the backwaters of America, but also in the hallowed halls of Congress. . . . And when you have a "birther" movement promulgating lies that Obama wasn't born in the United States, tea party protests with guns at its rallies, and a vicious right-wing contingent blocking the president of the United States from delivering an innocuous back-to-school speech encouraging America's children to stay in school, we are seeing efforts to delegitimize Obama's authority.[7]

Compare the story to a 2009 mainstream press story:

From Connecticut to California, the tea parties and tea bags being mailed to members of Congress are intended to evoke the spirit of the historic Boston event. That 1773 backlash was about taxes; this one is about what conservatives see as wasteful spending that helps the irresponsible at the expense of the diligent.[8]

The difference in how the tea party was interpreted is distinct. One may argue this was a massive oversimplification by black press; but, their inclusion of "historically consistent" added nuance to the villain myth and justified their interpretation. According to the black press, it was no coincidence the tea party, immediately following successes in the 2010 midterm elections, sought legislation intended to dismantle education integration—one of the earliest civil rights issues.

By not immediately dismissing white opposition to the United States's first black president, mainstream newspapers appear to have been fearful of continuing a tradition of instilling fear, anger, and resentment among whites and blacks. Whites, offended by the delegitimization of the tea party simply because its members disagreed with a black president, crafted a cultural resonance of resentment and fear of resource reallocation resulting from black political representation. Mainstream newspapers used the scapegoat and trickster myths, instead of the villain myth, because they weren't sure how to interpret the group. Journalists acknowledged that genuine racism probably played a part in some of the group's activities, but they also perceived that common party politics also played a part, along with actual fear that a supposedly liberal, African-American politician would steal resources and give them to others. Historically, this has been a tenuous story to tell for mainstream newspapers and they have traditionally leaned away from highlighting multicultural oppression when needed. The scapegoat and trickster myths, in the context of a changing culture that elected its first African-American president, enabled journalists to interpret the tea party dissent as one that was both possibly motivated by racism and by fear of higher taxes, higher spending, and resource reallocation.[9] It is not surprising the black press focused on the racial undercurrents of the tea party narrative; what is surprising is how quickly the black press was needed following President Obama's inauguration. Championing the causes of black communities is one of the black press's primary functions and, in the United States at least, there are still many causes for black communities to be championed. If the main-stream press is a reflection of mainstream society, then the United States is not nearly as inclusive as it would like to believe. Nearly 22 percent of the black press stories mentioning the tea party focused on race, compared to less than 1 percent of the mainstream newspapers articles mentioning the tea party focusing on race. In a digital media environment, with most diverse media growing, [10] the black press still fulfilled the role of narrating issues salient to nonwhites. Images of a mob of whites, carrying guns, with signs of President Obama as a monkey and a witch doctor, helped prompt the black press to interpret the group as a threat to the African-American community, to their ways of life.

The mainstream press, on the other hand, whose primary audience is white, did not interpret the tea party as a threat to white communities. The tea party was seen as a fringe group voicing its concerns, in an undemocratic fashion, about the government. In other words, the black press is more of a racial watchdog than mainstream media, which, in this narrative, was a racial lapdog. Left unchecked, we are concerned of the continued devastating con-sequences this lapdog could help unload on diverse communities.

Coupling the notion of racial solidarity with the indexing concept, we demonstrated the black press used more government sources than the main-stream press. The mainstream press included more tea party sources than the black press. These findings reflect the mainstream news's desire to be a governmental watchdog, not a racial watchdog—which isn't their stated pri-mary function. But if government begins addressing issues salient to diverse communities, the watchdog then becomes a white supremacist attack dog. The tea party, a group opposing the government, served as ample opportunity for the mainstream press to source what they perceived as a group trying to keep the government in check.

Demographics continue changing and more figures whose constituents are from diverse communities will likely hold political office in the future. These findings add an important nuance to the indexing hypothesis as we can expect the dynamic and sourcing patterns to change with the population. If diverse media continue growing and more diverse individuals are elected to office, it is possible those press outlets will be more indexed to the govern-ment than the mainstream press and consequently viewed as more credible by diverse communities but even more less credible by white communities. If government sources are still viewed as a vehicle for credibly and accurately disseminating news, and the mainstream press does not source nonwhite officials as much as diversity media, expect the mainstream press to continue losing influence and perceived credibility. The term "mainstream media" probably will not apply in the future; instead, a new term encompassing all minority media (including mainstream media) will emerge. This correlates with the concept that our society in the future will no longer have a demographic majority; the United States is expected to be comprised of multiple minority groups.[11]

Still serving its primary function is no small feat for the black press today. Its influence has diminished somewhat compared to its power historically.[12] As the United States becomes more multicultural, more pluralistic instead of relying on an assimilation model, and more diverse perspectives begin to have seats at the table of power, we anticipate even more policy debates and conflicts with race as undercurrents. Diverse presses such as the black press may become more influential because, as this book shows, the mainstream press tends, still, to ignore race as an important variable, and when they do cover race, they tend to use zero-sum conflict frames.

The black press viewed the tea party as a villain for a variety of reasons. One of the more prominent ones was the group opposed President Obama from the moment he took office, a figure the black press hoped would fight for issues pertinent to its primary audience. The mainstream press did not use this myth because the tea party was not viewed as a group posing a threat to their audience. Resonant myths uphold the status quo. From the mainstream press's perspective, the data in this book show issues and voices salient to nonwhites are still not yet all that important to white audiences. If that interpretation continues to prevail in the mainstream press, we anticipate an even further decline in readership. However, an understanding of narrative templates, myths, offers the mainstream press blueprints on how to effectively cover race while still appealing to its primary audience of white. The mainstream press will, eventually, need to vilify the policies disenfranchising diverse communities instead of the communities. To do that, they will need to understand those issues and provide substantive analyses of the impacts of the policies, not the superficial, glancing stories we occasionally find focusing on intent. For instance, a blend of the historically consistent villain myth and the scapegoat myth could help convey these stories to mainstream audiences. Non-minority media could have easily accomplished this by including more stories authored by black wire services, such as the NNPA, instead of relying mostly on Associated Press wire stories.

The black press, for future growth, does have work to do as well. The mainstream press reported more social interactivity with their news stories than the black press. The white press, on average, reported 40.2 Facebook shares and 5.3 retweets per story. The black press, on average, reported 0.84 Facebook shares and 0.19 retweets per story. We analyzed the differences with a one-way Anova and found these differences to be significant at $p<.001$. Given social media are an attractive platform for nonwhites,[13] obviously, then, simply having viable web sites is not enough if the black press hopes to recapture influence. Increasing their social media presence is a must for the black press because younger generations don't believe institutional racism exists or policies and legislation to combat previous and current racism are needed.[14] Research does show the black press is beginning to use Twitter as a vehicle for pleading their audiences' perspectives.[15] Diverse perspectives are needed on familiar platforms to educate new generations who may not be exposed to those viewpoints and history.

Increasing interactivity is not an easy task, but it is plausible. For instance, enhanced Search Engine Optimization (SEO) techniques could be deployed. This would not only help harness the diverse communities' collective intelligence, but it would help express their voices to a wider audience and increase understanding of issues salient to their readers. This includes using word clusters in stories, appearing more easily during online searches. Using links connecting to other popular websites can also improve their interactivity. Journalists for the black press, with sparse resources, may say they are not able to do more, adding more work for them is not feasible. However, some tools are available to help decrease their workload while increasing their online output. For instance, RSS aggregators can easily add content for their websites, freeing up time for them to increase their social media visibility. Partnerships with colleges eager to help minority media can also help the black press keep informed on new technologies adept at covering events in real time. Designing mobile apps, mostly drag and drop open/ no code at this point, is another area relatively easy to do and can attract more viewers.

A significant difference between black and mainstream press coverage was the black press essentially saw the tea party as a part of the Republican Party, not as anti-establishment outsiders who were trying to maverick the Republican Party. The black press interpreted tea partiers as the same villains they have previously resisted before, just with a different name. This point is even further illustrated by our first prediction demonstrating more implicit racial frames, both for President Obama and the tea party, existed in the black press than in the mainstream press. The mainstream press used the villain myth to tell the tea party's arc and used implicit racial frames as a key narrative device to tell that story.

One can reasonably argue a large portion of the black press coverage is explicitly racial because their role is to highlight issues salient to nonwhite communities. This book illustrates implicit racial frames, as currently defined by research, existed within this explicitly racial coverage. Two possible theoretical implications emerge from these findings. First, academia's definition of implicit racial frames in the mainstream press may be flawed. Second, accounting for a newspaper's overall mission should be part of the implicitness calculus. This book lays the groundwork for a more nuanced understanding of implicitness because current definitions of implicit racial frames posit a racial story is either implicit or explicit and don't consider there are degrees of implicitness. This book showed even newspapers explicitly covering racial issues contain implicit racial frames. It is also possible nothing implicit exists regarding issues connected to race, only awareness. Those unaware of diversity issues will not connect the racial dots embedded in a story. Those educated about diversity issues will see the story as explicitly about race regardless of the language used. However, priming research on the black press suggests implicit frames embedded in stories connected to race do affect readers. [16]

The existence of implicit racial frames, as they are currently defined by academia, pose interesting questions for the black press's role in President Obama's reelection. The majority of priming research suggests primes dampen white voter support for a nonwhite candidate; however, it can be argued the existence of these primes in the black press elevated support among the black press's audience. The nonexistence of the primes in the mainstream press aided President Obama in 2012 because their absence did not trigger race. [17] Thus, we argue both presses played an important role in President Obama's 2012 reelection through their narratives of the tea party with their usage and absence of implicit racial frames.

The mainstream press, while not including primes, also fell into the historically consistent routine of excluding racial discussions. By not focusing on the racial undercurrents of the tea party narrative, the mainstream press helped the group gain traction. It is highly probable had the tea party not gained traction, not experienced success in the 2010 midterms, and not spent time on dismantling programs pertinent to minorities, President Obama could have accomplished more during his first term. Instead of spending time and wasting energy providing his birth certificate, many times at the request of the tea party, his administration could have governed on more important issues, such as the economy (though, he was able to do that too but it is impossible to quantify how much more effectively he could have done his job).

In this sense, the mainstream press not only furnished the tea party a pass, but also opened the door for the party and others to make unsourced racial attacks while leaving much to be desired in terms of interpreting racial politics. Granted, mainstream press coverage of racial politics has improved some over the decades but this book shows the improvement is focused on covering nonwhite candidates. Covering whites, such as the tea party, who propose legislation and policies harmful to minorities needs improvement. A similar trend emerged during the 2016 presidential election. Mainstream news dedicated much space to the overtly racist, sexist, and islamophobic (among others, this list could continue for some time) statements made during the campaign but failed to focus on the substantive policy positions, or lack thereof.

This adds interesting propositions for future priming studies. Implicit racial frames in the mainstream press, and their effects, have been documented and predictions on election outcomes and policy debates have emerged from that research. However, little research exists testing priming theory in the black press. With society becoming more pluralistic and a more diverse media environment expected in the future, researching how implicit racial frames in nonwhite media, whose mission is to cover issues salient to their communities and are expected to mention race more than mainstream media, affect audiences is needed. If minority media continue growing and becoming more influential, as expected, their effects on audiences must be understood because they can shape future public opinion, elections, and policy.

To our knowledge, this is the only book coupling resonant myth and implicit racial frames. This book showed not all racial frames are the same. In the mainstream press, the few implicit racial frames actually used were episodic in nature, focusing mostly on candidates or an advocacy group. The two myths used in those stories, the scapegoat and the trickster, positioned the people in the stories as fringe members. They were not necessarily threats to the status quo. Instead, they were interpreted as individuals who were not abiding by the appropriate democratic rules for debate. The relative absence of implicit racial frames in the mainstream press made this storytelling possible.

In the black press, where many more implicit racial frames occurred, the myth used to construct the narrative was the villain. This continued the restless native model identified by Hall, but inverted. This implies the deployment of implicit racial frames fortifies the "us versus them" mentality upheld by the villain myth and the absence of racial frames in stories connected to race rely on myths such as the scapegoat and trickster that are social anomalies that will eventually work themselves out. In other words, an increase in racial frames in a narrative increases the chances of being interpreted as a villain, or a hero depending on one's audience. For instance, President Obama was positioned as a flawed hero in the black press stories because he symbolized black political representation for the black press's audience. Given the mainstream press's exclusion of racial discussions and the black press's use of the villain myth, discussing issues connected to race are still very challenging for society's storytellers. From a harnessing collective resonance perspective, one can reasonably argue the mainstream press ignored the racial aspects of the tea party narrative because that is how the mainstream press perceived its readers wanted the story told. Most white Americans do not centrally process race on a daily basis and this book posits white Americans don't want to think about race, period.

The types of stories including implicit racial frames varied greatly. In the mainstream press, the implicit racial frame stories barely mentioned race at all and ignored how the policies presented by President Obama and opposed by the tea party were connected to diverse groups. Historical context was lacking. In the black press, however, the implicit racial frame stories incorporated a great deal of historical context showing how the policy debates were connected to minority groups. Whether the tea party intended to hurt diverse groups is inconsequential from their perspective. The black press showed in their implicit racial frame stories the policies proposed by a possibly naïve tea party would hurt diverse communities regardless of motivation.

This book helps accomplish the three goals of improving multicultural media coverage.[18] It analyzes more diverse journalists, it provides educational material for journalists in school, and it documents minority media content to offer a more truthful account of race. Because myths are used to uphold hegemonic ideologies, the mainstream press's usage of the trickster myth following 2009, ignoring the racial connotations of the tea party's success, suggests expressing black voices is not perceived as an important value by the mainstream press. This book demonstrates the norms and routines of mainstream journalism must incorporate diversity much more vigorously as the nation's demographics change.

For future social movements, considering context is very important. If a movement's timing is off, even if the group has authentic concerns about society, the initial messages may occur during a time that may give rise to suspicions of racial intent. By all accounts, our country is increasingly becoming more pluralistic, with historical minorities gaining in numbers, and soon no majority group will exist. Thus, increased racial negotiations can be expected. This must be considered during an advocacy group's dissent. For instance, consider the issues the tea party dissented against (policies designed to erase barriers obstructing equality) and how those intersections were interpreted. Tea party participants "scripted" their "aggressive" actions to "agitate" and "challenge." Black newspaper articles interpreted the tea party as an obstructive, villainous group interested in defeating President Obama on every piece of legislation he tried to accomplish because in doing so, the group posed a threat to black interests. Their motives were conclusively stated in the black press and they were not portrayed as concerned citizens with actual issue agendas, but as confused antagonists with only one purpose—opposing America's first black president.

Some mainstream newspapers noted simply disagreeing with a black president doesn't necessarily make a group of white individuals racist. One columnist wrote, "the last resort of the liberal scoundrel is the false accusation of racism."[19] The *New Pittsburgh Courier* retorted:

"The last time I had to confront something like this was when I voted for the civil rights bill. At that time, we had a lot of Ku Klux Klan folks and White supremacists," . . . "I have seen this kind of hate before," . . . When people in town hall meetings decry "socialism," they're really using a code word for the N word, said MSNBC "newsman" Carlos Watson. Forty-five to 65 percent of those who protest Obamacare are motivated by racism, said Cynthia Tucker of the Atlanta Journal-Constitution . . . "It's about hating a Black man in the White House."[20]

According to black and mainstream newspapers, President Obama's policies did not, at the time, warrant such a response. This aspect of politics can assist deciphering complex narratives such as the events that unfolded in Ferguson, Missouri, where a white police officer killed an unarmed black man. The nation watched intensely as the local government investigated whether to charge the officer. Many protests emerged with some becoming violent, especially after a grand jury chose not to indict the officer. In a formulaic fashion, much discussion centered on confirming or denying racist intent. Mainstream press coverage focused on the violent actions of a few while the black press focused on humanizing people from a diverse neighborhood routinely killed by police officers. This formula continues as we write this book. The current president's Attorney General, Jeff Sessions, is instituting decades-old policies, such as his desire to crack down on drugs, which research shows disproportionately impacts black communities. Little, if any, mainstream press coverage highlights the historical context showing American society has already tried those solutions and know their effects.

Discussions related to race are never simple. Many layers to these narratives exist and incorporating a multifaceted cultural lens can help all press outlets more accurately report. Not understanding the many layers to diversity leads to misunderstanding, resentment, and friction. No better case exists today than response to the Black Lives Matter movement. Shortly after this movement gained traction, many naïve whites said "all lives matter," not understanding all lives can't matter until the legal system recognizes black lives matter too, not just white lives.

These struggles for power, for equal representation, and subsequent fears of resource allocation is traditionally narrated as a "zero-sum conflict" where someone must, and will, lose.[21] The use of the scapegoat and trickster myth in the mainstream press did allow the newspapers to, somewhat, avoid that conflict frame but at the expense of discussing the substance of the issues—subsequently re-normalizing some white supremacist ideologies. The villain myth in the black press, however, correlates with that frame fairly easily. Some scholars may point to this and argue the black press, actually, exacerbated the situation by relying on a mythic framework resembling mainstream press conflict frames, something the mainstream press are heavily criticized for by academics.[22] If they had solely relied on the villain myth, we may agree. The addition of the historically consistent precursor, one that is nearly always absent in mainstream newspapers, justified the usage of the myth. It is the black press's mission to correct perceived racial wrongs. This mission does not necessarily exist in the mainstream press, which probably is a large factor in their history of covering race. The examination of the myths used in these narratives can help future journalists, for both presses, cover racial politics because it provides a blueprint for being able to cover race by avoiding conflict frames while at the same time not entirely ignoring race.

This book argued as scholars struggle to accurately predict what media environment will emerge in the future as a result of new technologies and a changing field, it is intuitive to explore what resonant myths, one of the few narrative devices not fickle, are used by journalists as they attempt to maintain their profession and distinguish themselves from citizens who have access to the same technologies. Thus, digital content was the focus of this book because digital platforms are a major focus for mainstream and black newspapers looking to recapture their influence. This book showed during the tea party narrative storytelling did not change significantly from other previous news coverage of racial friction. The black press highlighted the racial undercurrents of the narrative through the villain myth and usage of implicit racial frames. The mainstream press virtually ignored the racial undercurrents of the tea party narrative and used the scapegoat and trickster myths as an attempt to show the status quo what happens when one doesn't abide by established democratic values. In other words, digital news did not engender drastically different storytelling techniques.

CONCLUSION

Electing African-American officials has often been viewed as an important step towards eradicating institutional racism. However, some argue, from a substantive legislation point of view, those nonwhite officials do not create drastically different legislation than their white counterparts. During President Obama's first term, one can reasonably argue he governed much like previous white Democratic presidents. The black press often criticized him for not representing their voices. But he was still, in the black press's tea party narrative, the hero, speaking to the power of President Obama's symbolic representation. President Obama will be the first president recalled from memory for an entire generation; the power of that symbolic representation cannot yet be fully and quantifiably measured. In this sense, from the black press's perspective, the symbolism of President Obama's administration, fortified by reelection in 2012, overrides his substantive representation.

This book asked many questions about interpreting racial politics. A main point serving as a conceptual umbrella was examining how journalists for black and white presses used resonant myth to transform episodic events into thematic narratives. As the data show, journalists from these two press organs interpreted the tea party much differently and used vastly different myths to construct their narratives. The data show the mainstream press, for the most part, relied on episodic coverage of the tea party, rarely connecting to history and political communication in a way to construct a thematic narrative exploring the many layers of race. The data show a thematic narrative, history, served as a precursor to the events the black newspapers covered. This historically consistent predecessor informed the thematic narrative that followed.

Because the mainstream press has a poor record of covering multiculturalism, many scholars have grappled with how to improve the coverage. One proposed solution is better education for journalists that arms them with knowledge that will lead to more diverse and sensitive reporting. My hope is that this book, by studying interpretative templates, can help future journalists cover racial politics. I'm not arguing that all white groups who oppose nonwhite officials should be interpreted as villains. However, I do believe that mainstream journalists should discuss historically consistent context more. Culture does not happen in a vacuum. Adding historical context will help journalists construct more intuitive and informative narratives instead of the episodic coverage today omitting history's influence on society. This suggestion is by no means a new revelation. But, with our society becoming increasingly diverse and more racial politics likely to emerge in the future, an awareness of all the groups' history will help journalists interpret the struggle for pieces of the American pie. This need shows the importance of multicultural courses in journalism programs.

Because the mainstream press virtually ignored the racial undercurrents of the tea party, I argue that mainstream press's interpretation of racial politics is still, for the most part, in an exclusionary phase.[23] A better understanding, and incorporation, of minority media can push the dialogue into a multicultural phase, where all groups are represented equally and their issues and interests discussed in a civil, informative manner. This applies to black press journalists as well. For instance, research shows that coalition building with white opponents is critical for black officials.[24] The black press condemned President Obama for trying to work with his Republican and tea party adversaries. It is quite probable that this coalition building contributed to his reelection in 2012. However, at the same time, President Obama did put minority interests on the back burner. This creates a paradox for nonwhite elected officials. In order to get reelected, they build coalitions with white audiences afraid of resource allocation changes. In the process, the minority officials don't represent or champion minority causes. Carol Swain may be correct when she argues that nonwhite officials don't offer substantively different legislation than their white counterparts, but, as this book shows, their symbolic representation may be more important at this point in time. This is an area that the black press could help improve by noting, when they are criticizing officials for working with adversarial groups, that coalition building is necessary if the official hopes to have a lengthy career in office.

Most scholarly research on the press has focused on mainstream media. Had this book not compared mainstream press coverage of the tea party to the narratives in the black press, my conclusions would be much different. We would probably commend the mainstream press for intricately discussing the racial undercurrents of the tea party; instead, compared to the black press, that discourse was minimal. We are not positing that all prior communication studies on the mainstream press are invalid; that would be obtuse. Instead, we are arguing that future research should incorporate a more thorough analysis of diversity media to better understand what the future media environment, and our society, will look like.

NOTES

1. Maurianne Adams, ed., *Readings for Diversity and Social Justice* (Oxfordshire, United Kingdom: Psychology Press, 2000).

2. Ibid., 77–78.

3. Ibid.

4. Ibid., 78–79.

5. Ibid.

6. Ibid., 143.

7. Monroe, "The Conversation America Won't Have on Race."

8. Hansen, "GOP Holds Tea Party Stimulus Protest in Vally."

9. LaPoe, "Crafting Narrative of Tea Party Dissent," 23–24.

10. Wilson et al., *Racism, Sexism, and the Media.*

11. Ibid.

12. Mia Moody, *Black and Mainstream Press' Framing of Racial Profiling: A Historical Perspective* (Washington, DC: University Press of America, 2008).

13. Wilson et al., *Racism, Sexism, and the Media.*

14. Ibid.

15. Benjamin LaPoe and Katie Lever, "The Black Press Tweets: How the Social Media Platform Mediates Race Discourse," Paper presented at Association for Education in Journalism and Mass Communication's (AEJMC) annual conference in San Francisco, Minorities and Communication Division (2015).

16. Benjamin LaPoe and Jas Sullivan, "The Black Press and Priming," in *Critical Black Studies Reader*, R. Brock and D. Stevenson, eds. (Bern, Switzerland: Peter Lang Publishing, 2017).

17. Seth K. Goldman and Diana C. Mutz, *The Obama Effect: How the 2008 Campaign Changed White Racial Attitudes* (New York, NY: Russell Sage Foundation, 2014).

18. Ibid.

19. Charles Blow, "Genuflecting to the Tea Party."

20. Talibah Chikwen, "Tea Party Marchers Far Right and White."

21. Entman and Rojecki, *Black Image in the White Mind.*

22. Ibid.

23. Wilson et al., *Racism, Sexism, and the Media.*

24. Hanks, *Struggle for Black Political Empowerment.*

Appendix

SELECTED AFRICAN-AMERICAN NEWSPAPERS—17

- *Arizona Informant*
- *Baltimore Afro-American*
- *Bay State Banner*
- *Cincinnati and Cleveland Call & Post*
- *Chicago Defender*
- *Florida Star*
- *Los Angeles Sentinel*
- *Michigan Chronicle*
- *Michigan Citizen*
- *New Pittsburgh Courier*
- *New York Amsterdam News*
- *Norfolk Journal and Guide*
- *Philadelphia Tribune*
- *Portland Skanner*
- *Sacramento Observer*
- *Tri-State Defender*
- *Washington Informer*

SELECTED MAINSTREAM NEWSPAPERS—15

- *Arizona Republic*
- *Atlanta Journal-Constitution*
- *Chicago Tribune*
- *Dallas Morning News*
- *Detroit Free Press*

- *Houston Chronicle*
- *Los Angeles Times*
- *New York Times*
- *Oregonian*
- *Orlando Sentinel*
- *Philadelphia Inquirer*
- *St. Petersburg Times*
- *Times-Picayune*
- *Seattle Times*
- *Washington Post*

Bibliography

Adams, Maurianne. *Readings for Diversity and Social Justice* (Oxfordshire, United Kingdom: Psychology Press, 2000).

A.I. Business Solutions. "Search Engine Optimization: The Key Elements." Retrieved June 1, 2011, at www.ai-bs.com.

Alpert, Bruce. "Debt Limit Deal Struck Mostly on Tea Party's Terms," *Times Picayune*, August 2, 2011. Accessed June 2, 2012. http://www.nola.com/politics/index.ssf/2011/08/debt_limit_deal_struck_mostly.html.

Altheide, David. *Qualitative Media Analysis* (Thousand Oaks, CA: Sage Publications, 1996).

"Americans Come Up Short in Debt Deal," *Chicago Defender*, August 4, 2011. Accessed June 1, 2012. http://www.chicagodefender.com/article-11486-americans-come-up-short-in-debt-deal.html.

Arrillaga, Pauline. "Three Years Later, What's Become of the Tea Party?" *Skanner*, April 16, 2012. Accessed Novebmer 15, 2012. http://www.theskanner.com/article/three-years-later-whats-become-of-the-tea-party-2012-04-16.

Associated Press. "Conservatives Protest Healthcare Reform in D.C.," *Skanner*, September 14, 2009. Accessed June 1, 2012. http://www.theskanner.com/article/Conservatives-Protest-Healthcare-Reform-in-DC-2009-09-14.

Associated Press. "GOP Field Shifts Right in First Presidential Campaign Since Tea Party Emerged," *Skanner*, May 30, 2011. Accessed June 1, 2012. http://www.theskanner.com/article/GOP-Field-Shifts-Right-in-First-Presidential-Campaign-Since-Tea-Party-Emerged-2011-05-30.

Associated Press. "Have Race Relations Improved in the Obama Era," *Dallas Morning News*, July 29, 2012. Accessed November 16, 2012. http://www.dallasnews.com/incoming/20120729-have-race-relations-improved-in-the-obama-era.ece.

Associated Press. "Texas Gov. Rick Perry Enters GOP Race for President," *Oregonian*, August 13, 2011. Accessed June 12, 2012. http://www.oregonlive.com/today/index.ssf/2011/08/texas_gov_rick_perry_enters_gop_race_for_president.html.

Associated Press. "2012 Super Tuesday: Ohio Voters Torn Between Hearts, Wallets," *Oregonian*, March 6, 2012. Accessed November 16, 2012. http://www.oregonlive.com/politics/index.ssf/2012/03/2012_super_tuesday_ohio_voters.html.

Aubry, Larry. "Obama's Twisting Blurs His Priorities," *Los Angeles Sentinel*, April 21, 2011. Accessed June 1, 2012. http://www.lasentinel.net/index.php?option=com_content&view=article&id=2487:obama-s-twisting-blurs-his-priorities&catid=95&Itemid=185.

Aubry, Larry. "Obama's Agenda and Rights' Attacks Interconnected," *Los Angeles Sentinel*, September 24, 2009. Accessed June 1, 2012. http://www.lasentinel.net/in-

121

dex.php?option=com_content&view=article&id=5200:obamaa-s-agenda-and-rights-at-tacks-interconnected&catid=95&Itemid=185.

Aubry, Larry. "Obama: Promises, Ratings and Vicious Attacks," *Los Angeles Sentinel*, December 3, 2009. Accessed June 1, 2012. http://www.lasentinel.net/index.php?option=com_content &view=article&id=4815:obama-promises-ratings-and-vicious-attacks&catid=95&Itemid=185.

Aubry, Larry. "President's Race Key Factor in New Forms of Racism," *Los Angeles Sentinel*, April 1, 2010. Accessed June 1, 2012. http://www.lasentinel.net/index.php?option=com_content&view=article&id=4390:presidenta-s-race-key-factor-in-new-forms-of-racism&catid=95&Itemid=185.

Aubry, Larry. "Race Matters: Post-Racial Society a Hoax," *Los Angeles Sentinel*, July 15, 2011. Accessed June 1, 2012. http://www.lasentinel.net/index.php?option=com_content&view=article&id=1974:race-matters-post-racial-society-a-hoax&catid=95&Itemid=185.

Bailey, A. Peter. "Bill O'Reilly's Obsession With Playing Race Card," *New Pittsburgh Courier*, April 28, 2010. Accessed June 1, 2012. http://www.newpittsburghcourieronline.com/index.php/opinion/1946-bill-oreillys-obsession-with-playing-race-card.

"Barack Obama sweeps to victory: First Black U.S. President," *Chicago Defender*, October 18, 2011. Accessed November 5, 2015. http://chicagodefender.com/2008/11/04/barack-obama-sweeps-to-victory-first-black-u-s-president/.

Barnett, Barbara. "Medea in the Media Narrative and Myth in Newspaper Coverage of Women Who Kill Their Children." *Journalism* 7, no. 4 (2006): 411–432.

Barnette, George. "National Urban League Supports Affordable Health Care as Today's Civil Rights Issue," *Baltimore Afro-American*, March 7, 2010. Accessed June 1, 2012. http://www.afro.com/sections/news/national/story.htm?storyid=67183.

Benford, Robert, and David A. Snow. "Framing Processes and Social Movements: An Overview and Assessment." *Annual Review of Sociology* (2000): 611.

Bennett, George. "Coffee Party Debuts in West Palm Beach as Anti Tea Party," *Palm Beach Post*, March 13, 2010. Accessed May 24, 2010. http://www.palmbeachpost.com/news/news/state-regional/coffee-party-debuts-in-west-palm-beach-as-anti-tea/nL5Pr/.

Bennett, Lance. "Toward a Theory of Press-State Relations in the United States." *Journal of Communication* 40, no. 2 (1990): 103–127.

Bennett, Lance, Regina Lawrence, and Steven Livingston. *When the Press Fails* (Chicago, IL: University of Chicago Press, 2007).

Berbrier, Mitch. "Half the Battle": Cultural Resonance, Framing Processes, and Ethnic Affectations in Contemporary White Separatist Rhetoric." *Social Problems* (1998): 431–450.

Berkowitz, Daniel. *Cultural Meanings of News: A Text-Reader* (Thousand Oaks, CA: Sage Publications, 2010).

Berkowitz, Daniel. *Social Meanings of News: A Text-reader* (Thousand Oaks, CA: Sage Publications, 1997).

Berkowitz, Daniel. "Suicide Bombers as Women Warriors: Making News Through Mythical Archetypes." *Journalism & Mass Communication Quarterly* 82, no. 3 (2005): 607–622.

"Better Ideas for Health Care Option," *Post and Courier*, August 18, 2009, A-10.

Biswas, Masadul, and Ralph Izard. "Viability of Online Outlets for Ethnic Newspapers." AEJMC Convention in Denver, Colorado, August 4–7, 2010.

Blow, Charles. "Genuflecting to the Tea Party," *New York Times*, August 12, 2011. Accessed June 12, 2012. http://www.nytimes.com/2011/08/13/opinion/blow-genuflecting-to-the-tea-party.html.

Bogle, Donald. *Blacks in American Films and Television: An Encyclopedia* (New York, NY: Simon & Schuster, 1989).

Boyd, Dan. "Tea Party Protestors Stir Things Up," *Albuquerque Journal*, April 16, 2009, A1.

Boyd, Danah. "Can Social Network Sites Enable Political Action?" *International Journal of Media & Cultural Politics* 4, no. 2 (2008): 241–244.

Bristor, Julia, Renee Gravois Lee, and Michelle R. Hunt. "Race and Ideology: African-American Images in Television Advertising." *Journal of Public Policy & Marketing* (1995): 48–59.

Brooks, David. "In Search of Deal Making, Not Partisan Warfare," *Seattle Times*, November 13, 2012. Accessed November 16, 2012. http://www.seattletimes.com/html/opinion/2019676450_brookscolumnpoliticsxml.html.

Brooks, Maxwell. *The Negro Press Re-examined: Political Content of Leading Negro Newspapers* (Los Angeles, CA: Christopher Publishing House, 1959).

Broussard, Jinx. *African American Foreign Correspondents: A History* (Baton Rouge, LA: Louisiana State University Press, 2013).

Broussard, Jinx. *Giving a Voice to the Voiceless: Four Pioneering Black Women Journalists* (London, England: Psychology Press, 2004).

Brown, Christopher. "WWW.HATE.COM: White Supremacist Discourse on the Internet and the Construction of Whiteness Ideology." *The Howard Journal of Communications* 20, (2009): 189–208.

Browne, Anthony P. "Obama Matters as a President and a Black Leader," *New York Amsterdam News*, April 7, 2011. Accessed June 1, 2012. http://www.amsterdamnews.com/opinion/obama-matters-as-president-and-a-black-leader/article_47b92291-f8e4-5d7c-92c9-89c84c254742.html.

Bunch, Will. "The South's Gonna Do It Again," *Philadelphia Inquirer*, April 12, 2011. Accessed June 2, 2012. http://www.philly.com/philly/blogs/attytood/the-souths-gonna-do-it-again.html.

Caliendo, Stephen, and Charlton McIlwain. "Minority Candidates, Media Framing, and Racial Cues in the 2004 Election." *The Harvard International Journal of Press/Politics* 11, no. 4 (2006): 45–69.

Campbell, Christopher. *Race and News: Critical Perspectives* (New York, NY: Routledge, 2012).

Campbell, Christopher. *Race, Myth and the News* (Thousand Oaks, CA: Sage Publications, 1995).

Caprariello, Peter, Amy Cuddy, and Susan T. Fiske. "Social Structure Shapes Cultural Stereotypes and Emotions: A Causal Test of the Stereotype Content Model." *Group Processes & Intergroup Relations* 12, no. 2 (2009): 147–155.

Carey, James W. *Communication as Culture, Revised Edition: Essays on Media and Society* (London: Routledge, 2008).

Carlton, Sue. "Pass the Tea and Stop the Manatee Insanity," *Tampa Bay Times*, July 15, 2011. Accessed June 2, 2012. http://www.tampabay.com/news.

Carter, Ulish. "He's Back: Santorum Runs for President," *New Pittsburgh Courier*, January 13, 2012. Accessed November 15, 2012. http://www.newpittsburghcourieronline.com/index.php/opinion/6268-hes-back-santorum-runs-for-president.

Chadwick, Andrew. *Internet Politics: States, Citizens, and New Communication Technologies* (New York, NY: Oxford University Press, 2006).

Chikwen, Talibah. "Tea Party Marchers Far Right and White," *New Pittsburgh Courier*, September 18, 2009. Accessed June 1, 2012. http://www.newpittsburghcourieronline.com/index.php/featured-news/national/359-tea-party-marchers-far-right-and-white.

Citrin, Jack, Donald Philip Green, and David O. Sears. "White Reactions to Black Candidates: When Does Race Matter?" *Public Opinion Quarterly* 54, no. 1 (1990): 74–96.

Clawson, Rosalee, C. Harry, and Eric N. Waltenburg. "Framing Supreme Court Decisions: The Mainstream Versus the Black Press." *Journal of Black Studies* 33, no. 6 (2003): 784–800.

Clay, William Lacy. "Republican Tea Party Out to Cripple Obama," *Skanner*, October 16, 2010. Accessed June 1, 2012. http://www.theskanner.com/article/republican-tea-party-out-to-cripple-obama-2010-10–16.

Cook, Timothy. "The News Media as a Political Institution: Looking Backward and Looking Forward." *Political Communication* 23, no. 2 (2006): 159–171.

Cook, Timothy. *Governing With the News: The News Media as a Political Institution* (Chicago, IL: University of Chicago Press, 1998).

Curran, James. "What Democracy Requires of the Media." *The Institutions of American Democracy: The Press* (2005): 120–140.

Curry, George. "Every Republican in Congress Fails Blacks," *Baltimore Afro-American*, May 4, 2012. Accessed November 15, 2012. http://www.afro.com/sections/news/national/story.htm?storyid=74903.

Curry, George. "Michele Bachmann: The John Wayne of Political Lies," *New Pittsburgh Courier*, July 8, 2011. Accessed June 1, 2012. http://www.newpittsburghcourieronline.com/index.php/opinion/4903-michele-bachmann-the-john-wayne-of-political-lies.

Curry, George. "President Carter Was Right to Raise Race Issue," *Skanner*, September 24, 2009. Accessed June 1, 2012. http://www.theskanner.com/index.php/article/President-Carter-Was-Right-To-Raise-Race-Issue-2009-09-24.

Curry, George. "Right-Wing Republicans Often Masquerade as Tea Baggers," *Chicago Defender*, March 31, 2010. Accessed June 1, 2012. http://www.chicagodefender.com/article-7478-right-wing-republicans-often-masquerade-as-tea-baggers.html.

Daniels, Lee A., and Stacey Patton. "Racism: The Monkey on the Tea Party's Back," *Skanner*, April 28, 2011. Accessed June 1, 2012. http://www.theskanner.com/article/racism-the-monkey-on-the-tea-partys-back-2011-04-28.

Dates, Jannette, and William Barlow. *Split Image: African Americans in the Mass Media* (Washington, DC: Howard University Press, 1993).

Detenber, Ben, Melissa R. Gotlieb, Douglas M. McLeod, and Olga Malinkina. "Frame Intensity Effects of Television News Stories About a High-Visibility Protest Issue." *Mass Communication & Society* 10, no. 4 (2007): 439–460.

Detweiler, Frederick. *The Negro Press in the United States* (Chicago, IL: University of Chicago Press, 1922).

Deuze, M. *Media Work–Digital Media and Society Series* (Cambridge: Polity Press, 2007).

Dines, Gail, and Jean M. Humez. *Gender, Race, and Class in Media: A Text-Reader* (Thousand Oaks, CA: SAGE Publications, Incorporated, 2002).

Dionne, E. J. "Facts Crash the Tea Parties," *Philadelphia Inquirer*, December 22, 2010. Accessed June 2, 2012. http://www.philly.com/philly/news/year-in-review/20100420_E_j_dionne_facts_crash_the_tea_parties.html.

Ditonto, Tessa, Richard R. Lau, and David O. Sears. "Amping Racial Attitudes: Comparing the Power of Explicit and Implicit Racism Measures in 2008." *Political Psychology* (2013).

Dolan, Mark, John Sonnett, and Kirk Johnson. "Katrina Coverage in Black Newspapers Critical of Government, Mainstream Media." *Newspaper Research Journal* 30 (2009): 34.

Du Bois, W. E. B. *The Souls of Black Folk* (Mineola, NY: Dover Publications, 1994).

Edelman, Murray. *The Politics of Misinformation* (Cambridge, England: Cambridge University Press, 2001).

Edney, Hazel Trice. "Despite Widespread Appeals, Obama Fails to Nominate Black Woman to Supreme Court," *New Pittsburgh Courier*, May 11, 2010. Accessed June 1, 2012. http://www.newpittsburghcourieronline.com/index.php/featured-news/national/2011-despite-widespread-appeals-obama-fails-to-nominate-black-woman-to-supreme-court.

Edney, Hazel Trice. "American Racial Temperature Rising," *Skanner*, June 14, 2010. Accessed June 1, 2012. http://www.theskanner.com/article/american-racial-temperature-rising-2010-06-14.

Ellison, Charles. "Culture Wars Imperil Obama," *Philadelphia Tribune*, February 12, 2012. Accessed November 15, 2012. http://www.phillytrib.com/newsarticles/item/2732-culture-wars-imperil-obama.html.

Entman, Robert. "Framing: Toward Clarification of a Fractured Paradigm."*Journal of Communication* 43, no. 4 (1993): 51–58.

Entman, Robert, and Andrew Rojecki. *The Black Image in the White Mind: Media and Race in America* (Chicago, IL: University of Chicago Press, 2001).

Ettema, James. "Crafting Cultural Resonance: Imaginative Power in Everyday Journalism." *Journalism* 6, no. 2 (2005): 131–152.

"False Protection," *Orlando Sentinel*, October 19, 2012. Accessed November 16, 2012. http://www.orlandosentinel.com/news/nationworld/sns-mct-editorial-false-protection-201210 19,0,4057539.story.

Farrar, Hayward. *The Baltimore Afro-American: 1892–1950* (Westport, CT: Greenwood Press, 1998).

Finkel, Steven, and John G. Geer. "A Spot Check: Casting Doubt on the Demobilizing Effect of Attack Advertising." *American Journal of Political Science* (1998): 573–595.

Finney, Leon, Jr. "The Future of Black Political Power?" *Chicago Defender*, January 7, 2012. Accessed November 15, 2012. http://www.chicagodefender.com/article-12324-the-future-of-black.html.

Fiske, Susan, Amy Cuddy, and Peter Glick. "Universal Dimensions of Social Cognition: Warmth and Competence." *Trends in Cognitive Sciences* 11, no. 2 (2007): 77–83.

Fletcher, Bill, Jr. "Black People With Guns?" *Chicago Defender*, April 28, 2010. Accessed June 1, 2012. http://www.chicagodefender.com/article-7691-black-people-with-guns.html.

"Former Congressman, Palin Blast Obama at Tea Party Gathering," *Baltimore Afro-American*, February 2, 2010. Accessed June 1, 2012. http://www.afro.com/sections/news/national/story.htm?storyid=67184.

"Fox News Flourishes in the Age of Obama," *Virginia-Pilot*, August 18, 2009, E-5.

Fram, Alan. "Health Care Lobbyists Target Returning Congress," *Washington Informer*, September 4, 2009. Accessed June 1, 2012. http://www.washingtoninformer.com/index.php/us/item/1594-health-care-lobbyists-target-returning-congress.

Franke-Ruta, Garance. "Carter Cites Racism Inclination in Animosity Toward Obama," *Washington Post*, September 16, 2009. Accessed May 15, 2010. http://voices.washingtonpost.com/44/2009/09/15/carter_cites_racism_inclinatio.html.

Gabriel, Trip. "In Tight Iowa Race, Romney Struggles to Excite GOP Base," *New York Times*, August 3, 2012. Accessed November 16, 2012. http://www.nytimes.com/2012/08/04/us/politics/in-iowa-grass-roots-republicans-are-still-not-sold-on-romney.hmtl.

Gale, Daryl. "He's Got Guts, but Not Much Heart," *Philadelphia Tribune*, July 13, 2012. Accessed November 15, 2012. http://www.phillytrib.com/localopinion/item/4879-he's-got-guts-but-not-much-heart.html.

Gale, Daryl. "Respect the Man? You Lie!" *Philadelphia Tribune*, April 6, 2012. Accessed November 15, 2012. http://www.phillytrib.com/localopinion/item/3563-respect-the-man-you-lie.html.

Gamboa, Suzanne. "GOP: Illegal Immigrants Taking Minorities' Jobs," *Bay State Banner*, March 10, 2011. Accessed June 1, 2012. http://www.baystatebanner.com/natl25-2011-03-10.

Goffman, Erving. *Frame Analysis: An essay on the Organization of Experience* (New York, NY: Harper & Row, 1974).

Goldman, Seth K., and Diana C. Mutz. *The Obama Effect: How the 2008 Campaign Changed White Racial Attitudes* (New York, NY: Russell Sage Foundation, 2014).

"GOP Wants to Attack, Not Help," *Lowell Sun*, August 23, 2009, Editorial.

Gormley, Michael. "Democrats Seize on Tea Party Candidates' Social Stances," *Skanner*, October 12, 2010. Accessed June 1, 2012. http://www.theskanner.com/article/democrats-seize-on-tea-party-candidates-social-stances-2010-10-12.

Habermas, Jurgen. *The Structural Transformation of the Public Sphere: An Inquiry Into a Category of Bourgeois Society* (Cambridge, MA: MIT Press, 1991).

Habermas, Jurgen. "Political Communication in Media Society: Does Democracy Still Enjoy an Epistemic Dimension? The Impact of Normative Theory on Empirical Research." *Communication Theory* 16, no. 4 (2006): 411–426.

Hall, Stuart. "Racist Ideologies and the Media." *Media Studies: A Reader* (2000): 271–282.

Hamilton, John Maxwell, Regina G. Lawrence, and Raluca Cozma. "The Paradox of Respectability: The Limits of Indexing and Harrison Salisbury's Coverage of the Vietnam War." *The International Journal of Press/Politics* 15, no. 1 (2010): 78–79.

Hanks, Lawrence. *The Struggle for Black Political Empowerment in Three Georgia Counties* (Knoxville, TN: University of Tennessee Press, 1987).

Hansen, Ronald. "Gop Holds Tea Party Stimulus Protest in Valley," *Arizona Republic*, April 3, 2009. Accessed June 2, 2012. http://www.azcentral.com/arizonarepublic/news/articles/2009/04/03/20090403teaparty0403.html?wired.

Hardin, George. "Tea Party Invoking Stale States' Rights Argument," *Tri-State Defender*, March 31, 2010. Accessed June 1, 2012. http://www.tsdmemphis.com/index.php/archives/23-commentaries/5233-.

Hartmann, Paul, and Charles Husband. *Racism and the Mass Media* (Lanham, MD: Rowman & Littlefield, 1974).

Haqq, Isaac Abdul. "GOP Pledges Tea Party Lynching," *Los Angeles Sentinel*, October 14, 2010. Accessed June 1, 2012. http://www.lasentinel.net/index.php?option=com_content&view=article&id=3507:gop-pledges-tea-party-lynching&catid=81&Itemid=171.

Hicks, Jonathan. "In Iowa and Beyond, Candidates Play the Race Card for Votes," *New York Amsterdam News*, January 8, 2012. Accessed November 15, 2012. http://www.amsterdamnews.com/opinion/columnists/jonathan_hicks/in-iowa-and-beyond-candidates-play-the-race-card-for/article_1330d284-389a-11e1-9d0e-0019bb2963f4.html?mode=story.

Hicks, Jonathan. "The Tea Party Downgrade and What's Behind It," *New York Amsterdam News*, August 11, 2011. Accessed June 1, 2012. http://www.amsterdamnews.com/opinion/columnists/the-tea-party-downgrade-and-what-s-behind-it/article_671262fc-c37c-11e0-a4e7-001cc4c03286.html.

Hicks, Jonathan. "Tea party: Distorting American History," *New York Amsterdam News*, February 18, 2011. Accessed June 1, 2012. http://www.amsterdamnews.com/opinion/tea-party-distorting-american-history/article_6e7b3b39-b224-50d8-9984-5d8e080c918c.html.

Hochschild, Jennifer. *Facing Up to the American Dream: Race, Class, and the Soul of the Nation* (Princeton, NJ: Princeton University Press, 1996).

Hurwitz, Jon, and Mark Peffley. *Perception and Prejudice: Race and Politics in the United States* (New Haven, CT: Yale University Press, 1998).

Hutchings, R. *A Free and Responsible Press* (Chicago: University of Chicago Press, 1947).

Hutchinson, Earl Ofari. "Black Tea Party Activists Say Don't Call Us Traitors," *Chicago Defender*, May 12, 2010. Accessed June 1, 2012. http://www.chicagodefender.com/article-7756-black-tea-party-activists-say-dont-call-us-traitors.html.

Hutton, Frankie. *The Early Black Press in America: 1827 to 1860* (Westport, CT: Greenwood Press, 1993).

"If GOP Beats Down President Obama Black American Crashes With Him," *Washington Informer*, November 25, 2010. Accessed June 1, 2012. http://washingtoninformer.com/index.php/component/content/article/102-national-archive/1742-harvard-scholar-gates-arrested-charges-later-dropped/.

Jackson, Raynard. "Tea-ed Off," *New Pittsburgh Courier*, April 7, 2010. Accessed June 1, 2012. http://www.newpittsburghcourieronline.com/index.php/opinion/1785-tea-ed-off.

Jackson, Jesse. "Fed-Run Health Care a Proven Success," *Los Angeles Sentinel*, September 17, 2009. Accessed June 1, 2012. http://www.lasentinel.net/index.php?option=com_content&view=article&id=5253:fed-run-health-care-a-proven-success&catid=90&Itemid=180.

Jackson, Jesse. "The GOP and the Vote: Return to Jim Crow," *Michigan Citizen*, August 5, 2012. Accessed November 15, 2012. http://www.michigancitizen.com/the-gop-and-the-vote-return-to-jim-crow.

Jackson, Jesse. "Great Civilizations Aren't Ruled by Guns," *Los Angeles Sentinel*, March 11, 2010. Accessed June 1, 2012. http://www.lasentinel.net/index.php?option=com_content&view=article&id=4569:great-civilizations-aren-t-ruled-by-guns&catid=90&Itemid=180.

Jamieson, Kathleen Hall. *Dirty Politics: Deception, Distraction, and Democracy* (New York, NY: Oxford University Press, 1993).

Jamieson, Kathleen Hall, and Joseph N. Cappella. *Echo Chamber: Rush Limbaugh and the Conservative Media Establishment* (New York, NY: Oxford University Press, 2008).

Jealous, Benjamin Todd. "Racism in the Tea Party Must End," *New York Amsterdam News*, July 14, 2010. Accessed June 1, 2012. http://www.amsterdamnews.com/opinion/editorials/racism-in-the-tea-party-must-end/article_1820eb14-5e40-591e-9454-6ef7a012924c.html.

Jensen, Klaus Bruhn. "The Complementarity of Qualitative and Quantitative Methodologies in Media and Communication Research," *A Handbook of Media and Communication Research*, Klaus Bruhn Jensen, ed. (London: Routledge, 2002), 272.

Johnson, Jason. "Reflections in Tea Time," *Chicago Defender*, April 22, 2009. Accessed June 1, 2012. http://www.chicagodefender.com/article-4032-reflections-in-tea-time.html.

Johnson, Jason. "Tea Party Serving Terrorism," *Chicago Defender*, March 31, 2010. Accessed June 1, 2012. http://www.chicagodender.com/article-7480-tea-party-serving-terrorism.html.

Johnson, Jason. "Tea Party Terrorism," *New Pittsburgh Courier*, March 31, 2010. Accessed June 1, 2012. http://www.newpittsburghcourieronline.com/index.php/opinion/1742-tea-party-terrorism.

Johnson, Stephon. "Obama's 40-Yard Dash for Health Care Reform," *New Pittsburgh Courier*, March 17, 2010. Accessed June 1, 2012. http://www.newpittsburghcourieronline.com/index.php/featured-news/national/1652-obamas-40-yard-dash-for-health-care-reform-.

"Justices Signal Trouble for Health Care Law," *Call and Post*, March 27, 2012. Accessed November 15, 2012. http://www.callandpost.com/index.php/news/national/1982-justices-signal-trouble-for-health-care-law.

Karpowitz, Chris, J. Quin Monson, Kelly D. Patterson, and Jeremy C. Pope. "Tea Time in America? The Impact of the Tea Party Movement on the 2010 Midterm Elections." *Political Science and Politics* 44, no. 2 (2011): 303.

Keever, Beverly, Carolyn Martindale, and Mary Ann Weston. *U.S. News Coverage of Racial Minorities: A Sourcebook, 1934–1996* (Westport, CT: Greenwood Press, 1997).

Kenski, Kate, Bruce W. Hardy, and Kathleen Hall Jamieson. *The Obama Victory: How Media, Money, and Message Shaped the 2008 Election* (New York, NY: Oxford University Press, 2010).

Kinder, Donald, and Lynn M. Sanders. *Divided by Color: Racial Politics and Democratic Ideals* (Chicago, IL: University of Chicago Press, 1996).

Knoke, David, George Bohrnstedt, and Alisa Mee. *Statistics for Social Data Analysis* (New York, NY: Wadsworth, 2002).

Krippendorff, Klaus. *Content Analysis: An Introduction to its Methodology* (Los Angeles, CA: SAGE Publications, 2012).

"Lacking Facts and Reason, Health Care Foes Use Fear," *Kansas City Star*, August 18, 2009, A-11.

LaPoe, Benjamin. "Crafting the Narrative of Tea Party Dissent: Unpacking Cultural Resonance, Myth, and Black Political Empowerment." Paper presented at the 2011 NCA annual conference in New Orleans, Political Communication Division.

LaPoe, Benjamin. "Death in the American Family: Framing of Health Care Reform After Senator Edward Kennedy's Death." Paper presented at the 2010 AEJMC annual conference in Denver, Mass Communication and Society Division.

LaPoe, Benjamin. *Gender and Racial cues During the 2008 Democratic Party's Presidential Candidate Nomination Process: Social responsibility in the 21st Century* (Ann Arbor, MI: ProQuest, 2008).

LaPoe, Benjamin, and Andrea Miller. "Supervising Public Opinion: Voices Diffusing Disaster Coverage of the Dalian Oil Spill in China." Paper presented at the 2012 SPSA annual conference in New Orleans, Internet, Technology, and Media Division.

LaPoe, Benjamin, and Jas Sullivan. "The Black Press and Priming." In R. Brock and D. Stevenson, eds., *Critical Black Studies Reader* (Bern, Switzerland: Peter Lang Publishing, 2017).

LaPoe, Benjamin, and Jinx Broussard. "Tea Party Trickster Resonates the 2010 Midterm Elections: Newspapers' Crafting of the Palin Myth." Paper presented at the 2012 Southern Political Science Association annual conference in New Orleans, Political Communication Division.

LaPoe, Benjamin, and Katie Lever. "The Black Press Tweets: How the Social Media Platform Mediates Race Discourse." Paper presented at Association for Education in Journalism and Mass Communication's (AEJMC) annual conference in San Francisco, Minorities and Communication Division (2015).

LaPoe, Victoria, Benjamin LaPoe, and Dan Berkowitz. "*Nurse Jackie* and *HawthoRNE* Stick it to the Mother Myth: Gender and Resonance Online." Paper presented at 2012 ICA annual conference in Phoenix, Ethnicity and Race in Communication Division.

Lessig, Lawrence. *Remix: Making Art and Commerce Thrive in the Hybrid Economy* (New York, NY: Penguin Press, 2008).

Lippmann, Walter. *Public Opinion* (Mineola, NY: Dover Publications, 2004).

Lowry, Rich. "Obama's Option Play May be Too Little Too Late," *Contra Coast Times*, August 19, 2009, Opinion.

Lule, Jack. *Daily News, Eternal Stories: The Mythological Role of Journalism* (New York, NY: The Guilford Press, 2001).

Malveaux, Julianne. "An All-White Senate," *New Pittsburgh Courier*, July 7, 2010. Accessed June 1, 2012. http://www.newpittsburghcourieronline.com/index.php/opinion/2470-an-all-white-senate.

Malveaux, Julianne. "A Sugar-Coated Satan Sandwich," *New Pittsburgh Courier*, August 3, 2011. Accessed June 1, 2012. http://www.newpittsburghcourieronline.com/index.php/opinion/5058-a-sugar-coated-satan-sandwich.

Malveaux, Julianne. "Debt Ceiling, What's That? And Why Does It Need to Be Raised?" *Tri-State Defender*, May 26, 2011. Accessed June 1, 2012. http://www.tsdmemphis.com/index.php/opinion/6604-debt-ceiling-whats-that-and-why-does-it-need-to-be-raised.

Malveaux, Julianne. "Should We Bank on Recovery?" *Chicago Defender*, March 8, 2011. Accessed June 1, 2012. http://www.chicagodefender.com/article-10197-should-we-bank-on-the-recovery.html.

Marcus, Lloyd. "Herman Cain: Runaway Slave," Tea Party Nation, October 18, 2011. Accessed January 5, 2012. http://www.teapartynation.com/profiles/blog/show?id=3355873%3ABlogPost%3A1568547&xgs=1&xg_source=msg_share_post.

Martin, Pharch. "Black Leaders Announce Move Against Conservative Attempt to Distort King's Dream," *New Pittsburgh Courier*, June 23, 2010. Accessed June 1, 2012. http://www.newpittsburghcourieronline.com/index.php/featured-news/national/2374-blacknleaders-announce-move-against-conservative-attempt-to-distort-kings-dream.

Mastin, Teresa, Shelly Campo, and M. Somjen Frazer. "In Black and White: Coverage of U.S. Slave Reparations by the Mainstream and Black Press." *Howard Journal of Communications* 16, no. 3 (2005): 201–223.

McCartney, Robert. "Tea Partiers More Wacky Mavericks Than Extremist Threat," *Washington Post*, April 18, 2010. Accessed June 2, 2012. http://www.washingtonpost.com/wp-dyn/content/article/2010/04/17/AR2010041702652.html.

McIlwain, Charlton. "Race for America 2008: Breaking Through on a Different Track." *Qualitative Sociology* 35, no. 2 (2012): 229–235.

McIlwain, Charlton, and Stephen M. Caliendo. *Race Appeal: How Candidates Invoke Race in U.S. Political Campaigns* (Philadelphia, PA: Temple University Press, 2011).

McIlwain, Charlton, and Stephen Caliendo. "Racial Frames and Potential Effects of Minority Candidates in the 2008 Presidential Election." In Annual Meeting of the Midwest Political Science Association, Chicago, Illinois, 2008.

McQuail, Denis. *McQuail's Mass Communication Theory* (London: Sage Publications Inc, 2005).

Mead, Walter Russell. "The Tea Party and U.S. Foreign Policy," *New York Times*, February 11, 2011. Accessed June 2, 2012. http://www.nytimes.com/2011/02/22/opinion/22iht-edrussel-mead22.html.

Mendelberg, Tali. *The Race Card: Campaign Strategy, Implicit Messages, and the Norm of Equality* (Princeton, NJ: Princeton University Press, 2001).

Mendelberg, Tali. "Racial Priming Revived." *Perspectives on Politics* 6, no. 01 (2008): 109–123.

"Michael Williams: Bow-Tied, Cowboy Boot-Shod Black Texan Carries Tea Party Backing in Run for Senate," *Baltimore Afro-American*, January 30, 2011. Accessed June 1, 2012. http://www.afro.com/sections/news/national/story.htm?storyid=70295.

Miller, Andrea, and Amy Reynolds. *New Evolution or Revolution?: The Future of Print Journalism in the Digital Age* (New York, NY: Lang Publishers, 2014).

Mintz, Steven. *African American Voices: A Documentary Reader* (Hoboken, NJ: Wiley-Blackwell, 2009).

Mitchell, Larry. "TV Dust Up Could Cost Herger His Obscurity," *Chico-Enterprise Record*, August 26, 2009, Local.

Monroe, Irene. "The Conversation America Won't Have on Race," *Bay State Banner*, October 1, 2009. Accessed June 1, 2012. http://www.baystatebanner.com/opinion58-2009-10-01.

Moody, Mia. *Black and Mainstream Press' Framing of Racial Profiling: A Historical Perspective* (Washington, DC: University Press of America, 2008).

Morial, Marc H. "Rand Paul Is On the Wrong Side of History," *New Pittsburgh Courier*, June 8, 2010. Accessed June 1, 2012. http://www.newpittsburghcourieronline.com/index.php/opinion/2263-rand-paul-is-on-the-wrong-side-of-history.

Morris, John Jack. "Textual Analysis in Journalism," in *Qualitative Research in Journalism*, Sharton Iorio, ed. (Mahwah, NJ: Lawrence Erlbaum, 2004).

Morozov, Evgeny. *The Net Delusion: The Dark Side of Internet Freedom* (New York, NY: PublicAffairs, 2012).

Muhammad, Askia. "Obamacare Now Really Means Obama Cares," *Washington Informer*, July 5, 2012. Accessed November 15, 2012. http://washingtoninformer.com/news/2012/jul/05/obamacare-now-really-means-obama-cares/.

Murray, Thomas, and Carmin D. Ross-Murray. *Mythical Trickster Figures: Contours, Contexts, and Criticisms* (Tuscaloosa: University of Alabama Press, 1996), 34.

Mutz, Diana. *Hearing the Other Side: Deliberative Versus Participatory Democracy* (Cambridge, England: Cambridge University Press, 2006).

Nagourney, Adam. "Tea Party Choice Scrambles in Taking on Reid in Nevada," *New York Times*, August 17, 2010. Accessed June 2, 2012. http://www.nytimes.com/2010/08/18/us/politics/18vegas.html.

"N.C. School Board Abolishes Integration Policy," *Baltimore Afro-American*, January 22, 2011. Accessed June 1, 2012. http://www.afro.com/sections/news/afro_briefs/story.htm?storyid=70020.

Nerone, John. *"Social Responsibility Theory." Last Rites: revisiting four theories of the press* (Illinois: University of Illinois Press, 1995).

"No Unemployment Extension," *Florida Star*, November 20, 2010. Accessed June 1, 2012. http://thefloridastar.com/?cat=6&paged=2.

Nuttall, Rebecca. "Obama Budget: First Cut Deepest," *New Pittsburgh Courier*, February 23, 2011. Accessed June 1, 2012. http://www.newpittsburghcourieronline.com/index.php/featured-news/national/3957-obama-budget-first-cut-deepest.

"Options are Public or Profit," *Palm Beach Post*, August 19, 2009, 10A.

Page, Benjamin. "The Mass Media as Political Actors." *Political Science and Politics* 29, no. 1 (1996): 20–24.

Page, Clarence. "Tea Party Myths and Mistaken Views," *Dallas Morning News*, April 19, 2010. Accessed June 2, 2012. http://www.dallasnews.com/opinion/latest-columns/20100419-Clarence-Page-Tea-Party-myths-8600.ece.

Pan, Zhongdang, and Gerald M. Kosicki. "Framing analysis: An approach to news discourse." *Political Communication* 10, no. 1 (1993): 55–75.

Pennington-Gray, Lori, Kiki Kaplanidou, and Ashley Schroeder. "Drivers of Social Media Use Among African Americans in the Event of a Crisis." *Natural Hazards* 66, no. 1 (2013): 77–95.

"Pennsylvania's School's Racial Segregation Feared a Trend," *Baltimore Afro-American*, February 5, 2011. Accessed June 1, 2012. http://www.afro.com/sections/news/afro_briefs/story.htm?storyid=70230.

Perry, Douglas. "The Kings and Queens of the Tea Party," *Oregonian*, November 2, 2010, Accessed June 2, 2012. http://blog.oregonlive.com/elections/2010/11/the_kings_and_queens_of_the_te.html.

Perry, Nick, and Susan Gilmore. "Protestors, Supporters Greet Glenn Beck as He Visits Seattle, Mount Vernon," *Seattle Times*, September 27, 2009. Accessed June 2, 2012. http://seattletimes.com/html/localnews/2009950835_beck27m.html.

Peters, Jeremy, and Brian Stetler. "For Debate Partners, An Unusual Pairing," *New York Times*, September 12, 2011. Accessed June 2, 2012. http://www.nytimes.com/2011/09/13/us/politics/13cnn.html.

Petri, Alexandra. "Biden's Terrorist Gaffe," *Washington Post*, August 1, 2011. Accessed June 2, 2012. http://www.washingtonpost.com/blogs/compost/post/bidens-terrorist-gaffe/2011/08/01/glqakmtgol_blog.html.

Pitts, Leonard, Jr. "Candidate Says Good-Bye to Enmity, and the GOP," *Detroit Free Press*, April 10, 2012. Accessed November 16, 2012. http://www.freep.com/apps/pbcs.dll/article?aid=2012204100323.

Pitts, Leonard, Jr. "Hooray for Common Sense: Tea Party in Decline," *Detroit Free Press*, August 16, 2011. Accessed June 12, 2012. http://www.freep.com/apps/pbcs.dll/article?aid=2011108160307.

Polman, Dick. "Dick Lugar's Departure a Sign of Washington Paralysis," *Philadelphia Inquirer*, May 19, 2012. Accessed November 16, 2012. http://www.philly.com/philly/columnists/20120518_Dick_Lugar_rsquo_s_departure_a_sign_of_Washington_paralysis.html.

Poole, Sheila, Craig Schneider, and Jim Tharpe. "Health Care Rallies Attract Lively Crowds," *Atlanta Journal Constitution*, August 17, 2009. Accessed June 2, 2012. http://www.ajc.com/news/news/local/health-care-rallies-attract-lively-crowds/nQLZy/.

Portney, Kent. "Civic engagement and sustainable cities in the United States." *Public Administration Review* 65, no. 5 (2005): 579–591.

Postman, Neil. *Amusing Ourselves to Death: Public Discourse in the Age of Show Business* (New York, NY: Penguin Books, 1985).

Pride, Armistead, and Clint C. Wilson. *A History of the Black Press* (Washington, DC: Howard University Press, 1997).

Prince, Zenitha. "Federal Election Voter ID Sought by house republican," *Baltimore Afro-American*, June 21, 2012. Accessed November 15, 2012. http://afro.com/sections/news/afro_briefs/story.htm?storyid=75364.

Prince, Zenitha. "Newly-Elected Black Republicans vs. CBC," *Arizona Informant*, November 10, 2010. Accessed June 1, 2012. http://www.azinformant.com/index.php?option=com_content&view=article&id=277%3anewly-elected-black.

Prince, Zenitha. "Joint Center Report: Black Vote Possible Key to Democrat Victory," *Baltimore Afro-American*, October 16, 2010. Accessed June 1, 2012. http://www.afro.com/sections/news/afro_briefs/story.htm?storyid=69025.

"Protestor's Anger Could Lead to Probe," *Detroit Free Press*, December 12, 2011. Accessed June 2, 2012. http:www.freep.com/apps/pbcs.dll/article?aid=2011112120400.

"Protests are About Obama, Not Health Care," the *State*, August 18, 2009, A-0.

"Public Radio, Ethnic Media Sound Alarm of Growing Right Wing Extremism," *Michigan Chronicle*, April 1, 2010. Accessed June 1, 2012. http://www.michronicleonline.com/index.php/2011-08-04-18-06-26/rss-feeds/180-news-briefs/642-public-radio-ethnic-media-sound-alarm-of-growing-right-wing-extremism.

Rau, Alla Beard. "Arizona's 'Birther' Bill Faces Legal Challenges," *Arizona Republic*, April 16, 2011. Accessed June 2, 2012. http://www.azcentral.com/arizonarepublic/news/articles/20110416arizona-birther-bill-legal-challenges.html.

Reeves, Keith. *Voting Hopes or Fears?: White Voters, Black Candidates & Racial Politics in America* (New York, NY: Oxford University Press, 1997).

"Reform as Intended," *Washington Times*, August 18, 2009. Accessed February 12, 2011. http://www.washingtontimes.com/news/2009/aug/18/reform-as-intended/.

Reich, Walter. *Origins of Terrorism: Psychologies: Ideologies, Theologies, State of Mind* (Washington, DC: Woodrow Wilson Center Press, 1998).

"Republican Strategy Depends on Low Minority Turnout," *Washington Informer*, October 29, 2010. Accessed June 1, 2012. http://www.washingtoninformer.com/php/.../2786-republican-strategy-depends-on-low-minority-turnout.

Richardson, Laurel. *Writing Strategies: Reaching Diverse Audiences* (Thousand Oaks, CA: SAGE Publications, Incorporated, 1990).

Robinson, Sue. "SOMEONE'S GOTTA BE IN CONTROL HERE: The Institutionalization of Online News and the Creation of a Shared Journalistic Authority." *Journalism Practice* 1, no. 3 (2007): 305–321.

Rodman, George. *Mass Media in a Changing World* (New York, NY: McGraw-Hill, 2010).

Rogers, Everett. *Diffusion of Innovations* (New York, NY: Free Press, 2003).

"Romney Draws Boos from NAACP Crowd," *Philadelphia Tribune*, July 11, 2012. Accessed November 15, 2012. http://www.phillytrib.com/newsarticles/itemlist/obamacare.html.

Ruth, Daniel. "West Channels His Inner Joe McCarthy," *Tampa Bay Times*, April 13, 2012. Accessed November 16, 2012. http://tampabay.com/opinion/columns/article1223719.ece.

Rutten, Tom. "Birther Blather Lives On," *Los Angeles Times*, April 30, 2011. Accessed June 2, 2012. http://www.latimes.com/news/opinion/commentary/la-oe-0430-rutten-20110430,0,6735231.column.

Said, Edward. *Covering Islam: How the media and the experts determine how we see the rest of the world* (New York, NY: Random House, 1997).

"Sarah Palin's Myth of America," *Time Magazine*, 2008. Accessed October 20, 2010. http://www.time.com/time/politics/article/0,8599,1840388,00.html.

Scheufele, Dietram, and David Tewksbury. "Framing, Agenda Setting, and Priming: The Evolution of Three Media Effects Models." *Journal of Communication* 57, no. 1 (2007): 9–20.

Scheufele, Bertram, and Dietram A. Scheufele. "Framing and Priming Effects." *The International Encyclopedia of Media Studies* (2013).

Schudson, Michael. "How Culture Works." *Theory and Society* 18, no. 2 (1989): 153–180.

Schudson, Michael. *The Sociology of News* (New York, NY: Norton, 2003).

Sears, David, Colette Van Laar, Mary Carrillo, and Rick Kosterman. "Is It Really Racism?: The Origins of White Americans' Opposition to Race-Targeted Policies." *The Public Opinion Quarterly* 61, no. 1 (1997): 16–53.

Sears, David, and Patrick J. Henry. "The Origins of Symbolic Racism." *Journal of Personality and Social Psychology* 85, no. 2 (2003): 259–275.

Semuels, Alana. "Barbara Boxer Calls for Enforcement of Voting Rights Laws," *Los Angeles Times*, September 27, 2012. Accessed November 16, 2012. http://articles.latimes.com/2012/sep/27/news/la-pn-barbara-boxer-doj-voting-rights-20120927.

Senna, Carl. *The Black Press and the Struggle for Civil Rights* (New York, NY: F. Watts, 1993).

Shaw, Todd, Kasim Ortiz, James McCoy, and Athena King. "The Last Black Mayor of Atlanta?" *Research in Race and Ethnic Relations* 18 (2013): 201–230.

Sheinin, Aaron Gould. "Tea Party Turns Up the Heat on GOP," *Atlanta Journal-Constitution*, December 8, 2011. Accessed June 2, 2012. http://www.ajc.com/news/news/local-govt-politics/tea-party-turns-up-the-heat-on-gop/nqpmd.

Sheinin, Aaron Gould, and Kristina Torres. "Governor Vetoes Sunset Bill, Angering Tea Party Activists," *Atlanta Journal-Constitution*, May 4, 2012. Accessed November 16, 2012. http://www.ajc.com/news/news/local-govt-politics/governor-vetoes-sunset-bill-angering-tea-party-act/nqtz9.

Shirky, Clay. *Here Comes Everybody: Revolution Doesn't Happen When Society Adopts New Technology, It Happens When Society Adopts New Behaviors* (New York, NY: Penguin Books, 2008).

Sidoti, Liz. "Obama: Get the Dread Out of Tax Deadline Day," *Chicago Defender*, April 15, 2009. Accessed June 1, 2012. http://www.chicagodefender.com/article-3899-obama-get-the-dread out-of-tax-deadline-day.html.

Siebert, Fred Seaton, Theodore Peterson, and Wilbur Schramm. *Four Theories of the Press: The Authoritarian, Libertarian, Social Responsibility, and Soviet Communist Concepts of What the Press Should Be and Do* (Champaign, IL: University of Illinois Press, 1956).

Sigelman, Carol, Lee Sigelman, Barbara J. Walkosz, and Michael Nitz. "Black Candidates, White Voters: Understanding Racial Bias in Political Perceptions." *American Journal of Political Science* (1995): 243–265.

Simmonds, Yussuf. "Budget D-Day Avoided," *Los Angeles Sentinel*, August 4, 2011. Accessed June 1, 2012. http://www.lasentinel.net/index.php?option=com_content&view=article&id=1864:budget-d-day-avoided&catid=81&Itemid=171.

Simmons, Curtis. "Down But Not Out: Black Democrats Lose Committee and Subcommittee Chairmanships With House Loss," *New York Amsterdam News*, November 10, 2010. Accessed June 1, 2012. http://www.amsterdamnews.com/news/down-but-not-out-black-democrats-lose-committee-and-subcommittee/article_68b52e2a-8ee5-5689-a7ee-9be3d53d0262.html.

Slater, Wayne. "Front-Runner Romney Hardly a Tea Party Favorite," *Dallas Morning News*, January 9, 2012. Accessed November 16, 2012. http://www.dallasnews.com/news/politics/perry-watch/headlines/20120109-front-runner-romney-hardly-a-tea-party-favorite.ece.

Sloan, William. *The Media in America: A History* (Hammond, IN: Publishing Horizons, 1993).

Smith, John. *Collective Intelligence in Computer-Based Collaboration* (Hillsdale, NJ: Lawrence Erlbaum Associates, 1994).

Smith, Robert. "Recent Elections and Black Politics: The Maturation or Death of Black Politics?" *Political Science and Politics* 23, no. 2 (1990): 160–162.

Sniderman, Paul, and Edward G. Carmines. *Reaching Beyond Race* (Cambridge, MA: Harvard University Press, 1997).

Sniderman, Paul, and Michael Gray Hagen. *Race and Inequality: A Study in American Values* (Chatham, NJ: Chatham House, 1985).

Sniderman Paul, and Thomas Leonard Piazza. *The Scar of Race* (Cambridge, MA: Belknap Press of Harvard University Press, 1993).

Sonenshein, Raphael. "Can Black Candidates Win Statewide Elections?" *Political Science Quarterly* 105, no. 2 (1990): 219–241.

Sonmez, Felicia. "Rep. Carson: Tea party Wants to See African Americans 'Hanging on a Tree,'" *Washington Post*, August 30, 2011. Accessed June 2, 2012. http://www.washingtonpost.com/blogs/2chambers/post/.../glqafztmqj_blog.html.

"Sorry About the Birth Certificate," *Chicago Defender*. Accessed July 30, 2017. https://chicagodefender.com/2011/05/03/sorry-about-the-birth-certificate-i-rsquo-ve-been-hunting-osama/.

Steinhauer, Jennifer. "In Iowa and Beyond, Redrawn Districts Test Favorites of Tea Party," *New York Times*, October 4, 2012. Accessed November 16, 2012. http://www.nytimes.com/2012/10/05/us/politics/tough-tests-for-steve-king-and-other-tea-party-favorites.html.

Stelter, Brian. "CNBC Replays its Reporter's Tirade," *New York Times*, February 22, 2009. Accessed June 2, 2012. http://www.nytimes.com/2009/02/23/business/media/23cnbc.html.

Stout, Christopher, and Katherine Tate. "The 2008 Presidential Election, Political Efficacy, and Group Empowerment." *Politics, Groups, and Identities* 1, no. 2 (2013): 143–163.

Sullivan, Jas. "Race, Identity, and Candidate Support: A Test of Implicit Preference." In Tasha S. Philpot and Ismail K. White, eds., *African-American Political Psychology: Identity, Opinion, and Action in the Post-Civil Rights Era* (New York, NY: Palgrave Macmillan, 2010).

Swain, Carol. *Black Faces, Black Interests: The Representation of African Americans in Congress* (New York, NY: University Press of America, 2006).

Taylor, Andrew. "Time Short, Tempers Flare in Budget Showdown," *Philadelphia Tribune*, March 28, 2011. Accessed June 1, 2012. http://www.phillytrib.com/delawarecountrymetros/105-inthenews/inthenews/18309-time-short-tempers-flare-in-budget-showdown.html.

"Tea Party Favorite Storms Castle in Delaware Primary; O'Donnell Latest 'Outsider' to Defeat GOP Establishment," *Washington Times*, September 15, 2010, A1.

"Tea Party's Big Money," *New York Times*, September 23, 2010. Accessed June 2, 2012. http://www.nytimes.com/2010/09/24/opinion/24fri2.html.

Terkildsen, Nayda. "When White Voters Evaluate Black Candidates: The Processing Implications of Candidate Skin Color, Prejudice, and Self-Monitoring." *American Journal of Political Science* (1993): 1032–1053.

Terkildsen, Nayda, and David F. Damore. "The Dynamics of Racialized Media Coverage in Congressional Elections." *Journal of Politics* 61 (1999): 680–699.

Thiessen, Mark. "Palin Endorses GOP Challenger in Alaska Senate," *Seattle Times*, August 24, 2010. Accessed June 2, 2012. http://seattletimes.com/html/politics/2012011400_apusalaskasenatepalinendorsement.html/.

Thompson, Bankole. "Race-Baiting," *Michigan Chronicle*, February 8, 2012. Accessed November 15, 2012. http://www.michronicleonline.com/index.php/local/top-news/5455-race-baiting.

Trammell, Kaye, and Ana Keshelashvili. "Examining the New Influencers: A Self-Presentation Study of A-List Blogs." *Journalism & Mass Communication Quarterly* 82, no. 4 (2005): 968–982.

Tripp, Bernell. *Origins of the Black Press: New York: 1827–1847* (San Ramon, CA: Vision Press, 1992).

Tuchman, Gaye. *Making News: A Study in the Construction of Reality* (New York, NY: Free Press, 1978).

Tuchman, Gaye. "Objectivity as Strategic Ritual: An Examination of Newsmen's Notions of Objectivity." *American Journal of Sociology* (1972): 660–679.

Urbina, Ian. "Beyond Beltway, Health Care Debate Turns Hostile," *New York Times*, August 7, 2009. Accessed June 2, 2012. http://www.nytimes.com/2009/08/08/us/politics/08townhall.html.

Valentino, Nicholas, Michael W. Traugott, and Vincent L. Hutching. "Group Cues and Ideological Constraint: A Replication of Political Advertising Effects Studies in the Lab and in the Field." *Political Communication* 19, no. 1 (2002): 29–48.

Valentino, Nichalos, Vincent L. Hutchings, and Ismail K. White. "Cues That Matter: How Political Ads Prime Racial Attitudes During Campaigns." *American Political Science Review* 96, no. 1 (2002): 75–90.

Valle, C. "Communication, technology and power." *Media Development* 4 (2009): 17–21.

Van Laer, Jeroen, and Peter Van Aelst. "Cyber-Protest and Civil Society: The Internet and Action Repertoires in Social Movements." *Handbook of Internet Crime* (2009): 230–254.

Vigdor, Neil. "Rabble-Rousers Target Himes' Town Hall Meetings," *Connecticut Post*, August 18, 2009.

Walters, Ron. "Republican Radicals Reject Unemployment Fund Extension," *New Pittsburgh Courier*, June 30, 2010. Accessed June 1, 2012. http://www.newpittsburghcourieronline.com/index.php/opinion/2414-republican-radicals-reject-unemployment-fund-extension.

Walters, Ron. "Tea Party, Coffee Party: Why Not a Black Party?" *New Pittsburgh Courier*, March 17, 2010. Accessed June 1, 2012. http://www.newpittsburghcourieronline.com/index.php/opinion/1642-tea-party-coffee-party-why-not-a-black-party.

Walters, Ron. "Tea Party Racism," *New Pittsburgh Courier*, February 11, 2010. Accessed June 1, 2012. http://www.newpittsburghcourieronline.com/index.php/opinion/1398-tea-party-racism.

Warren, John. "The Necessity of the African American Vote in 2012," *Norfolk Journal and Guide*, July 11, 2012. Accessed November 15, 2012. http://www.thenewjournalandguide.com/commentary/item/1219-the-necessity-of-the-african-american-vote-in-2012.

Washburn, Pat. *The African American Newspaper: Voice of Freedom* (Evanston, IL: Northwestern University Press, 2006).

Waters, Enoch. *American Diary: A Personal History of the Black Press* (Chicago, IL: Path Press, 1987).

Wemple, Erik. "Vetting Errors: ABC News and the Rush to Get it Wrong," *Washington Post*, July 25, 2012. Accessed November 16, 2012. http://www.washingtonpost.com/blogs/erikwemple/post/.../gjqayuqp9w_blog.html.

"We Must Vote," *New Pittsburgh Courier*, October 27, 2010. Accessed June 1, 2012. http://www.newpittsburghcourieronline.com/index.php/opinion/3270-we-must-vote.

"Who's Who in the Tea Party," *Ottawa Citizen,* November 3, 2010, A7.

Williams, Damon. "State Reps. Decry Voter Id Law," *Philadelphia Tribune*, March 18, 2012. Accessed November 15, 2012. http://www.phillytrib.com/newsarticles/item/3527-statereps-decry-voter-id-law.html.

Williamson, Vanessa, Theda Skocpol, and John Coggin. *The Tea Party and the Remaking of Republican Conservatism* (New York, NY: Oxford University Press, 2011).

Wilson, Clint, Félix Gutiérrez, and Lena Chao. *Racism, Sexism, and the Media: The Rise of Class Communication in Multicultural America* (Los Angeles, CA: Sage Publications, Incorporated, 2013).

Wimmer, Roger, and Joseph R. Dominick. *Mass Media Research: An Introduction* (New York, NY: Wadsworth Publishing Company, 2006).

Wolseley, Roland. *The Black Press U.S.A.* (Ames, IA: Iowa State University Press, 1971).

Wright, James. "Jobs Top Priority for One Nation Marchers," *Arizona Informant*, October 4, 2010. Accessed June 1, 2012. http://azinformant.com/index.php?option=com_content&view=article&id=255:jobs-top-priority-for-one-.

Young, Dannagal G., and Russell M. Tisinger. "Dispelling late-night myths: News consumption among late-night comedy viewers and the predictors of exposure to various late-night shows." *Harvard International Journal of Press/Politics* 11, no. 3 (2006): 113–134.

Zaller, John. *The Nature and Origins of Mass Opinion* (Cambridge, England: Cambridge University Press, 1992).

Zelizer, Barbie, and Stuart Allan. *Journalism After September 11* (London, England: Taylor & Francis, 2011).

Index

About the Authors

Benjamin Rex LaPoe II, Ph.D., is a visiting assistant professor at Ohio University teaching political communication and race in Scripps College of Communication. He currently serves as director of the Political Communication certificate in the School of Communication Studies; he is also the adviser for Ohio University's Political Communication Student Group. Previously, LaPoe was an assistant professor in interactive storytelling at Western Kentucky University (WKU). At WKU, Ben served as adviser for WKU's Multicultural Student journalists group, assisting in its growth by fivefold during his time. He also headed WKU's School of Journalism & Broadcasting's Diversity Committee. He is a past and current officer within the Association for Education in Journalism and Mass Communication (AEJMC)'s Minority and Communication's division currently serving as the division's newsletter editor. He is coauthor of the book *Indian Country: Telling a Story in a Digital Age,* where he wrote about the history of media and minority press. LaPoe has also been published within several books addressing politics, media, and race with key political, media, and African-American scholars such as Dr. Jinx C. Broussard ("A History of the New Orleans *Times-Picayune.*" In *News Evolution or Revolutions? The Future of Journalism in the Digital Age*) and Dr. Jas Sullivan ("The Black Press and Priming." In *Critical Black Studies Reader*). LaPoe earned his Ph.D. in media and public affairs, with a concentration on race and political communication from Louisiana State University's Manship School in 2013. LaPoe received a B.A. in English in 2003 and a M.S. in journalism in 2008, both from West Virginia University (WVU). Prior to the Ph.D. program, LaPoe worked in the WVU's Dean's office writing and producing content for the alumni magazine.

Victoria L. LaPoe is an assistant professor in Ohio University's Scripps School of Journalism. Previously, she served as broadcasting and film coordinator and assistant professor at Western Kentucky University's School of Journalism and Broadcasting. She received her Ph.D. from Louisiana State University in 2013. She is coauthor of *Oil and Water: Media Lessons from Hurricane Katrina and the Deepwater Horizon Disaster*, which explores the visuals and narratives associated with both disasters. She also co-authored *Indian Country: Telling a Story in a Digital Age*, which evaluates how digital media impact storytelling within Native communities. *Indian Country* contains interviews with more than forty Native journalists around the country. Victoria is also the American Indian Editor for the Media Diversity Forum. She is vice president of the Native American Journalists (NAJA) and a NAJA lifetime member. She has co-run the Native American Journalists Association Fellows student newsroom for multiple years. She is a current AEJMC officer for both the Minorities and Communication division and Commission on the Status of Women. Prior to work in academia, she was an awarding-winning television journalist who worked in the industry for more than ten years.

Lightning Source UK Ltd.
Milton Keynes UK
UKOW01n2054080218

317584UK00001B/31/P

9 781498 566858